# Diasporas of Australian Cinema

## Dedication

This book is dedicated to those we have lost:

Christine Elizabeth Jones (1954-2008)
Bernadette Anne Carstein (1954-2007)

And those we have gained:

Appolonia Gigi Bernard (27 March 2008)

# Diasporas of Australian Cinema

Edited by
Catherine Simpson, Renata Murawska and Anthony Lambert

**intellect** Bristol, UK / Chicago, USA

First published in the UK in 2009 by
Intellect Books, The Mill, Parnall Road, Fishponds, Bristol, BS16 3JG, UK

First published in the USA in 2009 by
Intellect Books, The University of Chicago Press, 1427 E. 60th Street, Chicago,
IL 60637, USA

A catalogue record for this book is available from the British Library.

Cover designer: Holly Rose
Copy-editor: Sue Jarvis
Typesetting: Mac Style, Beverley, E. Yorkshire

ISBN 978-1-84150-197-0

Printed and bound by Gutenberg Press, Malta.

# CONTENTS

# ACKNOWLEDGEMENTS

This book has been an incredibly enjoyable collaborative and scholarly journey. To our contributors listed in the index, thank you for the privilege of working with your amazing ideas, and for your patience. Our gratitude goes to a number of institutions and individuals without whose support this book would not have been possible. Institutionally we would like to acknowledge Macquarie University's Divisional Research Fund, especially Anne Cranny-Francis, Peter Doyle and the Departments of Media and Critical and Cultural Studies. In addition, we would like to thank Simon Drake at the National Film and Sound Archive (Sydney and Canberra) and the Menzies Centre for Australian Studies, King's College London. There are also a number of people whose generosity with additional reviewing of papers extended beyond the call of duty and they include Ina Bertrand, Felicity Collins, Maree Delofski, Grisha Dolgopolov, Susie Khamis, Leonard Janiszewski and Effy Alexakis. We are indebted to all the film-makers and artists whose work is mentioned in the following pages; in particular, for their generous donation of materials and time, we would like to thank Gosia Dobrowolska, Sophia Turkiewicz, Tom Zubrycki, John Weiley, Michael Bourchier and Blink films. Our gratitude goes to Intellect for their professionalism, to the anonymous reviewers of this book and in particular to the very efficient Melanie Harrison. Also to Toby Miller, thanks for your 'provocation'. Finally, Catherine and Renata's sincere thanks to Anthony Lambert, who came on board just as the chapters were rolling in. Without his rigorous editing, inspiration and dedication to deadlines, we would probably still be working on this book!

We would all like to pay special tribute to long-suffering family and friends. In particular, Anthony would like to acknowledge his partner Matthew, parents Les and Brigid, sister Pauline, brother Daniel and their families, as well as the children and grandchildren of his late sister Bernadette Carstein, who passed away as this book was coming together. Renata would like to acknowledge the support from Jasiu and Mum Basia. Catherine is eternally grateful to her partner Bruce, to Mona and to daughters Ayesha and Rahni.

# PREFACE: *DIASPORAS OF AUSTRALIAN CINEMA – A PROVOCATION*

## *Toby Miller*

Diasporic hybridity, the organizing concept of this exciting volume, is at once a tribute to the tenacity and pugnacity of diasporic groups to sustain cultural formations, and a recognition of the inevitability of messy, abject, mixed cultural forms. In this preface, I would like to consider population issues theoretically and numerically, ending with some ideas for textual analysis. It is some time since I have been an informed student of Australian cinema, but what follows has enriched my memory, updated my present knowledge and stimulated me to consider the theoretical and political issues that animate this bold and innovative book. We inhabit a worldwide crisis of belonging, a population crisis of who, what, when and where. More and more people feel as though they *do not* belong; more and more people are *applying* to belong; and more and more people are not *counted* as belonging. Australian multiculturalism, the concept that underpins and is questioned by this book, was an attempt to deal with the beginnings of this crisis to ensure two things: labour peace, against the risk of restive unions, and racial peace, against the intolerance of European-descended white people. The screen texts spawned by the cultural side to this policy have been manifold and manifest, often critical of the idea of multiculturalism as well as its programmatic implementation.

So where did this global crisis come from? It began in the 1960s and has continued since, because of:

■ changes in the global division of labour, as manufacturing left the First World and subsistence agriculture was eroded in the Third;

- demographic growth, through unprecedented public-health initiatives;
- increases in numbers of refugees, following numerous conflicts amongst satellite states of the United States and the former Soviet Union;
- transformations of these struggles into intra- and trans-national violence, after half of the imperial couplet unravelled;
- the associated decline of state socialism and triumph of finance capital;
- vastly augmented trafficking in human beings;
- the elevation of consumption as a site of social action and public policy;
- renegotiation of the 1940s–70s compact across the West between capital, labour, and government, reversing that period's redistribution of wealth downwards;
- deregulation of key sectors of the economy; and
- the development of civil-rights and social-movement discourses and institutions, extending cultural difference from tolerating the aberrant to querying the normal and commodifying the result.

The dilemmas that derive from these changes underpin political theorist John Gray's (2003) critique of 'the West's ruling myth…that modernity is a single condition, everywhere the same and always benign', a veritable embrace of Enlightenment values. Modernity is just as much to do with global financial deregulation, organized crime, and religious violence as democracy, uplift, and opportunity; just as much to do with neoliberalism, religion and authoritarianism as freedom, science and justice (2003: 1–2, 46). The essays in this book illustrate how the struggle for the redefinition and redeployment of these ideas, ideals and realities plays out on screen in a white-settler colony under erasure through difference.

Australia is typical rather than aberrant in having to deal with these questions. Of the approximately 200 sovereign states in the world, over 160 are culturally heterogeneous, and they comprise 5000 ethnic groups. Between 10 and 20 per cent of the world's population currently belong to a racial/linguistic minority in their country of residence. Nine hundred million people affiliate with groups that suffer systematic discrimination. Perhaps three-quarters of the world system sees politically active minorities, and there are more than 200 movements for self-determination in nearly 100 states (Miller 2007). Even Australia's mythic site of origin and contemporary dominant fraction, the Northern Hemisphere's 'British-Irish archipelago', once famed 'as the veritable forge of the nation state, a template of modernity', has been subdivided by cultural difference as a consequence of both peaceful and violent action and a revisionist historiography that asks us to note its emergence from the millennial migration of Celts from the steppes; Roman colonization; invading Angles, Saxons, Jutes, Frisians and Normans; attacking Scandinavians; trading Indians, Chinese, Irish, Lombards and Hansa; and refugee Europeans and Africans (Nairn 2003: 8).

There are now five key zones of world immigration – North America, Europe, the Western Pacific, the Southern Cone, and the Persian Gulf – and five key categories: international refugees, internally displaced people, voluntary migrants, the enslaved and the smuggled. The number of refugees and asylum-seekers at the beginning of the twenty-first century was

21.5 million – three times the figure 20 years earlier. The International Organization for Migration estimates that global migration increased from 75 million to 150 million people between 1965 and 2000, and the United Nations (UN) says 2 per cent of all people spent 2001 outside their country of birth, more than at any other moment in history. Migration has doubled since the 1970s, and the European Union has seen arrivals from beyond its borders grow by 75 per cent in the last quarter-century (Miller 2007). This mobility, whether voluntary or imposed, temporary or permanent, is accelerating. Along with new forms of communication, it enables unprecedented levels of cultural displacement, renewal and creation between and across origins and destinations.

There are simultaneous tendencies towards both open and closed borders in response to these trends. Opinion polling suggests sizeable majorities across the globe believe their national ways of life are threatened by global flows of people and things. In other words, their cultures are under threat. At the same time, they feel unable to control their individual destinies. In other words, their subjectivities are under threat. Majorities around the world oppose immigration, largely because of fear. No major recipient of migrants has ratified the UN's 2003 International Convention on the Protection of the Rights of All Migrant Workers and Members of their Families, even though they benefit economically and culturally from these arrivals (Pew Research Center for the People and the Press 2003 and 2004; Annan 2003).

What is the problem with all this mingling? Bonnie Honig (1998) has shown that immigrants and their cultures have long been *the* limit-case for loyalty, as per Ruth the Moabite in the Jewish Bible/Old Testament. Such figures are both perilous for the sovereign state (where does their fealty lie?) and symbolically essential (as the only citizens who make a deliberate decision to swear allegiance to an otherwise mythic social contract). There have been many outbursts of regressive nationalism, whether via the belligerence of the United States, the anti-immigrant stance of Western Europe or the crackdown on minorities in Eastern Europe, Asia and the Arab world. The populist outcome is often violent – race riots in 30 British cities in the 1980s; pogroms against Roma and migrant workers in Germany in the 1990s and Spain in 2000; the *intifadas*; migrant-worker and youth struggles in France in 1990 and 2005; the Cronulla Beach cell-phone conspiracy in Sydney, Australia – on it goes. The two most important sites of migration between the Third World and the First – Turkey and Mexico – see state and vigilante violence alongside corporate embrace in host countries, and donor nations are increasingly recognizing the legitimacy of a hybrid approach to citizenship.

Australia's immigration program was very Anglo-Irish from the time of Federation until after World War II, when a reserve army of labour was welcomed from Eastern and Southern Europe to build manufacturing industries on the cheap that could quickly be militarized in the event of attack – something that had been lacking before World War II. There was very little cultural accommodation of these new arrivals, while Aboriginal people were regarded as occasional textual signs rather than authors, historians and custodians. Of course, cinema in general took unpaid long-service leave for two decades after the war. By the time of its return, there were also pressures to reform Australian immigration to lessen the culture's racialized consistency.

When added to refugee arrivals from Vietnam, by the late 1970s the nation was changing swiftly. The advent of SBS signified how poorly Australian broadcasting and film had addressed the country's emergent demography and the renewed political visibility of First Peoples. The country's project of nationalism was rethought and reinvigorated in a model that was neither entirely mixed nor entirely sectarian, but somewhere in between.

I want to suggest that Australia's future may well be something like that of Latin America, as newer and older populations continue to intermingle. Consider the history of *mestizaje*, which began a century ago as the mythology of an entirely new type of person that would be forged from intermingling after the Spanish and Portuguese colonized then were sent packing by independence movements. The valorization of the *mestizo* is best exemplified by José Vasconcelos' *La Raza Cósmica* (1925), which took the *mestizo* as the race of the future, shaped by aesthetic plasticity. In contrast to Europe, a hybridized and syncretized culture alongside nineteenth century Romanticism went on to constitute a key foundation of Latin American continental and national identity, albeit precariously. Then it was embraced, or coopted, by populist states in the early to mid-twentieth century. Now it is an everyday norm – frequently used to mask the continued economic, political and cultural hegemony of light-skinned people. That said, at an ideological level it remains a progressive force.

Hybridity is both a norm and a strength of progressive forces. Pondering the global data with which I began, Bruno Latour (with Kastrissianakis 2007) thinks the interdependence generated by life in today's migrant world may shift us 'from a time of succession to a time of co-existence', a site where historicity and commonality prevail and we are all mixed in a self-conscious and self-confident way that transcends the bigotry of nationalism.

This also suggests the need for a more hybrid means of interpreting cultural objects, as per Latour's investigations into cars, laboratories, devices, photographs and theories. Images and icons are not just signs to be read; they are not just coefficients of political and economic power; and they are not just industrial objects. Rather, they are all these things: hybrid monsters, coevally subject to rhetoric, status and technology – to text, power, and nature – all at once, but in contingent ways (Latour 1993). Cultural historian Roger Chartier (1989) proposes a tripartite approach to analyzing texts, *viz.* reconstruction of 'the diversity of older readings from their sparse and multiple traces'; a focus on 'the text itself, the object that conveys it, and the act that grasps it'; and an identification of 'the strategies by which authors and publishers tried to impose an orthodoxy or a prescribed reading on the text' (1989: 157, 161–3, 166). This grid directs us beyond traditional aesthetics. Because texts accrete and attenuate meanings on their travels as they rub up against, trope and are troped by other texts and the social, we must consider all the shifts and shocks that characterize their existence as cultural commodities – their ongoing renewal as the temporary 'property' of varied, productive workers and publics, and the perennial 'property' of businesspeople. It seems to me that this is the way to inhabit diasporic hybridity as a denizen and a reader. Both the texts analyzed in this book and the way they are understood serve as a model.

# PART ONE: THEORIES

# 1

# Introduction: Rethinking Diaspora – Australian Cinema, History and Society

*Catherine Simpson, Renata Murawska and Anthony Lambert*

The inspiration for *Diasporas of Australian Cinema* emanates from the diverse range of films dealing with diasporic experience produced in Australia over the past century. The vital relationship between migration and the moving image is often melancholically invoked, as in films such as Michael Bates' acclaimed short film *The Projectionist* (2002), in which a projectionist traipses through Sydney's darkened laneways as haunting memories flash across the surface of city buildings. Sergei Rachmaninoff's symphonic poem *Isle of the Dead* accompanies this 'gallery of ghostly visions' that includes images of migrant workers, a 'woman in pain', a 'man in despair' and refugees who have been forcibly displaced (Much Ado Films 2002). Using the live-action animation technique of 'Pixilation', these poetic images render urban Sydney an uncanny space, while at the same time hinting at both the animated origins of cinema and the imminent death of the cinema projectionist – a last vestige of modernity. *The Projectionist* exemplifies the ways film can evoke memories of things past, but shows how it can also be a way to make sense of the present and to imagine the future. In this case, the migrant projectionist's origins are never named. He is the modern Everyman who embodies the traumas of the twentieth century, and the subsequent cultural formations that have developed within a specifically Australian context. While these images haunt the projectionist, they are also liberating as they are cast out and shared with others, a diasporic visibility that becomes part of our collective memory.

This collection necessarily springs from Australia's specificity as an immigrant society, simultaneously celebrated and suppressed in the Australian social and cinematic imaginary.

A comprehensive list of films that reflect the ethnic diversity of directors' backgrounds, as well as filmic representations, now spans hundreds of titles, some of which we capture in Garry Gillard and Anthony Lambert's annotated 'Diasporic Filmography' at the back of this volume. The commercial success of films such as *They're A Weird Mob* (Michael Powell 1966), *Strictly Ballroom* (Baz Luhrman 1992), or *The Wog Boy* (Aleksi Vellis 2000) attest to the popular appeal of films representing non-mainstream Australian cultures. Also, the critical appeal of films such as Clara Law's *Floating Life* (1995) or Ana Kokkinos's *Head On* (1997) is evidenced by an ever-expanding body of intellectual work devoted to them (e.g. Siemienowicz 1999; Yue 2000; Mitchell 2003; Berry 1999; Bennett 2007). The less-celebrated genres of documentary, short and experimental film-making have nonetheless been the most prolific in dealing with diasporic identities, and this book attempts to attend to their relative absence from critical attention with half the chapters addressing these formats.

Few entire collections deal with diaspora in cinema, and fewer still engage with specific diasporic national cinemas. In his influential *Accented Cinema*, Hamid Naficy (2001) considers how displacement affects film-makers, predominantly from the developing world, who move (by necessity or voluntarily) to developed countries. Naficy makes a distinction between three types of accented films/film-makers: exilic, diasporic and postcolonial ethnic. He argues that exilic film-makers tend to define homeland in political terms in their early films, while diasporic film-makers have a sense of collective identity. On the other hand, postcolonial ethnic film-makers are those born to non-white, non-western parents since the 1960s and emphasize ethnic identity *within* their host country. Naficy argues that the artisanal production mode and stylistic tendencies of 'accented film-makers' include such things as the 'accented' use of speech; asynchronous sound and multilinguality; the textual presence of the lost homeland; an emphasis on journeying, border subjectivities and hybrid identities; a split relationship with the body; epistolarity as potential conflict/disruption in the narrative; and the self-inscription of the film-maker within the film's text.

Likewise, Laura Marks in *Under the Skin of the Film* (2001) focuses on the techniques used in 'intercultural cinema'; this has emerged 'from the new cultural formations of Western metropolitan centres which in turn have resulted from global flows of immigration, exile and diaspora' (Marks 2001: 1). Intercultural films embrace the proximal as a means of embodying knowledge and memories through 'haptic visuality', which focuses on things such as the texture, tactility and sensuality of objects, 'as if touching a film with one's eyes' (Marks 2001: 162). This moves the viewer closer to the body/human sensorium and is a way of representing memories or longing which many intercultural film-makers negotiate in their displacement.

Naficy's and Marks' theories of 'accented' and 'intercultural' cinema complement one another by arguing that diasporic films and film-makers conform to/seek out a set of formal and stylistic tendencies. Subsequent collections such as Rueschmann's (2003) *Moving Pictures, Migrating Identities* further suggest radically different trajectories of diasporic experience in the cinema. This in itself marks the limited capacity of such work to locate the diasporic within the Australian cinematic and cultural context, beyond the identification of conditions that produce embodied responses to exilic displacement. A 'danger' of diaspora as an organizing principle of visual culture is, according to Mirzoeff (1999b: 8), the promotion of 'a new universalism in contrast to the formal structures of national culture'. The interstitial conditions that produce a third cinema and film-makers from the developing world are not interchangeable with those in Australia.

The Australian diasporic context is not, however, uncharted critical terrain, and much recent work addresses at least some aspects of diasporic identity and multiculturalism in Australian film-making (e.g. Conomos 1992; O'Regan 1996; Turner 1997; Rattigan 1998; Ang et al. 2000; Ang 2001a; Gilbert, Khoo and Lo 2000; Cunningham and Sinclair 2000; Bertone, Keating and Mullaly 2000; Hynes 2000; Madan 2000; Lee and Tapp 2004; Rutland 2005; Carniel 2006; Smaill 2006; Bennett 2007; Rando 2007). However, none of the notable books on Australian cinema allows for any substantial focus on the significant role diasporic qualities have played in Australian cinema's history and industry. *Diasporas of Australian Cinema* is the first volume to do so. This collection of essays is not intended to be an exhaustive treatment of the subject but to open up the critical terrain and present fresh insights into some of the diasporic aspects of Australian cinema, offering foundations for future discussions on the topic.

## Cinema and the diasporic society

Defining Australian cinema has proven a challenging task for theorists, critics and government financiers. With those films that sit at national borders – in terms of origins of creative talent, cast and crew, themes, locations and financing – definitions of the national are fluid with respect to the constant movement of capital and personnel. Deciding where Australian cinema ends and international cinema starts is not the concern of this book. By their diasporic nature, many of the films examined in this volume sit at the borders of Australian and other national cinemas. For this reason, we have adopted a similar approach to Tom O'Regan (1996), where we regard 'Australian cinema' as a loose category that is not overly prescriptive in definition. In his landmark text, *Australian National Cinema*, O'Regan breaks open the national cinema category, positioning Australian cinema as inclusive and inherently diverse.

As a postcolonial immigrant society, contemporary Australia has come a long way from its British penal colony origins. The federation of five states and two territories into a nation in 1901 coincided with the fostering of a British-derived identity and ethnicity through the *Immigration Restriction Act 1901*. This Act, widely known as the 'White Australia' policy, sought to limit the immigration of 'non-Europeans' and 'coloured races' to Australia (Stratton and Ang 1994). Such thinking impacted on the representation and treatment of Asian characters in the early cinema, a racism evidenced in well-known films such as *A Girl of the Bush* (Raymond Longford 1921) and Phil K. Walsh's now infamous *The Birth of White Australia* (1928), which ends with Anglo-Celtic lovers framed by the plait of a Chinese man, presumably scalped on the goldfields.

The policy was progressively dismantled after World War II, with increased migration (predominantly from war-torn Europe) encouraged, although it persisted until the early 1970s. In order to cope with the diversifying population, a policy of cultural assimilation governed

*[handwritten margin note: History of Australia]*

official rhetoric during the post-war period, arguing that 'new Australians' would be absorbed socially and culturally into the mainstream Anglo-Australian community.

At the 1968 Citizen Convention, Polish immigrant Professor Jerzy Zubrzycki first advocated multiculturalism, a proposal later consolidated in his Department of Immigration submission *Australia as a Multicultural Society* (AEAC 1977). Multiculturalism emerged from the perceived failure of assimilation and was a pragmatic response to a society that could no longer sustain national identity dependent on the myth of British origin (Stratton and Ang 1994). The cultural diversity of contemporary Australia belies its own origins in the United Kingdom's historical inability to meet Australia's growing workforce demand, especially in the second half of the twentieth century (Jupp 2001: 62–6). This led to the first official national policy of multiculturalism in 1978 and government endorsement in 1989 of the report *National Agenda for a Multicultural Australia*, which contained principles of 'cultural identity', 'social justice' and 'economic efficiency' with the aim being to 'promote an environment that is tolerant and accepting of cultural and social diversity' (ACMA 1989). However, Australian multiculturalism differs from that of countries such as the United States in its concern with the synthesizing of unruly and unpredictable cultural identities and differences into a harmonious unity-in-diversity, which serves to protect the nation-state of many cultures (Stratton and Ang 1994). Commentators have since begun to replace multicultural ideals with those of a transient, diasporic collective affiliated with the Australian state (Hugo 2006). With this conceptual revision of state and identity came more prolific filmic representations of the non-core (non-British originated) Australians. The boundaries of Australian national cinema have evolved to reflect and encompass these changes and, as this collection demonstrates, the maturing diasporic hybridity of its constituents.

Extending O'Regan's (1996) understanding of Australian cinema as messy and diverse, an even more significant dialogical contribution to this book's theoretical framework is his conceptualization of four pathways for Australian nationhood and its filmic translations: as a European-derived society; a settler society; a New World society; and a diasporic society (O'Regan 1996: 305). The first two pathways imply a Eurocentrism reflective of the persistence of the 'White Australia' policy well into the 1970s, while the third – despite its attempts to de-emphasize ethnicity through its 'melting pot' definition of Australian society – no longer reflects the cultural dominance of an ethnically unnamed Australian core. The diasporic pathway to Australian nationhood, O'Regan notes, is also wrought with problems. On the one hand, almost consistently throughout Australian history since white settlement, around one-quarter of the Australian population have been born overseas (with the exception of the 1940s), with another quarter having at least one parent born overseas. On the other hand, the most significant number of new or second-generation Australians come from the United Kingdom, suggesting a continuing Anglo-Celtic bias in line with the cohesive rather than diversified concept of nationhood implied by the term 'diasporic'. Additionally, O'Regan argues that claiming the predominance of a diasporic cinema as a conceptual framework for Australian cinema could lead to the neglect of 'Australia's indigenous people or the absurdity of calling a "diaspora" people of several ancestries who [do not identify diasporically and] are now in their tenth generation in the country' (O'Regan 1996: 305), a claim further problematized by various intra-Australia migrations, or micro-diasporas, of its Aboriginal peoples (Harrison 2003). Labelling Australia and its cinema as *primarily* 'diasporic' misrepresents both in the same way as the approach that focuses predominantly on an ethnically unnamed 'settler' or New World 'Australian' culture. The subsection of Australian cinema that *can* loosely be categorized within a diasporic framework is the focus of this book.

## From diasporas to diasporic hybridity

In the first instance, this volume relies on three particular characteristics of the term *diaspora*: the scattering of a people (forced or unforced, asylum-seekers or economic migrants) across different new homelands; the maintenance of real or imaginary relations with homeland; and the shared self-awareness of belonging to a dispersed people as its members remain collectively away from their original homeland for beyond one generation (Butler 2001: 192). Homeland can be a micro-location, such as a particular town or settlement, and a macro-location, such as a nation (Butler 2001: 192–6). We complement these understandings with Zygmunt Bauman's claim that the greatest identity challenge of this new century is not how to subscribe to a particular identity, but which one(s) to choose (Bauman 2001: 147).

In Australia towards the end of the twentieth century, emphasizing diasporic origins started to serve an authenticating objective, partly as a backlash against the discriminations suffered by children of immigrants in previous decades, and partly because of the opening up of Australia to non-assimilationist ideas of national integration embedded in multiculturalism. Consequently, multilayered identities have the potential to do away with the fixity of a singular ethnicity or homeland (Kalra 2005: 16) and the exclusion of other forms of identity (cf. Ang 2003: 145). More interestingly, the category 'diasporic people' superimposes a network of transnationalities on to a territorially bound nation-state. These networks do not negate a nation-state as much as adding a dimension of diversity to it that simultaneously enriches and unsettles its more habitual assimilationist sense of identity (Cohen 1997: x). Thus, as Brubaker (2005: 12) observes, 'diaspora can be seen as an *alternative* to the essentialization of belonging, but it can also represent a non-territorial form of essentialized belonging' as 'a category of practice'. This explains the contrasting impulses evident in celebrating and suppressing the awareness of diasporic contributions to Australian cinema mentioned earlier.

Within an understanding of identity as multi-layered, Australianness is complemented and complicated by one or more diasporic points of reference, which are in conversation with one another. This use of diaspora is exemplified by Stuart Hall's (1990: 31) seminal essay 'Cultural Identity and Diaspora', in which he famously argues that diasporic identity is 'defined, not by essence or purity, but by the recognition of a necessary heterogeneity and diversity'. Hall adds that 'diaspora identities are those that are constantly producing and reproducing themselves anew through transformation and difference' (1990: 31).

Previously, the types of identities encompassed in this volume may have been described as 'multicultural', 'minority' '(im)migrant', 'ethnic', 'transnational' or simply 'hybrid'. As Ien Ang (2001) writes, 'the terms "migrants" and "ethnics" as such are strangely distancing, as if these people were, *en bloc*, a category apart, not really a part of Australian culture and society' (2001: 14). David Callahan (2001) also emphasizes patterns of victimization and alienation inherent in representations of 'ethnics' in Australian film (2001: 95–107). The term 'ethnicity', especially within the context of multiculturalism, maintains an ontological assumption of ethnic purity (Gilroy 1994: 54–5), through its popular use as a differentiator from the ethnically unnamed Australian core. 'Minority' often implies relegation to the margins of socio-cultural power, 'transnationalism' denies the possibility of loyalty to the residential homeland, neglecting the positioning of 'transnationals' within a culture or a nation-state (Rueschmann 2003: ix–xi) and 'multiculturalism' unwillingly homogenizes the diversity that is this term's main constituent.

The discursive limits of diaspora are likewise notable concerns within critical explorations of cultural identities. Ien Ang (2003) argues that the discourse of diaspora is fundamentally proto-nationalist and essentialist, and as such 'feeds into a *transnationalist nationalism* based on the presumption of internal ethnic sameness and external ethnic distinctiveness' (2003: 145). While Ang prefers the term 'hybridity' in place of 'diaspora' because it 'confronts and problematises boundaries' (2003: 149), that concept also 'remains problematic insofar as it assumes the meeting or mixing of completely separate and homogenous cultural spheres' (Barker 2004: 89–90). This is further evidenced by the deployment of hybridity in the analysis of identity markers, in particular those studies that centre on differences such as gender within groups of migrants (e.g. Clifford 1999; Wolska, Saggars and Hunt 2004).

In the climate of calls for renewed cultural homogenization in Australia at the beginning of the twenty-first century, the discussion of such critical tensions within the use of diaspora is especially important. In this way, our collection necessarily prefers and deploys 'diasporic hybridity' as an organizing principle, engaging with the debates and the possibilities that both terms embody and the cultural messiness that their combination allows and celebrates. Diasporic hybridity in Australian culture and cinema refers to the multi-layered (that is, hybrid) nature of Australianness, complemented and complicated by diasporic points of reference in constant conversation with one another. As many of the essays in this volume reveal, diasporic identity can be the site of 'support and oppression, emancipation and confinement, solidarity and division' (Ang 2003: 142).

### Introducing the chapters: *Diasporas of Australian Cinema*
For those readers navigating this book with little knowledge of Australian film-making, the following section is an attempt to sketch a rough history of Australian cinema's most significant moments and/or eras, and survey some key (diasporic) films, some of which may or may not be mentioned in the chapters. In addition, we use this opportunity to introduce the chapters that follow this Introduction and group them with their historical, thematic and/or narrative context in mind. For this reason, the chapters as they are described here are not in the order that they appear in the book.

Since its early years, Australian film-making has been produced by, and featured people from, diverse cultural backgrounds. Australia's first feature film celebrated the 'true-life' tale of infamous Irish-Australian bushranger Ned Kelly, on the run from police in *The Story of the Kelly Gang* (1906). The film's resonance with local audiences meant it was in distribution for 10 years. However, in the early years of Australian cinema many films were clearly in the service of the state, in particular its World War I and II efforts, such as Alfred Rolfe's *The Hero of the Dardanelles* (1915) or Charles Chauvel's *Forty Thousand Horsemen* (1940). These films are discussed in Chapter 7, 'Anzac's 'Others': "Cruel Huns" and "Noble Turks"'. Antje Gnida and Catherine Simpson argue that, while 'war films are not an obvious starting point for the exploration of Australia's diasporic cinema', film-making from and about the time of both world wars demonstrates shifts in the construction of Turkish and German identities in the service of an Australian nationalism. Read in a contemporary light, these films are also part of a discourse around the development of migration programs to Australia from both countries.

Australia had a thriving silent film industry in first decades of the twentieth century. However, during and since World War I, the story of Australian cinema has been one of 'boom' and 'bust', as the local industry succumbed to the pressure of the increasing dominance of the American market. By the middle of the twentieth century, lacking government support, Australian film-making had been reduced to the famed series of interwar newsreels and a small number of important feature films and documentaries, such as those by Harry Watt, Charles Chauvel, Ralph Smart and Lee Robinson.

Even within the context of a flagging cinema, diasporic subjects provided a specific locus for film-making and national self-reflection. Alongside the older government promotional films are landmark post-war docudramas such as *Mike and Stefani* (Ron Maslyn Williams 1952) that depicts the journey of a Ukrainian couple reuniting in a displaced persons (DP) camp in Germany and their subsequent journey to Australia. The film draws attention to 'the neglect of enforced displacement as a major theme of twentieth-century history' that 'demonstrates a reluctance to think beyond conventional histories and ideas of home and nation' (Webster 2006: 662). The final scenes, depicting gruelling selection interviews, upset Australian censors and saw the film limited to a governmental library release. One of the most popular documentaries of this postwar period of assimilation is the *Back of Beyond* (John Heyer 1954), which featured not only iconic mailman/bushman Tom Kruse on the world's longest mail run but other characters in the isolated outback, such as Bejah Dervish, the Afghan camel driver who 'fought the desert by compass and by Koran'.

One notable post-war diasporic film-maker from this 'hiatus' period is Italian migrant Giorgio Mangiamele. His experimental films *The Contract* (1953), *The Brothers* (1958) and *The Spag* (1962) were followed by his 1965 feature *Clay*, selected for competition at the Cannes Film Festival. Conomos (1992: 12) argues that Mangiamele and Ayten Kuyululu are 'mandatory figures to be negotiated', and have often been erased in orthodox histories of Australian cinema 'because they pose many unsettling questions about Anglo-Australian colonialism ... and theoretical frameworks for representing cultural otherness'.

The absence of local feature films on cinema screens during the 1950s and 1960s prompted agitators to declare that Australians had 'no daydreams of our own' (Weir 1958: 141). Renewed government and public interest in film-making, film funding, film scholarship and the training of film-makers in the late 1960s led to what is now known as the 'revival' or 'renaissance' of Australian film-making in the 1970s, a period which produced some of the most famous Australian films of all time including *Picnic at Hanging Rock* (Peter Weir 1975) and *My Brilliant Career* (Gillian Armstrong 1979).

The decade or so after the revival of the film industry has been noted for its reticence in exploring ethnic diversity and in reifying a 'more singular, monocultural Anglo-Australian definition of national identity' (Rattigan 1998: 23). Notable exceptions include five dramatic features that explore Greek, Turkish, Italian and Maltese Australian identities in various ways: Tom Cowan's *Promised Woman* (1975); Ayten Kuyululu's *The Golden Cage* (1975); Paul Cox's *Kostas* (1979); Donald Crombie's *Cathy's Child* (1979); and Michael Pattinson's *Moving Out* (1983).

The larger history of migration has meant that directors from non-English speaking origins are now credited for some of the most important films since the Australian cinema revival (O'Regan 1996: 352). George Miller, born of Greek immigrants who Anglicized their surname (Miliotis) to Miller, directed the seminal *Mad Max* (1979). Yoram Gross, a Polish Jew, is well known as a prolific animator and creator of the popular children's film *Dot and the Kangaroo* (1977). Nadia Tass, born Tassapolous in Greek Macedonia, made the popular and quirky *Malcolm* (1986). Rolf de Heer, of Dutch origin, has directed the celebrated films *Bad Boy Bubby* (1992), *The Tracker* (2002) and *Ten Canoes* (2006).

Of these 'renaissance' film-makers, it is Cox whose work has most consistently examined diasporic themes. In Chapter 11, '"A European Heart": Exile, Isolation and Interiority in the Life and Films of Paul Cox', Marek Haltof offers a historical location for Cox's early work. Cox's self-description as a homeless, 'exilic film-maker' is used to frame the stylistic choices and thematic concerns that shape *Lonely Hearts* (1982), *Man of Flowers* (1983) and *My First Wife* (1984), in addition to the aforementioned *Kostas*. As 'interior films', Cox's early works are found to construct personal and urban interiors that are simultaneously Australian and European.

Yet if 1970s film-making seemed resistant to diasporic experience, film-makers now routinely explore and deploy a range of genres, technologies and film-making styles in the communication of culturally complex phenomena. This is especially visible in the number of contemporary documentaries and short films that investigate cross-cultural tensions and the renewed public interest in the politics of migration post 9/11. The chapters by Susie Khamis and Sonia Tascón in this volume show how film-makers such as Tom Zubrycki use the range of genres, forms and techniques to explore prejudices attached to migrants, post-diasporic generations (Khamis) and those seeking asylum (Tascón) in Australia. In Chapter 13, 'Lebanese Muslims Speak Back: Two Films by Tom Zubrycki', Khamis places *Billal* (1996) and *Temple of Dreams* (2007) within what she terms the 'third-wave turmoil' of Lebanese Muslim migrants. Khamis moves from the films' negotiations of institutional bigotry and 'revved-up masculinity' to find an agency that tests the limits of 'diaspora' as a critical category. The politics of cross-cultural contact take an ethical turn in Chapter 4, '"I'm Falling in Your Love": Cross-cultural Romance and the Refugee Film', where

Tascón critically interrogates cross-cultural romances in Zubrycki's (2003) *Molly and Mobarak* and Karen Hodgkins' *Amanda and Ali* (2003) using a Levinasian ethical framework. The films work from an ethical perspective that seeks to overcome the undermining of multicultural imperatives that prevailed during the Howard era (1996–2007) of Australian government.

While Zubrycki's and Hodgkin's films articulate the political context of intimate cross-cultural relations in Howard's Australia, they also recall what is possibly the first prominent cross-cultural/diasporic romance in Australian cinema, featured in Michael Powell's classic post-migration comedy *They're a Weird Mob* (1966). Based on the novel by John O'Grady, *Weird Mob* explores Italian cultural difference in a Sydney setting. The film offers an anthropological take on Australianness from the perspective of Nino, an Italian immigrant who eventually settles down with an Anglo-Australian woman. Nino's emulation of working-class Australian behaviour highlights the 'weirdness' of many Australian customs, which he overcomes to start his new life. In contrast, Ayten Kuyululu's *The Golden Cage* (1975) features an unsuccessful cross-cultural romance between an Australian woman and a Turkish migrant. Unlike the romantic happy ending of *They're a Weird Mob*, a dystopian image of 1970s Australia emerges from this little-known film, which contrasts the experiences of two recently migrated Turkish men.

In the 1980s, following the success of micro-budget, independently financed genre film *Mad Max* (1979), the government encouraged investment in the film industry by introducing lucrative tax incentives (Division 10BA of the *Taxation Act*). This sparked a boom in production and a subsequent debate about the quality of films emerging from Australia. The scheme was substantially wound back in the late 1980s. Films dealing with cultural difference seem to have been relatively rare during the 1980s, but one recipient of the 10BA tax incentives was *Silver City* (1984), Sophia Turkiewicz's story of post-war Polish immigration set in the tin huts of a migrant compound. Renata Murawska notes in Chapter 12, 'Sophia Turkiewicz: Australianising Poles, or "Bloody Nuts and Balts"' in *Silver City*', that the film was seen to be 'anti-Australian' (see Rattigan 1991). Murawska finds that the cynically assimilationist Australia seen through the eyes of Polish post-war refugees was difficult to accept in the climate of an official insistence on multiculturalism, which saw European immigrants more agreeably positioned within the post-British Australian imaginary. Murawska's analysis of *Silver City* witnesses the merging of two worlds, Polish and Australian, and Turkiewicz's own attempts to inhabit the world of diasporic hybridity.

The situation changed significantly in the early 1990s, when cultural difference was celebrated in films such as the top-grossing romantic comedy *Strictly Ballroom* (Baz Luhrmann 1992), with its Spanish-Australian heroine, the avant-garde *BeDevil* (Tracey Moffatt 1992), the reconciliatory *The Crossing* (George Ogilvie 1990), the critically acclaimed *Nirvana Street Murder* (Aleksi Vellis 1990) and popular black comedy *Death in Brunswick* (John Ruane 1991).

Alongside these celebratory films, a darker vision of Australian multiculturalism emerged, voicing a critique of racist and unsympathetic attitudes towards diasporic figures and groups. Geoffrey Wright's (1992) *Romper Stomper* features Neo-Nazi white supremacists engaging in brutally violent attacks on members of Melbourne's Vietnamese community. A lesser known but equally compelling drama, *Aya* (Solrun Hoaas 1992), explores the deterioration of a bicultural marriage between a Japanese war bride and an Australian veteran over a 20-year period. The relationship descends into violence and bitterness, but Aya starts a new life for herself in Hobart and the film, as with *Romper Stomper*, ends on a note of hope for the future.

A number of films of this same period explore non Anglo-Australian teenage angst. Michael Jenkins' *The Heartbreak Kid* (1993) depicts a relationship between a Greek-Australian high school teacher (Claudia Karvan) and her student (Alex Dimitriades) while Ana Kokkinos's award-winning *Head On* (1997) sees a 19-year-old Greek-Australian negotiating sex, drugs and cultural heritage in the back streets and clubs of Melbourne (see Bennett 2007). In Chapter 10, 'Other Shorelines or the Greek-Australian Cinema', John Conomos uses the latter film to demonstrate the way 'certain film-makers of Greek-Australian descent have made films that delineate important aesthetic, cultural, exilic, gender, historical and political complexities, themes and stylistic configurations'. The film and Kokkinos herself are shown to form part of a larger network of films and film-makers in the past few decades dealing with Greek-Australian experience on and in film. In Conomos's mapping of such work, cultural and historical contexts dialogue with the 'always fluid Australian identity' explored by such films.

The complexities of cultural heritage and teenage self-discovery have continued to inform millennium films about the descendants of migrant families, such as the popular coming-of-age drama, Kate Woods' *Looking for Alibrandi* (2000). Based on Melina Mechetta's best-selling book, the film features a teenage Italian-Australian girl coming to terms with the sudden appearance of a father who never knew she existed, along with the suicide of her school sweetheart against the backdrop of her final year at a Sydney Catholic high school.

Themes of alienation, confusion and cultural traditions in transition and tension had already shaped the work of film-makers, and the representation of characters, from Asian countries. Hong Kong director Clara Law produced her first Australian feature, *Floating Life* (1995), after migrating to Melbourne in the early 1990s. It continues to attract an extraordinary level of critical commentary on its exploration of the transnational Chinese diaspora and Hong Kong pre-takeover angst (e.g. Kraicer 1996; Yue 2000; Teo 2001; Stein 2002; Mitchell 2003). Like *The Golden Cage*, *Aya* and *Silver City* before it, *Floating Life* is directed by a female film-maker and deals with the process of migration and first arrival – in this case, a diasporic Chinese family from Hong Kong. Spoken predominantly in Cantonese and German, *Floating Life* was Australia's first non-English speaking (NES) feature; it has been followed progressively (though cautiously) by the release of subtitled films that feature non-English speaking characters in an Australian setting.

Two such films, *Japanese Story* (Sue Brooks 2003) and the short film *The Last Chip* (Heng Tang 2006), are analyzed in this volume by Rebecca Coyle and Audrey Yue respectively. Coyle, in Chapter 9, 'Now You Blokes Own the Place', charts shifts within the Australian-Japanese relationship by contrasting Brooks' *Japanese Story* with Rachel Lucas's (2004) multi-generic surf film *Bondi Tsunami*. As generational moments of Australian-Japanese contact and identification, the films are found to 'offer perspectives on Australian attitudes to cultural difference and belonging, on notions of diasporic cultures and Australian "identities"' reflective of a chequered history of wars, migration, capitalism and tourism. Similarly marking generic shifts as reflective of social change and cultural contact, Audrey Yue explores the 'minor transnationalism' of the short film *The Last Chip* in Chapter 3. The film imports aspects of the Hong Kong gambling comedy to reread and revise Chinese identity, women's friendship and risk-taking in Australian cinema. Deploying an 'ethics of ethnic identity' (drawn from Chow and Foucault), Yue locates the global focus of the locally made short film as revealing the structures of subordination producing the female (especially Chinese) migrant in Australian film and culture.

*The Last Chip*'s politicized fusion of comedy genres is an identifiable feature of films from the early 2000s, especially evident in the return of 'wog comedies' such as *The Wog Boy* (Aleksi Vellis 2000) and *Fat Pizza* (Paul Fenech 2003). These features have their genesis in the popular stage show *Wogs out of Work* and the television comedy *Pizza* (Paul Fenech 2000–5), a series made for SBS, a free-to-air government-supported multicultural television channel. Felicity Collins combines an analysis of both films with *They're a Weird Mob* in Chapter 6, 'Wogboy Comedies and the National Type'. Collins unsettles the 'tolerant society' with respect to all three 'landmark comedies' that 'have turned the comic spotlight on "Australian ethnicity" as a work-in-progress'. Collins notes that these wog comedies 'reconfigure the Australian ocker' (via Speed 2005) as a hybrid cinematic figure, but she questions the extent to which such characterizations leave the 'key characteristics' of the 'longstanding national type' undisturbed.

It is this combination of changing ethnicity and 'traditional' Australian masculinities that has become a defining feature of many films in the 2000s. In *Footy Legends* (Khoa Do 2006), Vietnamese-Australian director Khoa Do features Mediterranean and Asian figures in a film about culturally disparate males lacking opportunities who are drawn together through football. The popular documentary *The Bra Boys* (Sunny Abberton and Macario De Souza 2007) soon followed, profiling a surfer 'tribe' in Maroubra, Sydney in the wake of violent 2005 race riots that took place around Sydney's Cronulla Beach between white nationalists and Australians of so-called 'Middle Eastern appearance'.

Within this post-9/11 context of the beach/border as contested space came *Lucky Miles* (James Michael Rowland 2007), a comedy about illegally transported male refugees from Indonesia, Cambodia and Iraq. The film takes the cinematic preoccupation with masculinity and ethnicity into a critique of recent immigration and border control practices. In Chapter 2, 'Tinkering at the Borders: *Lucky Miles* and the Diasporic (No) Road Movie', Catherine Simpson marks the ways the film speaks to 'the history of migration and its associated regulation of diasporic difference', while situating the film within a broad taxonomy of interrelated types of diasporic Australian films. Taking her lead from the film's promotion, Simpson uses the themes of 'difference, distance and dud maps' to gauge the film's embodiment of Australian film-making traditions as well as its mobilization of a diasporically gendered politics of place.

The regulation of male refugees' difference finds its counterbalance in the conflation of diasporic femaleness with forms of neurosis. Since *Floating Life*, which depicts the neurotic and depressed protagonist Bing, several releases feature emotionally unstable mothers: *La Spagnola* (Steve Jacobs 2001), *Romulus My Father* (Richard Roxburgh 2007), *The Home Song Stories* (Tony Ayres 2007) and *Clubland* (Cherie Nowlan 2007). Their madness in most cases is implied as a 'loss of control' over their environment in response to the process of migration and its consequential alienation, a theme explored by Anthony Lambert in Chapter 5, 'White Aborigines: Women, Space, Mimicry and Mobility'. Attending to the absence of Indigenous Australians from discussions of diaspora, Lambert explores the mimicry of Aboriginality by British and American women in *Journey Among Women* (Tom Cowan 1977) and *Over the Hill* (1992) as a displacement brought on by a crisis in the perception of space. The films thus contextualize the transgressions of Indigenous space by migrating western women in recent films such as *Jindabyne* (Ray Lawrence 2006). For Lambert, such crises are emblematic of a confused and contentious white postcolonial feminism.

At the same time, as *Floating Life* and *Home Song Stories* have shown, this kind of 'madness' or psychosis is not limited to Anglo-Celtic women. Gregory Dolgopolov argues in Chapter 7, 'Excess in Oz: The Crazy Russian and the Quiet Australian', that female 'excess' is often a characteristic associated with Russian women and to a lesser extent Russian men, in order to normalize the 'non-ethnically marked' Australian. Dolgopolov surveys a range of films and observes that 'Russians are rarely represented as a community of loyal, settled migrants; worthy members of Australia's seemingly cohesive multicultural community'. Even the most endearing of Russian excesses become 'symbolically integrated' into Australian norms and Australian life, losing the 'un-Australian difference' in their processes of cultural and narrative assimilation.

Definitions of Australian and non-Australian are simultaneously underwritten by the complexities of cultural contact and film-making practice. Ben Goldsmith and Brian Yecies, in the final chapter 'Sejong Park's *Birthday Boy* and Korean-Australian Encounters', explore Korean-Australian film-making, positioning *Birthday Boy* (2004) as an 'exemplar of both the artisanal and collective modes of production that for Naficy mark out diasporic film-making'. Extending this focus to production work on *Musa* (Kim Sung-su 2001) and *Shadowless Sword* (Kim Young-jun, 2005), the authors explore Australian-Korean collaborations that do not speak directly to the Korean diaspora but instead 'form part of a complex, creative, transnational intercultural dialogue which is little remarked either in Australia or Korea'. The flow of film work between countries productively confuses cultures, identities and technological processes. Locating the diasporic in contemporary film-making is, again, a process of comprehending diaspora as 'a category of practice' (Brubaker 2005: 12).

**Conclusion**

As these descriptions suggest, the focus of this volume is on the role of film-makers and representations in forming the diasporas of Australian cinema. The chapters in this book are subsequently organized and presented with reference to their specific diasporic focus: *theories* (Simpson, Yue, Tascón, Lambert); *representations* (Collins, Dolgopolov, Gnida and Simpson, Coyle, Conomos); and *film-makers* (Khamis, Haltof, Murawska, Goldsmith and Yecies).

The diasporic ontologies in Australian cinema addressed throughout the following chapters encourage inclusive rather than exclusive modes of identity formation, explicitly referencing migrants, their descendants and the cultural products they inspire or initiate. This volume fosters an imaginative and critical space not only for national cultural heterogeneity, but also for multiplicity within the construction of individual identities, which does not assume an a priori conflict between 'Australian' and diasporic points of identification.

The chapters in this book focus on popular as well as lesser known films, including dramatic feature films, documentaries and a range of short films, all important in understanding the formation and insistent reassembling of the diasporic identities of Australian cinema (of filmic figures and film-makers, reflective of the available definitions and experiences of Australianness). The editors and individual authors of this volume are most interested in the cross-cultural points of intersection that constitute and critique the Australian diversity exemplified by filmic texts and by particular film-makers. What this book does not do, and what would constitute an equally fascinating field of inquiry to complement this content, is to address industrial factors of Australian cinema impacting on its diasporic aspects, such as film policy, funding, distribution or exhibition. We hope that such studies will soon appear, as will dialogical extensions of the following discussions of diasporas of Australian cinema.

Like the projected shadows that meet the central figure of Michael Bates' The Projectionist, this book represents a negotiation of past and present, old and new, here and there, persistence and possibility. The confronting images in Bates' film form the context for the diasporic subject where diaspora 'can be taken as a figure for modern, spectral subjectivity, homeless and self-haunted' (Davis 2006: 341). Yet, while images and memories linger, they do not limit movement, as diasporic experience is also a negotiation with the space of the local. The essays assembled in Diasporas of Australian Cinema are projections on a path that is not only haunted, but enlivened. They understand Australian cinema and culture 'in a dynamic, fluid sense' which, as Mirzoeff (1999a: 131) has argued, 'offers a way to analyze the hybrid, hyphenated, syncretic global diaspora in which we live'.

# 2

# Tinkering at the Borders: *Lucky Miles* and the Diasporic (no) Road Movie

## Catherine Simpson

Warm are the still and lucky miles,
White shores of longing stretch away ...
Restored! Returned! The lost are borne
On seas of shipwreck home at last ...

(W.H. Auden (1939) 1966: 238–39)

During the late 1990s and early 2000s, independent political documentaries, including Clara Law's *Letters to Ali* (2004) and Tom Zubrycki's *Molly and Mobarak* (2003), contested the prevailing anti-asylum-seeker discourse in Australian media. Australian feature film-making, however, had been noticeably silent on this issue until the release of Michael James Rowland's debut, *Lucky Miles* (2007). This film revolves around the quest of three exiles to seek civilization, resist capture and survive in the desert after being abandoned by an Indonesian fishing vessel in remote Western Australia. Pursued by an Army Reservist unit that seems more interested in fishing and football than the (seemingly impossible) task of maintaining border integrity, the three exiles become more and more lost as they wander deeper into the desert.

This chapter dialogues directly with the introduction of this book, further theorizing diasporic hybridity in the Australian cinematic landscape and simultaneously engaging with broader discussions around the concept of multiculturalism. I argue that diasporic hybridity has manifested in specific ways in Australian national cinema, and that extant theories of transnational and diasporic cinemas (Naficy 2001; Marks 2000) cannot be unproblematically transplanted and grafted on to the Australian context. A unique set of conditions constitutes the contextual development of Australian society and cinema, such as the history of migration and its associated regulation of diasporic difference; the domination of the 'White Australia' policy for the majority of the twentieth century followed by state-sponsored policies of assimilation and multiculturalism since 1977; Australia's status as a new world and a settler society, as well as its geographic isolation and position as 'south of the west' (Gibson 1993); and the impact of government funding on the Australian film industry. All of these issues shape the kinds of films produced in Australia. Without being intentionally prescriptive, I outline a taxonomy of some of the films, broadly labelled 'diasporic', that have been produced in Australia since the revival. Through the example of *Lucky Miles*, this chapter then makes a case for a distinctive type of diasporic film-making in Australia, one that is rooted within identifiable Australian cultural traditions.

*Lucky Miles* could be considered part of an expanding international genre of festival films which Yosefa Loshitzky labels 'journeys of hope' – films portraying migration from the homeland to the host country and the associated struggle and suffering endured along the way (Loshitzky 2006: 745). Internationally, since Xavier Koller's *Journey of Hope* – about a group of ill-fated Turkish Kurds seeking asylum in Switzerland – won Best Foreign Film at Cannes in 1990, an ever-growing number of high-profile festival films focus on the issue of forcibly or voluntarily displaced persons and their quest for asylum, such as *Borders* (Mostafa Djadjam 2001), *In this World* (Michael Winterbottom 2002) or *Baran* (Majid Majidi 2001). Loshitzky argues that this genre subverts the dominant public discourse which dehumanizes and criminalizes migrants.

Very few films have attempted to explore such journeys of hope with a playful and humorous tone, as *Lucky Miles* does. The film is marketed as a comedy about 'difference, distance and dud maps' (LuckyMiles.com), and it is these three tropes, both in the film and in Australian cinema and culture more broadly, that structure this chapter. *Lucky Miles* is one of the first Australian feature films to let diasporic 'others' into the 'heartland' (Collins and Davis 2004: 100) of Australian cinema. Exploring the recurring tropes, narratives and cultural metaphors of such diasporically hybrid cinema, this chapter marks the relationship of migration and diaspora to shifting notions of Australianness, while emphasizing the cinematic reiteration of dominant settler conceptions of Australianness, especially those that are rooted in a sense of place.

### Difference: 'We decide who comes to this country and the circumstances in which they come.' (Prime Minister John Howard at Liberal Party conference, 31 October 2001, cited in Manne 2004: 41)

At the dawn of the twenty-first century, despite record numbers of émigrés from non-English speaking backgrounds (NESB), John Howard's government (1996–2007) made direct attacks on the ideals of multiculturalism and returned Australia to an era of assimilation. Many argued that the 2004 election was won on the basis of the 'children overboard' saga and the *Tampa* crisis, with the Prime Minister proclaiming with 'great bravado and little irony' (Hage 2006) that: 'We decide who comes to this country and the basis upon which they come.' While this proclamation came in the context of the perceived threat of asylum-seekers illegally gaining access to the country on boats from Indonesia through its limitless uncharted borders, it was also an ideological attack against the 20 or so years of multiculturalism.

Throughout the 1980s and 1990s, multiculturalism – as Geoffrey Brahm Levey states – had acquired powerful symbolic significance in what it meant to be Australian (Levey 2007: 199). The multicultural conceptualization of Australian nationhood became a familiar concept in the 1980s as a set of policies and a cultural ideal that critiqued prevailing monocultural views of national identity, and opened up the possibilities for Australian cinema and culture more broadly. Multiculturalism was the cornerstone of Paul Keating's government's *Creative Nation* policy document in 1994, and until the early 2000s this had been the dominant framework within which to theorize ethnic difference. This vision of Australian cultural diversity facilitates a special institutional space for various NESB communities (both diasporic and Indigenous) within Australian life. However, as a state-sanctioned discourse, multiculturalism came under attack from a range of political and cultural theorists for its perceived inability to account for Australian social realities. It was also seen as tokenistic, pigeonholing ethnic cultures so they remained apart from the mainstream, while strengthening the notion of an Anglo-Australian cultural core.

From a political science perspective, Brian Galligan and Winsome Roberts (2003) in their paper, 'Australian Multiculturalism: Its Rise and Demise', argue that multiculturalism is now a poor description of what we have in Australia because:

> migrants are for the most part geographically dispersed; they educate their children in English along with other Australian school children; and those children have a high propensity to marry out of their parents' ethnic group. Australia does not have cultural groups that endure in any significant way. Boxing up the cultural differences that first generation migrants bring and the declining remnants that endure to the second and third generation makes little conceptual sense. (Galligan and Roberts 2003)

The implication of Galligan and Roberts' argument here is that identity is something that is fixed rather than fluid, and that geography necessitates a sharp break with historical and cultural practices which will only 'endure' as the 'declining remnants' of a past life. Such thinking does not reflect the changes that may occur over the duration of a lifetime, nor even the public/ private divide within a person's daily experiences. That the children of migrants generally speak English in ways indistinguishable from their ethnically unnamed Australian peers is, as Ien Ang argues, 'a sign of integration in the dominant culture ... [but] it belies the fact that at home, they often partake in a very different cultural world' (Ang 2001a: 14). This comes particularly to the fore in *Hybrid Life,* a 13-part series of short films and documentaries produced by SBSi and screened on SBS in 2001. Kuranda Seyit's short from this series, *Always a Visitor* (2000), shows that while growing up in outer Western Sydney's Emu Plains, it was detrimental for the Turkish-born Seyit to identify as such amongst his peer group. Nevertheless, his Turkish fluency enables him to move fluidly between the worlds of the Turkish diaspora and the mainstream Australian community. While he speaks 'Aussie' English in a way indistinguishable from his peers (which enables him to take a leading role in the growing Muslim community in Sydney), a relationship to both (past) cultural heritage and (present) cultural hybridity endures.

The assimilationist logic of Galligan and Roberts' argument represents the discursive justification of the Howard government's push for a focus on 'Australian values', citizenship and language tests, and the de-funding of culturally specific institutions and agencies. While hackneyed and insular visions for the nation-state prevailed at government levels throughout the Howard years, portrayals of diasporic subjectivity and cultural diversity have became an unremarkable aspect of the Australian filmic landscape. In contrast to Galligan and Roberts, the dominant discourse evident from across the Australian cinema archive is not necessarily one of assimilation. When a character is featured who is *not* from the dominant ethnically unnamed Australian culture, that person's difference is almost uniformly defined through their ethnic origin. On cursory inspection, more than half the 17 Australian features and documentaries represented at the 2007 Sydney Film Festival displayed non-Anglo Celtic central characters, and *Lucky Miles* won the audience award for most popular film. However, as James Bennett claims, the mere fact that diasporic 'others' feature more frequently in Australian cinema by no means equates to unproblematic depictions of multicultural identities (Bennett 2007: 64).

Another critique of the multicultural project in practice is that it has led to a cultural location of various ethnic communities that reduces their capacity to influence a hegemonically unnamed Australian ethnicity, with the exception of the commodification and consumption of food, music and dance. Cultural theorist Sneja Gunew (1994) claims that 'multiculturalism in Australia is acceptable as a celebration of costumes, customs and cooking' (1994: 22). While the public funding of the multicultural project meant the establishment of institutions and funding for NESB communities such as SBS, Australia's multicultural broadcaster, it has also meant that anything labelled 'ethnic' is not seen as the domain of the mainstream population, nor is it regarded as of interest to the ABC, the national public broadcaster, which sees its support base as representing this 'core' group; it is therefore relegated to the viewership of the SBS, with its comparatively low audience numbers (Simpson 2000: 60–63).

In her article on diasporic subjectivity in contemporary Australian documentary, Belinda Smaill (2006) makes the argument that it is through the mainstream television documentary that we have seen the most prolific number of diasporic representations. However, unlike the films examined by Hamid Naficy and Laura Marks, which for the most part are located within the rubric of experimental and artisanal mode of fiction film-making, Smaill points out that these local films adhere to the established conventions and codes of the TV documentary.

Hamid Naficy's and Laura Marks' theories of 'accented cinema' and 'intercultural cinema' respectively complement one another by broadly arguing that diasporic film-makers conform to/seek out a particular set of formal and stylistic tendencies that enable them to be spoken about together (such as their artisanal and experimental production mode, their emphasis on journeying, their multilinguality, their haptic visuality and their use of 'accented' speech and epistolatory). In most cases, the institutional context which governs the production of these independent documentaries (they are funded through collaborative arrangements with the government film-funding bodies such as the Australian Film Commission, the Film Finance Corporation and sometimes the various state film bodies), combined with the projected expectations of the public service television audience, means that they 'narrativise diasporic experience' (Smaill 2006: 272).

In *Lucky Miles*, as well as the vast majority of Australian feature films, diasporic experience also manifests through the storytelling process rather than any experimentation with form and style, as I attempt to show in the taxonomy of post-revival film-making below. The institutional arrangements governing the making of documentaries related by Smaill also govern the production of most feature film-making in Australia. So, perhaps unlike other aspects of identity, to a large extent diasporic identity has become regulated and institutionalized through the government funding of an industry which demands that its feature films, given audience expectations, be made within a fairly traditional mode of storytelling. The revival of the Australian film industry also came at a time when multiculturalism was becoming the dominant discourse for imagining the nation (Bennett 2007: 61). Admittedly, many of the directors of these films listed below are not, and/or do not necessarily identify as, diasporic. Nonetheless, a taxonomy in a book such as this gives readers unfamiliar with Australian film output a broad brushstroke of the kinds of films which deal with ethnic difference in the Australian context. This taxonomy is one of criticism rather than production, and evidently there is also a lot of bleed between categories. Nonetheless, those films which experiment with form and style in category six below constitute a fraction of the output and for the most part, I would argue, are short films such as *The Projectionist* (Michael Bates 2002).

## Six types of diasporic Australian film

### *1. Migratory self-inscription*
This category has been adapted from Belinda Smaill's (2006) excellent discussion of diasporic TV documentaries, and has been expanded to include all films in which the film-maker has an intimate connection with his or her subjects. It could be that they are representing their own sense of difference or ethnicity, or that the material is about themselves – their life story. They are often about the process of migration and settling in for first-generation migrants. While *Lucky Miles* concerns the exile's journey, it is not the film-maker's own story; it therefore does not fit into this category, which includes the documentaries Smaill notes and in addition *Floating Life* (Clara Law 1996), *Silver City* (Sophia Turkiewicz 1984), *My Mother India* (Safina Uberoi 2001), *Aya* (Solrun Hoaas 1990), *Letters to Ali*, *Romulus My Father*, *The Home Song Stories* (Tony Ayres 2007) and *Fistful of Flies* (Monica Pellizzari 1996), as well as the short films *Sadness* (Tony Ayres 1999), Monica Pellizzari's *Rabbit on the Moon* (1987) and *Just Desserts* (1993), Christina Andreef's *Excursion to the Bridge of Friendship* (1993), Laleen Jayamanne's *A Song of Ceylon* (1985) and *Birthday Boy* (Sejong Park 2004). (Many of these films, such as Jayamanne's and Pellizzari's, use experimental techniques, which means they would fit into category six as well).

### 2. Wog comedies

These are films in which send-ups of ethnicity or cultural tendencies, and stereotypes often become the prime inspiration for comedy. Leslie Speed (2005) has coined these films 'wogsploitation'. They often rely on crass humour and a propensity for exploring the Australian vernacular, as well as focusing on masculinity – examples include *They're a Weird Mob* (Michael Powell 1966), *Nirvana Street Murder* (Aleksi Vellis 1990), *Death in Brunswick* (John Ruane 1991), *Fat Pizza* (Paul Fenech 2003), *Wog Boy* (Aleksi Vellis 2000), *Footy Legends* (Khoa Do 2006), *Spank!* (Ernie Clark 1999), *Greeks Bearing Guns* (John Tatoulis 2000), *La Spagnola* (Steve Jacobs 2001). *Lucky Miles'* focus on masculinity and comic ethnic stereotypes (particularly Indonesian but also Indigenous-Australian) enables it to fit into this category. In some of these films, such as *Footy Legends* and *Bra Boys* (Sunny Abberton 2007), sport is seen to bridge the gap between belonging and masculinity. Felicity Collins discusses this 'genre' extensively in Chapter 6 of this book.

### 3. Coming of age through ethnicity

This set of films often exemplifies conflict between NESB youth and their parents' (sometimes) rigid ideas of cultural maintenance. The theme of being trapped between two cultures is dominant. However, as Collins and Davis have argued, many of these films resist the 'nostalgic tendency in the coming-of-age story' and instead demand an acknowledgement of shame and injury in the present in a way that is enabling (Collins and Davis 2004: 169). Examples include *Looking for Alibrandi* (Kate Woods 2000), *Heartbreak Kid* (Michael Jenkins 1993), *Beneath Clouds* (Ivan Sen 2004), *Strictly Ballroom* (Baz Luhrmann 1992), *Head On* (Ana Kokkinos 1998), *Moving Out* (Michael Pattinson 1983), *Jewboy* (Tony Krawitz 2005), *Serenades* (Mojgan Khadem 2001), and the short films *Only the Brave* (Ana Kokkinos 1992), *Always a Visitor* (Kuranda Seyit 2000) and *Delivery Day* (Khoa Do 2000).

### 4. Fleeting representations (bit parts)

These films have non-Anglo-Celt Australians as minor characters employed to move the story along. They often perform the role of emphasizing the dominance of ethnically unnamed Australian. They may be vice/foil/or comic relief in a number of Australian films. Often these characters are presented as an unremarkable part of the landscape of Australian society – for example, the Chinese nudist restaurateur in *Love Serenade* (Shirley Barrett 1996), the Lebanese neighbour in *The Castle* (Rob Sitch 1997), the Russian Jewish father in *Shine* (Scott Hicks 1996), the Vietnamese gang and German mother of Davey in *Romper Stomper* (Geoffrey Wright 1992), Eastern European father in *Soft Fruit* (Christina Andreef 1999), *Dogs in Space* (Richard Lowenstein 1987). Some of these films also emphasize the 'melting pot' definition of Australian identity. The centring of the three non-Australians is in no way 'fleeting' in *Lucky Miles*.

### 5. The tourist

These are films in which a foreign tourist/traveller is indeed out of place, needing an Aussie (usually ethnically unmarked) offsider as a guide in the new culture/country – examples are *Heaven's Burning* (Craig Lahiff 1997), *Japanese Story* (Sue Brooks 2003), *Goddess of 1967* (Clara Law 2000), *Howling III: The Marsupials* (Philippe Mora 1987), *Lantana* (Ray Lawrence

2001), *Crocodile Dundee* (Peter Faiman 1986), *My Brilliant Career* (Gillian Armstrong 1979), *Razorback* (Russell Mulcahy 1984), *Wolf Creek* (Greg McLean 2005), *Travelling Light* (Kathryn Millard 2003), *Lucky Miles* and *Dallas Doll* (Ann Turner 1994). There is only rarely a sense that the tourist is going to become a permanent fixture of Australian society, unless of course they die (as in *Wolf Creek*, *Razorback*, *Lantana*, *Japanese Story*, *Dallas Doll*)! They are mostly just passing through.

## 6. Experimental diasporic diversity

Often, these films experiment with form and style. They have a strong aesthetic focus where the diasporic hybridity is part and parcel of innovation in form and style. These films come closest to what Naficy describes as accented cinema, although they may not adhere to all the characteristics he describes – examples are *Letters to Ali* (Clara Law), *Beneath Clouds* and Tracey Moffatt's *BeDevil* (1993). There are also a number of short films such as *The Projectionist*, *Excursion to the Bridge of Friendship* and *A Song of Ceylon* which fit this classification. *Lucky Miles'* fairly conventional road movie quest structure means it does not fit into this category.

In addition to these categories, there is also an emerging group of films in which ethnic difference is evident, such as *Little Fish* (Rowan Woods 2005), Paul Cox's films, *Romulus, My Father, Soft Fruit* and *Finished People* (Khoa Do 2003), but does not become a structuring narrative (or otherwise) device in the film. In other words, these films reflect a 'melting pot' notion of Australian life where the difference is accepted as simply another (non-contested) aspect of Australian culture.

As illustrated by this taxonomy, within the critical organization of films whose themes and content could broadly be labelled 'diasporic' or 'multicultural', the theoretical frameworks of both Marks and Naficy are limited in their capacity to account for the Australian context. *Lucky Miles* demonstrates this through its fairly traditional narrative and road movie 'quest' structure, which I further elaborate upon in the final two sections of this chapter. The film speaks differently to the institutionalization of diasporic hybridity through both its contemporary relevance and its movement beyond the singular function of 'narrativizing of diasporic experience'.

In 1998, Ghassan Hage critiqued Australia's state-sanctioned multiculturalism because, he argued, it promoted ethnic difference as something enriching for the Anglo-Celtic core. It became an:

> established power structure which always positions the migrant or Asian in the position
> of the Other, the tolerated rather than the tolerator … where White Australia as occupiers
> of the national space control, tolerate, enjoy and manage difference, diversity and
> ethnicity (Smith 2004: 3, 9).

James Bennett (2007) argues that most representations of multicultural Australianness (in feature film-making at least) have been tackled by (male) white Australian directors (2007: 62). *Lucky Miles* is a film in which a space for the 'other' is *created* and defined by the dominant group, an observation that does not necessarily refer to the ethnic origin of the scriptwriters nor the production context (the government funding) of the film. In fact, *Lucky Miles* involved intense collaboration and consultation between the Khmer, Iraqi and Indonesian communities in its writing and pre-production, and according to the director this is the first Australian feature since Peter Weir's *The Year of Living Dangerously* (1982) to feature Indonesian characters. However, within the film itself we learn little about the cultures and places from which these characters have come. While some sense of diasporic difference emanates from the characters' interactions and conflict in the film, in the long run it is subjugated to and concerns the universal focus of the story: the men's survival in a harsh, foreign environment. Director Michael James Rowland emphasizes the universality of the story when he comments: 'We know the back stories of these guys; we know where they come from and where they go after they come into our society.' (McFarlane 2007: 26) This leads to another possible reading: that any performance of cultural particularity is instead relegated to the characters' overriding quest for survival in the harsh, isolated Kimberley region. To attract funding for the film, *Lucky Miles*' creators used the pitch 'three men lost in the desert looking for a liberal western democracy'. In this sense, understanding their present place, rather than their ancestry or diasporic difference, is far more important. The remaining sections of this paper attempt to engage with how this film positions the (migrant) quest(s) for survival in ways that work to extend previously established, non-Indigenous, relationships with the land(scape) as threatening.

**Distance: 'If you stop, you're stuffed.'** (Sandy in *Japanese Story*, Sue Brooks 2003)

Within these 'journeys of hope', Loshitzky (2006) signals the dialectical relationship between the gaze of the tourist/spectator on the one hand and that of the refugee on the other (2006: 752). The two films, *'In This World* and *Journey of Hope* deprive the spectator of the scopophilic "touristic" pleasure, subordinating his or her gaze to the refugees gaze in the pursuit of survival' (2006: 752). Likewise, in *Lucky Miles*, there are few sweeping long shots portraying the drama and sublime beauty of the iconic Australian landscape. In fact, the director tried to foreground the 'banality of their [the exiles'] existence' (McFarlane 2007: 24). In *Lucky Miles*, the camera succumbs to the gaze of the displaced asylum-seekers as they traverse the inhospitable and scrubby desert terrain before them, in pursuit of a road to either Broome or to Perth. The alienation of the asylum-seekers is further emphasized by the physical environment and objects and spaces within it. At one point they chance upon a little shanty in the middle of the desert, only to find it deserted, containing only a few tins of food and an abandoned car wreck.

Australia's 'tyranny of distance' made it a difficult territory to colonize, and colonization came relatively late. As a result, it is now a difficult territory to access for those seeking asylum, unlike other 'desirable' countries such as the United States and the nations of Europe, which share land borders with many countries. While Geoffrey Blainey originally used the phrase 'tyranny of distance' to describe Australia's relationship with the Europe, particularly the United Kingdom, it is now more often used to describe the situation *within* Australia – Australians' distance from one another, dotted around the huge continent. This isolation, or 'tyranny of distance', takes on added significance in the context of émigrés and asylum-seekers. Distance from the rest of the world has compelled (as a matter of survival) most diasporic communities in Australia to integrate quickly into the broader community, more so than in the United States and Europe. This, combined with a government-sanctioned policy of multiculturalism and a government-funded film industry, has spawned a series of diasporic films which often say more about the new country, Australia, and its existing hegemonic tropes than the old. *Lucky Miles* seems typical in this regard.

As well as contributing to the distinctive Australian genre of the 'no road' film, as discussed below, *Lucky Miles* also exhibits a fascination with the car and mobility, which I have described elsewhere as 'antipodean automobility' (Simpson 2006). The isolation of Australia's country roads and long distances between major urban centres means Australians depend on their cars not only for mobility but also for survival. Outside major urban centres, alternatives to car-based travel rarely exist. If a vehicle breaks down or crashes in a remote area, there is a possibility that no one will offer aid: 'a crash in the bush, in the outback, reduces us all to nothing ... and plugs into our deepest fears and desires' (Kitson 2003: 68). This car-survival (or not) has provoked a number of film-makers to abandon or maroon their protagonists through car crashes, breakdowns or boggings in the outback or in 'hick' country towns, to explore this auto-*immobility* (Simpson 2006). For example, in *Shame* (Steve Jodrell 1988), Asta's motorbike breaks down then she gets stuck in the redneck town of Ginborak; in *High Tide* (Gillian Armstrong 1987), Liligets stuck in Eden after her Valiant breaks down and she loses her job; in *Japanese Story* (Sue Brooks 2003), the central characters are marooned in the bush after their Landcruiser gets bogged; in *Walkabout* (Nicolas Roeg 1971), two children are abandoned in the bush by their suicidal father who sets his VW Beetle alight; and in *Wolf Creek* (Greg McLean 2005), a gruesome fate awaits three backpackers left at the mercy of a local madman after their dodgy Falcon breaks down in the outback (Simpson 2006).

While not strictly a car crash, the opening shot of *Lucky Miles* sees the characters marooned on the national border by an Indonesian fishing boat, that liminal, interstitial space between land and sea, between Australia and *not* Australia. But *Lucky Miles*' 'antipodean automobility' is not limited to its diasporic figures. The army reservists also have to get their car going to survive. Finally, to show how thoroughly adapted to their new environment the lost exiles have become, a humorous scene close to the end of the film displays the Iraqi 'qualified engineer' getting an abandoned car wreck going, echoing those *mutikars* from the ingenious *Bush Mechanics* series (Clarsen 2002). These exiles' ability to survive in Australian cinema's heartland, the desert – a place where 'real' Australians live (Collins and Davis 2004: 100) – means they've legitimately earned the title 'Australian' if they so desire it – or at the very least, the right to refuge.

**Dud maps: 'It's a road movie without a road; it's uniquely Australian.'** (Director Michael James Rowland in conversation with Brian McFarlane) (McFarlane 2007: 26)

For the majority of *Lucky Miles*, the exiles are lost, traversing by foot the harsh desert terrain. While they possess a map, even Western cartographers' lines don't mean a thing if you can't *read* the land or find a road. This is not the first film to be described as 'a road movie without roads'. *Lucky Miles* could in fact be considered an extension to the subgenre which Fiona Probyn has labelled the 'no road' film. The 'no road' film pays tribute to Stephen Muecke's ficto-critical text, *No Road: Bitumen All the Way* (1997). To date, 'no road' films include *Rabbit Proof Fence* (Phillip Noyce 2002), *The Tracker* (Rolf de Heer 2002), *One Night the Moon* (Rachel Perkins 2001), *Beneath Clouds* (Ivan Sen 2002) and *Wind* (Iven Sen 1999), amongst others. The 'no road' film has a few defining characteristics, such as being without bitumen (read: colonized) roads and in includes 'different epistemological traces' to the traditional road movies that, unless you're an Indigenous tracker, you 'might not be able to know from the inside' (Probyn 2005). The Australian 'no road' film denies the nihilism of the traditional US road movie, or the 'freedom on the road to nowhere' as Timothy Corrigan typifies the genre, because in:

> postcolonial Australia … the road does not lead to 'nowhere' with its connotations of *terra nullius* … rather it leads into, on to and through, someone else's already culturally inscribed land … the no road films illustrate above all the 'somewhere-ness' of place in contrast to the Nowhereness of unbounded, unmapped 'space' (Probyn 2005).

So in all these 'no road' films, the tracker is central, performing the vital function guiding the non-Indigenous Australians on the road, or the 'no road' as the case may be where there are no maps, or rather just 'dud maps'. Interestingly, the only redeeming, fully functioning character in *Lucky Miles* is one of the Indigenous Army Reservist who is sensible, technologically savvy and gets his team out of many sticky situations. In a minor way, he performs the role of the guide in the film. However, his role is further complicated by the presence of the other, less obvious Indigenous Army Reservist, whose lack of tracking expertise is the source of much humour which in effect de-essentializes the 'noble savage' mystical tracker stereotype.

The film also exhibits some of the characteristics of the hegemonic European sensibility towards Australian space. Even the title of the film, *Lucky Miles*, adapted from the W.H. Auden poem, reflects that familiar laconic nihilistic relationship to country which denies the bush or the outback a cultural value and reinscribes that idea of it being 'an empty expanse, a tabula rasa' (Dargis, cited in Cohen and Hark 1997: 1) – or, in Australian terms, a *terra nullius*. The director reflects this when he says: 'When you come to Australia, you walk inland, thinking, "Surely there'll be something there." But there's nothing but the desert.' (McFarlane 2007: 26)

And the humorous laconic tone of *Lucky Miles* which emanates from that very European sensibility towards the landscape invokes the famous scene from *Gallipoli* (Peter Weir 1981), when Archy and Frank walk over the expansive salt-pan in Western Australia on their way to enlist for World War I. They meet a camel driver whose isolation is such that he hasn't even found out a war is going on. When Archy and Frank confront him with the idea that Australia might be invaded by the Germans, the camera follows his gaze to reveal a vast 'empty' tract of land, and he responds: 'They can bloody have it.' Likewise, to the would-be asylum-seeker to Australia, even the title of the film – *Lucky Miles* – seems to be posing the question: 'Do you *really* want to come *here*, to the "lucky" country?'

In the context of the 'no road' film, *Lucky Miles* contemplates the positionality of non-Indigenous non-Australians within both the land and dominant Australian cultural tropes. Are they an extension of the settler relationship with land? Do they inherit the legacy of dispossession and the same conquistadorial perspective on land(scape) to which Ross Gibson (1993) has alluded? The fact that these characters react in the same way that countless non-Indigenous Australians have before indicates the prevailing dominance of this perspective. The director reinforces this: 'It's the story of Burke and Wills updated to reflect immigration patterns of recent years. We've shamelessly reworked a national myth to sell to the world.' (McFarlane 2007: 26)

At the same time, the presence of a key Indigenous characters points to further cultural and critical possibilities, as Stephen Muecke (1997) indicates in *No Road*, that come from seeing and understanding the country/land differently, particularly in relationship to Aboriginal sovereignty over the land, meaning that non-Indigenous people (and some Indigenous people, if this film is anything to go by) might have to 'leave the bitumen, to leave the roads and finally to get lost and maybe to find a way again' (Muecke 1997: 133)

## Conclusion

> It is precisely our encounters at the border – where self and other, the local and the global, Asian and Western meet – that make us realize how riven with potential miscommunication and intercultural conflict these encounters can be (Ang 2003: 149).

In 2005, Richard Dyer spoke of a tendency in film studies which saw theorists ask questions of a film based on an academic agenda rather than being focused on the concerns of the films themselves (Bennett 2007: 63). *Lucky Miles* playfully and self-consciously reinscribes those tropes that countless academics have described as hegemonic tropes of national identity. Through its terms of 'difference, distance and dud maps', this film seems to be signifying more than just a wink and a nod to the Australian film archive. The explicit intertextual referencing and continuities of film-making themes and traditions suggest a self-conscious relationship to the academic study of Australian cinema.

In the Australian context, most portrayals of non-British émigré experience have rarely ventured beyond the urban and suburban confines of the major cities. Recently, films like *Love's Brother* (Jan Sardi 2004) and *Romulus My Father* (Richard Roxburgh 2007) have shown the country as tentatively open to émigré experience. But portrayals of the non-Anglo-Celtic and non-Indigenous exiles in the extreme outback are extremely rare.

While *Lucky Miles* attempts a liberal-humanist questioning of the inhumane anti-refugee, anti-multicultural, pro-assimilationist, 'relaxed and comfortable' stance of John Howard's Australia, it doesn't do much more than just tinker at the borders. While this is one of the first Australian films to let diasporic 'others' into the 'heartland' (Collins and Davis 2004: 100) of Australian cinema, it doesn't really attempt to negotiate the bigger questions of diasporic hybridity with which Australian culture is grappling. The action of the film takes place on the geographic and sovereign borders of Australia and its critical exploration of the relationship between identity, mobility and Australian space is suspended and contained at the periphery.

This chapter has attempted to engage with some of the debates within the broader spectrum of Australian culture and politics and relate them to their particular impact on Australian film-making. On the one hand, since multicultural policy became a dominant feature of the Australian cultural and artistic landscape, the representation and articulation of diasporic experience has to a large extent been regulated. This is not necessarily a reflection on the film-makers' desires, but rather a comment on how film-making milieu create or suppress stylistic innovation and storytelling, and how film-makers themselves may self-censor in order to gain the funds necessary to make a feature film with broad appeal. Film-maker and executive producer at SBSi Franco di Chiera has said we should be aiming for diversity at all levels: 'A healthy film and television industry in Australia, in my view, would have a diversity of content, diversity of culture, diversity of format, diversity of genres...diverse storytelling.' (quoted in Tuccio 2006: 132)

# 3

# ETHICS AND RISK IN ASIAN-AUSTRALIAN CINEMA: *THE LAST CHIP*

*Audrey Yue*

Ethics and risk are central to the discourse of gambling and its impact on migration and diasporic communities because they raise crucial questions about moral conduct and social threat. In representations of ethnic gambling, these questions are foregrounded in social welfare stories on addiction and family dysfunction, media sensationalism about toddlers locked in cars while their parents gamble the night away at the casino, and moral panics from the international student gambling plague.

Ethics and risk underpin these liberal appeals to regulate and reform the problem ethnic gambler, the representation of which has an established pattern in Australian cinema. As early as *Satan in Sydney* (Beaumont Smith 1918), *The Menace* (Cyril Sharp 1927) and *The Birth of White Australia* (Philip Walsh 1928), and as recently as *Little Fish* (Rowan Woods 2005) and *The Home Song Stories* (Tony Ayres 2007), this representation follows the dominant discourse of ethnic gambling as deviant, and as a consequence of the alienation of migration, social isolation and low income. This chapter returns to the concepts of risk and ethics to reconsider the representation of ethnic gambling in a recent short film, *The Last Chip* (2006), by emerging Malaysian-born Chinese Australian film-maker Heng Tang.

Tang is a Melbourne-based film-maker who migrated to Australia in 1989 with his family. In 1999, his self-financed and experimental avant-garde film about a Chinese schoolboy in Australia becoming aware of his cultural identity and homosexual desires (Yue 2000) won the

Special Mention Prize at the 1999 Venice Film Festival. After graduating from the Australian Film and Television School in 2000, he worked on many local projects, including the films of Cate Shortland, and as assistant director in *The Home Song Stories*. His second film, *The Last Chip*, is a black comedy about a day in the lives of three middle-aged Asian women and their penchant for gambling. The film is not a didactic narrative on the moral or psychological effects of gambling on the Asian-Australian community; rather, it celebrates how going to the casino is a form of sociality for lonely migrant women, and how gambling is a creative form of added income for the working-class migrant.

This chapter examines two ways *The Last Chip* can be considered diasporic. First, it critically examines how the film evinces minor transnationalism (Lionnet and Shih 2005) by consciously importing and translating the gambling action genre of Hong Kong cinema, a little-known genre in the West. Second, it evaluates the film's shift from the hybridity of ethnic identity to the ethics of ethnic identity by subverting available discourses surrounding gambling in Australian film culture as inherently bad (and especially so when attached to non-white characters), or exclusively white (as a strategy of nationalism and a legacy of colonialism), or solely the domain of men (white or non-white).

### Minor transnationalism: The award-winning short film and Hong Kong gambling comedy

*The Last Chip* is a minor film. As a short film, its format is subordinate to the full-length feature film in running time, often functioning as 'a calling card' for exposure within, and entry into, the film industry (Martin 2001). As a story about ethnic gambling, its narrative is also peripheral to dominant stories of mateship and suburbia in Australian national cinema. Although the short film genre has marginalized Tang in Australia, it also has enabled him to bypass the thematic/canonical concerns of (local) national cinema as he achieves transnational recognition.

The short film is usually considered a precursor to a director's first feature. In terms of production, it is usually low budget and non-commercial. *The Last Chip* took eight years to secure the A$200,000 funding it received from the Australia Film Commission. When casting the film, the film-maker was unable to find professional middle-aged female Asian actresses in Australia. He found the non-professional cast by walking the streets of Chinatown in Sydney and chancing upon a Chinese opera club on the fourth floor of a non-descript building; it was there that he met May Chan (Madam Fang, an ex-cabaret singer), and was later introduced to May Chan's singing buddy Gabby Chan (Sister Ah Lan, a seamstress) and Queenie Vuong, a doctor (Mrs Nguyen, a waitress). The short film's devalued status (Martin 2001) has contributed to the slow recognition of Tang in Australia, as the critical success of *Boy Serpentine* at the 1999 Venice Film Festival was barely noted in Australian media reports. Over the last eight years, Tang has become more internationally known. In 2002, he was awarded the coveted New Director's Residence at the Cannes Film Festival, the same mentoring program that launched the careers of Quentin Tarantino and Stephen Soderbergh.

Since its release in 2006, *The Last Chip* has similarly received minimal media coverage and limited mainstream distribution, despite winning international awards. It won the Grand Jury prize at the 2006 Clermont Ferrand International Short Film Festival in France, the most prestigious film festival celebrating the short film. It was nominated for the Best Foreign Film at the Los Angeles International Short Film Festival, and collected the Asia International Best Film prize before going on to win the Grand Prix of the 2006 Sapporo International Short Shorts Film Festival in Tokyo. The film was further screened at film festivals in Taiwan, Thailand, Singapore, Korea, Canada and South America, and sold to Jupiter TV in Japan.

In Australia, it won the Special Broadcasting Services (SBS) Television Award at Melbourne's St Kilda Film Festival and the Best Film Award at the Westgarth Film Festival. At the Shorts Fest in Adelaide, it also received the Best Film Award. Initially rejected by the Melbourne International Film Festival (MIFF), it was only reinvited after its success at Clermont Ferrand. The MIFF's cultural cringe and belated recognition are reflective of the general attitude towards the short film in Australia, a reluctance compounded by the film's focus on the highly charged topic of ethnic gambling. Although successful on the short film festival circuit and recognized internationally and nationally, The Last Chip received a short one-week limited release at The Classic cinema in Melbourne and was broadcast only once on SBS, the country's multicultural television service.

The film's marginalized status is characteristic of the development of Asian-Australian cinema as ethnic minority or multicultural cinema within Australian national cinema. Where such films previously portray migrant communities through cultural enclaves – for example, My Tiger's Eyes (Teck Tan 1992), New Gold Mountain (Ziyin Wang, 1987) and My Sister (Yen Ooi 2004) – or diversity multiculturalism – such as Aya (Solrun Hoaas 1990), China Dolls (Tony Ayres 1997), Wahori Days (Joseph Wong 2003) or Footy Legends (Khoa Do 2006) – an emerging trend in more recent films like The Finished People (Khoa Do 2003), Letters to Ali (Clara Law 2004), Lucky Miles (Michael Rowland 2007) and The Home Song Stories (Tong Ayres 2007) explicitly uses the transnationality of the diaspora to make films that are more subterranean, regional and international rather than national. Where the earlier films represent the diaspora as minor and exclusive to multiculturalism, more recent films represent the diaspora as global and exclusive of the nation-state. Whether or not it is the diaspora's excentrism (or its off-centre location) from institutional funding, supported formats or sanctioned genres, diaspora has become an ontological and epistemological starting point in these films – through self-funding, the digital video format or co-production with other national cinemas. In The Last Chip, the transnational reference to the genre of the Hong Kong gambling action comedy has contributed to the film's popular reception internationally.

The Last Chip is a black comedy that relies on the humor generated by witty and funny one-liners in the Cantonese dialogue, reminiscent of Hong Kong comedy. The following table details the opening five-minute scene that introduces this humor in the phone conversation between two of the three protagonists, Madam Fang, a superstitious former cabaret singer who frequents the casino to ease her loneliness and to escape her unhappy marriage, and Mrs Nguyen, a struggling yum cha waitress. Madam Fang is in the middle of a tai-chi class at a studio when her phone rings:

**Table 3.1:** Opening sequence of *The Last Chip*.

| Vision | Audio | In Point |
|---|---|---|
| Madam Fang answers the phone | Madam Fang:<br>Hello? Hello? | 01:28 |
| Mrs Nguyen at Yum Cha | *Mrs Nguyen:*<br>Hey. It's seniors night at the casino tonight.<br>All-you-can-eat $2.95 international buffet. Let's go. | 01: 30 |
| Madam Fang on the phone | *Madam Fang:*<br>Aiya! What's the bloody hurry? I hate being rushed<br>at tai-chi! What do you think this is? Salsa? I'm serious<br>about losing weight. | 01:37 |
| Madam Fang on phone | *Mrs Nguyen:*<br>Lose weight? Ha! |  |
| Mrs Nguyen at Yum-cha | You have enough fat stored … to last me three lifetimes.<br>I finish at three. Come pick me up. | 01:52 |
| Madam Fang on phone | *Madam Fang:*<br>Huh! Pick you up? You should cycle to the casino … and<br>shed a few kilos yourself! | 02:02 |
| Mrs Nguyen at yum-cha | *Mrs Nguyen:*<br>Just drag your fatty dragonfly arse over here … and pick<br>me up! | 02:05 |

Between the 1970s and the 1990s, the genre of gambling comedy was popularized in Hong Kong cinema as part of the wider rubric of action cinema. Films such as *Games Gamblers Play* (Michael Hui 1974) and the successful *God of Gamblers* series directed by comedy director Wong Jing (*God of Gamblers* 1989; *God of Gamblers 2* 1990; *God of Gamblers Part 3: Back to Shanghai* 1991; *God of Gamblers Return* 1994; *The Saint of Gamblers* 1995) showcase a star cast combination of Chow Yun Fatt, Andy Lau and Stephen Chow, and feature the well-dressed tuxedo-clad gambler as the outlaw anti-hero capable of outwitting his higher standing opponents at the casino. Its melodramatic effect follows the action cinema style of John Woo, with its stylized portrayal of the suffering and doing male protagonist, but it also transforms this genre by parodying the John Woo style with its humour. This humour, especially through the linguistic hybridity of Stephen Chow, uses a local vernacular to champion the common person (or the 'little' person) as a 'rags-to-riches' outlaw who will succeed in his economic quest. Chow's linguistic hybridity, mixing Hong Kong Cantonese with Mandarin and English, has been theorized as a genre of 'nonsense' (Lai 2001) that differentiates postmodern Hong Kong Cantonese from other Cantonese spoken in the greater Chinese diaspora. Likewise,

From left to right: Mrs Nguyen (Queenie Vuong), Sister Ah Lan (Gabby Chan), Madam Fang (May Chan) in *The Last Chip* (Heng Tang, 2006). Image courtesy of Heng Tang.

humour is also evident in action sequences that use special effects to accentuate the requisite gambling skills. The opening sequence in Table 3.1 demonstrates this deployment of linguistic hybridity, where Hong Kong Cantonese is mixed with accented and 'broken' English to create the nonsensical parlance. The melodrama of the action genre is also evident in the film's aesthetics of stillness and motion – the former in the emotive tentativeness of Sister Ah Lan, and the latter in the spectacle of the casino and the excitement of gambling. As Adrian Martin (2001) concurs, the short film's aesthetics of 'astonishment' and 'shock' are central to its 'strength' and 'impressions'.

Comedy was popular in Hong Kong during the crisis-laden decades before its 1997 handover to China. Chris Berry (1992/93), writing about Hong Kong comedy in the 1980s, suggests that comedy functioned as a transgressive space and provided a fantasy outlet for the anxious people of the colony. The gambling comedy action genre reflects two tendencies of 1980s Hong Kong: while laughter provided escapism in the form of popular entertainment, the themes of the outlaw anti-hero and the chance of gambling and luck resonated with people in the colony who were wanting to make money quickly and leave. The recourse to chance and luck also spoke to Hong Kong's fate and destiny. The gambler is the perfect metaphor for the Hong Kong common people. Ackbar Abbas (2001) uses the term 'hedging' to refer to the people's penchant for economic speculation, and how this form of speculation – the practice of hedging – is also Hong Kong's way of asserting its trans-localism through co-locating itself with the forces of Chinese postsocialism, local indigenization, inter-Asia regionalism and global capitalism.

By consciously importing and translating the Hong Kong generic style, *The Last Chip* demonstrates the new minor transnational trend in Asian-Australian cinema that uses the diaspora as ontology and epistemology. As ontology, it relies on a popular genre from the 'homeland' to challenge the dominant modes of storytelling about ethnic gambling; as epistemology, it also uses the intelligibility of this genre among the global Asian audience to enable its easy crossover and cultivate its wide transnational appeal. Tang confirms this reconfiguration in an interview: 'I referenced the frenetic pace of Hong Kong screwball comedies but made it relevant to an Australian setting.' (Yue 2006) The Hong Kong gambling genre is minor in terms of the way it is categorized generically between the romantic male action of John Woo and the action comedy of Jackie Chan. These gambling films have never been picked up by the new Hong Kong cinephilia in the West, the long tail transnational distribution circuits of Miramax or the local Australian-based Asian cinema distributor, Madman Entertainment. Rather than the major transnationalism of Hong Kong cinema's globalization, the subterranean alliance occurs because of the director's migrant cultural location: he grew up watching these films, and in Australia watches his parents watch these films. Diasporic memory and mediated homeland roots are central to its minor transnationality.

*The Last Chip*'s transnational reference to Hong Kong action shows a mediated style and an emerging successful genre for the diasporic film-maker – mediated because it consists of localizing a film form through the use of diasporic media and memory, and emerging because it is the first of its kind in Australia to explore the social issue of gambling with comedy. This genre is attributed as a key factor in the global success of the film:

> The film has been received much better overseas than in Australia, especially in Japan where it won Best Asian and Best International Film at Short Shorts Tokyo, qualifying it for Oscar pre-selection and was immediately purchased by Jupiter TV (our only TV foreign sales so far). Asian audiences in Asia are curious about stories of Asians living in the West...In North America, the film has been popular with many Asian American film festivals because it portrays sassy older Asian women. In South America, it's been screened at the Developing Nation Poverty Convention for the socio-politico content. All in all, the blend between black comedy with social issues has made the film accessible to a broad audience. (Tang, in Yue 2008)

Although the film-maker has been around for the last eight years, this is the film that has marked 'his arrival on the Australian film scene' (Safran 2006). The film's minor transnationalism has connected minor and regional alliances, and produced shared cinematic styles that bypass the canon of national cinema. Its cultural translation and localization of gambling as a social issue have also provided another theoretical platform to rethink the theorization of hybrid ethnic identity in Australian national cinema.

### From ethnics to ethics: The commodification of gendered labour

Dominant representations of gambling in iconic Australian films such as Raymond Longford's *The Sentimental Bloke* (1919), Charles Chauvel's *Forty Thousand Horsemen* (1940), Fred

Zinnerman's *The Sundowners* (1960) and Gillian Armstrong's *Oscar and Lucinda* (1997) portray gambling as practices of leisure and bonding between Anglo-Australian men. These positive representations reveal the struggle of working class 'battlers' as they challenge economic uncertainty and the power of authority. Gambling is used to shore up the moral reform of the male character through the themes of mateship and camaraderie (Pike and Cooper 1980; Moran and O'Regan 1985; O'Regan 1996; Nicoll 2001). In representations of ethnic gambling, the racialized stereotype of the ethnic gambler is used to negatively portray gambling as an extension of deviant otherness. Early films such as *Satan in Sydney* (Beaumont Smith 1918) and *The Menace* (Cyril Sharp 1927) associate Chinese men with gambling as an imported vice, and these connotations are used to exaggerate the threat of the 'Asian invasion' and rationalize the 'White Australia' migration policy. Recent films such as *The Home Song Stories* (Tony Ayres 2007) extend this stereotype to show ethnic gambling among alienated Chinese migrants as a form of imagined community and sociality. In these films, gambling is represented through men, and the foci are national civility, colonial legacy or the ghettoization of ethnicity. *The Last Chip* departs from these dominant representations by showing ethnic gambling from the perspectives of female migrants. In its portrayal of female ethnic gamblers, it does not moralize these representations of gambling or valorize the alterity of the migrant's difference. Rather, it critiques the ethics surrounding the liberal claims to ethnic gambling, and shows how the female migrant is produced by the truth-claims of such discourses.

Theorizations of ethnic cultural identity as hybridity have been criticized in recent times for their idealization of otherness, which is at the heart of identity politics. In *Diaspora: Negotiating Asian-Australia*, the editors caution that 'the uncritical celebration of hybridity runs the risk of collapsing the heterogeneous experiences of diaspora into the fetishized display and consumption of Otherness in ways that not only mask but also preserve the status quo' (Gilbert, Khoo and Lo 2000: 5). Not surprisingly, Ien Ang's (2001) concept of cultural hybridity as together-in-difference abandons the ethnic by assimilating the specificity of the diaspora into the universality of the city. This, too, is problematic, for it is precisely within the hegemonic spaces of the multicultural city that the materiality of ethnic hybridity comes to fore, as an effect of unequal exchange. A critique of idealism, Rey Chow (1998) suggests, requires an ethics where tactics of reading may not conform to such idealizations but yet still enable the other to emerge in their full complexity:

> Such a reading practice must carry with it a willingness to take risks, willingness to destroy the submission to widely accepted, predictable and safe conclusion. This risk-taking, destructive process is what I associate with *ethics*, a term I use in contrast to mores and its cognates *morality* and *moralism*... To propose a kind of ethics *after* idealism is thus not to confirm the attainment of an entirely independent critical direction, but rather to put into practice a supplementing imperative – to follow, to supplement idealism doggedly with non-benevolent readings, in all the dangers that supplementarity entails. (Chow 1998: xxii, emphasis in original)

Chow uses an anti-humanist concept of ethics to advocate a critical reading practice that exposes the strategies of benevolence in discourses such as the liberal, humanist, multicultural and universal claims to diversity, otherness, rights and tolerance. Ethics, she argues, is necessarily practised from within a restricted position because it is historically constituted by the forces of contact and subordination: 'Rather than being the occasion for benevolent philosophizing, then, ethics in this restrictive position involves an understanding of subordination, of irresolvable social and cultural antagonisms, and of finding oneself negotiating at the limits of possibilities even as life must go on.' (Chow 2004: 686) Chow's reading practice will be deployed in this section to critically consider how the film interrogates the benevolent celebration of ethnic hybridity.

Discourses of benevolent tolerance are central to studies on ethnic gambling in Australia. Emanating predominantly from the disciplines of social work, social planning, public health and criminology, the problem ethnic gambler is constructed as a migrant from Chinese, Vietnamese and Arabic backgrounds whose propensity to gamble is a consequence of the immigrant experiences of readjustment, unemployment, under-employment and low self-esteem (Driscoll 1996; Brown et al. 1998; Hallebone 1999; Marshall and Baker 2001). Some studies even take a culturalist perspective to associate immigrant gambling with homeland traditions such as superstition, spirituality and luck (Yamine and Thomas 2000; Nattaporn, Jackson and Thomas 2004). These studies call for the moral rehabilitation of the problem ethnic gambler by appealing to the social welfare of the alienated migrant community. In the quest to enlighten and correct the problem ethnic gambler, these studies inadvertently support the liberal claims on the part of the reformed white society that continue to reinvest its white privilege by appropriating the emancipating claims to ethnic cultural difference as both differentiation and discrimination. Echoing Chow, Alain Badiou (2001) dismisses such ethics of difference or the concern of the other as the insistence of the other's sameness within the self: they are 'nothing more than the infinite and self-evident multiplicity of human-kind' (2001: 26).

Chow's concept of ethics departs from dominant postcolonial studies that discuss ethics through morality and otherness. These studies celebrate the alterity of hybrid ethnic identity by valorizing and universalizing cultural difference as freedom. Her deployment is more aligned with Foucauldian ethics as the negotiated practices of freedom. Foucault (1997) examines these practices through subjectivation as a process of understanding how the self gains knowledge and uses this knowledge to conduct its relationship to others. George Yudice (2003) applies Foucauldian ethics to refer to how minority groups are not only governed by policy discourses that demand their conformity to dominant representations, but also how they self-stereotype in their representations in order to make claims in their demands for cultural resources. Anthony Appiah (2005) extends this theorization of ethics to refer to the cultivation of individuality.

Common to these theorizations is the focus on the ways ethnic subjects gain their freedom through various biopolitical practices of regulation and self-regulation. Rather than the hybridity of ethnic identity that celebrates the emancipation of the subject through the recognition of cultural difference, the ethics of ethnic identity highlights the constraints by which migrants and diasporic groups construct their self-presence and self-autonomy. By showing how the self is governed through individual cultivation, group management and/or official representation, it emphasizes how identity is governed, how resources are distributed and how cultural power functions. In *The Last Chip*, this practice of ethics is evident in the commodification of ethnic labour.

Where ethnicity refers to foreignness, the links between ethnicity and labour are unavoidable. Migrants are most commonly found in low paying service jobs, and it is through this form of labour that they are interpellated as ethnics. It is also through performing such labour that the ethnic is recognized and rewarded as such (e.g. the model minority, or the welfare recipient). In the film, Mrs Nguyen works as a yum-cha waitress in a Chinese restaurant. Sister Ah Lan sews clothes in a sweatshop factory. Madam Fang is a former cabaret singer. These sites of labour – the Chinese restaurant, the sweatshop factory and the entertainment hall – are spaces of contact in the Asian-Australian diaspora. Their affective modes of work – hostessing, waitressing and sewing – are defined by the foreignness and feminization of ethnicity, which at once determines and differentiates the country's hierarchical division of labour. At the level of group management and official representation, these women are ethnicized because they have either performed or continue to perform work that commodifies them. In other words, they have to pay for their living by performing work that reduces them to ethnic foreigners. These practices are also evident in the portrayal of the film's two Anglo-Australian croupiers – an anonymous woman and a male protagonist, Craig. They are both 20-something university graduates unable to find work and are forced to work at the casino. Their labour is also ethnicized – they have to service the customers by speaking Cantonese. As the film's official press release states: 'Everyone seems to be working to live, not living for work.' Where work provides freedom (e.g. financial mobility), it is also through this type of labour that regulates how the self is constructed as ethnic and as alienated labour. Here capital accumulates through labour as a site for the marking of boundaries. In these instances, labour has become an incisive site to expose the benevolent, racialized and racist interpellation of the Asian-Australian subject.

This biopolitics is given support by gambling as a form of risk taking to the ontological insecurity of late modernity (Beck 2006). In the film, orientations to fear and luck provide the basis for constructing the 'chance' of gambling. In the penultimate closing sequence, Sister Ah Lan is implored to accept a chip by an anonymous gambler under the toilet door. It is said that the last chip from a losing gambler will bring fortune to the one who is given the chip. When Sister Ah Lan refuses (she is religious and superstitious), the gambler breaks out in violent hysterics. The gambler is never seen except through the red-chipped polished nails of a wrinkled hand and the ankles of a pair of garish golden high heels. The gambler has a loud but low Australian accented voice. From this, it can be inferred the gambler is of Anglo-Australian background, although the gender is not specific. In fright, Sister Ah Lan accepts the last chip and rushes out to find her friends. As more savvy gamblers, they seize upon the potential good fortune the last chip will bring. They begin to bet. Round after round at the roulette table, their fortunes multiply. This sequence is shot from the point of view of the panic-stricken Sister Ah Lan. It is heightened with swirling and dizzying camera angles, and juxtaposed with quick edits and jump cuts of the neon glitter from the poker machines. At this stage, the sequence veers into the realms of the supernatural with little gremlin-like devils invading the casino, crawling under the tables and wrapping themselves around their legs. It ends abruptly when Sister Ah Lan, unable to maintain her composure, vomits on the table. In the concluding scene, the three dishevelled women walk out of the casino at dawn, with the camera zooming out until an establishing shot of the monumental casino is in full frame. In a corner, a golden high-heeled shoe floats on the river.

The orientations to chance and risk in the film show how the narrative of gambling foregrounds contemporary Australian society as a risk culture. Using gambling to supplement their meagre income and in the hope of finding fortune, the three women are risk-taking entrepreneurs. Their practices recall Abbas's concept of hedging, for it is these forms of risk-taking that produce the supplementarity and materiality of creative diasporic survival and intolerant multicultural coexistence. This culture, while functioning in the film as a form of escape from routine, loneliness and alienation, also demonstrates, through the space of the casino, its rationalization, commercialization and commodification (Reith 1999). The play with chance and uncertainty, and the increasing management of risk, involves the same logic that saw the southern migration of Chinese risk-taking entrepreneurs to the Australian goldfields in the nineteenth century and the subsequent biopolitics of the 'White Australia' policy. It also parallels the current logic of late Australian modernity and its shameful border-protection policies.

## Conclusion

The Last Chip is an example of a group of recent Asian-Australian films that explicitly use the diaspora to cultivate global circulation and engage international audiences. Rather than being subsumed under the rubric of minority or multicultural cinema, these films are excentric in their modes of production, distribution and representation. In The Last Chip, the film's minor transnationality is both enforced and strategic. Although constrained by the devalued status of the short film and restricted by the dearth of professional middle-aged female Asian actresses in the country, the short film has enjoyed international critical acclaim by strategically borrowing from the popularity of the Hong Kong gambling comedy, utilizing its regional intelligibility and translating it with a local social sensibility. Its story about female friendships from migrant Hong Kong, Malaysian and Vietnamese backgrounds is also a narrative about the subterranean transnationalism of the Asian-Australian diaspora. The film is also diasporic in its subversion of dominant colonial, national and benevolent representations of gambling.

This chapter has also deployed a critical reading practice using the concept of ethics to un-celebrate the preoccupation with the hybridity of diasporic ethnic identity. Central to this is the aim of devalorizing benevolent discourses on ethnicity as universal (diversity) and local (difference). Ethics also refers to the negotiated practices of freedom that govern the biopolitical production of the female migrant subject. In this film, the commodification of ethnic and gendered labour is a crucial site to reveal the structures of subordination that shape the gendered ethnicity of the female migrant subject. Rather than the hybridity of ethnic identity, the ethics of ethnic identity provide a more pertinent platform to critically consider risk-taking in film reading strategies, the risk cultures of gambling and the risk management of diasporic immigration. In the diasporas of Australian cinema, it is precisely these supplementary moments of risk-taking that have also enabled minor film-makers to creatively tell stories that are more global and less national.

# 4

# 'I'M FALLING IN YOUR LOVE': CROSS-CULTURAL ROMANCE AND THE REFUGEE FILM

*Sonia Tascón*

Love is one of the primary processes of cinema, not just at the level of representation (of which it occupies a central role in a great many films), but also ... that cinema deals with, and constantly returns to, love locates it as part of a cultural order. (Fuery 2000: 94)

## Introduction: Love, ethics and multiculturalism

In Australia during the early 2000s, a number of films appeared, such as *Fish Sauce Breath* (Nguyen 2003), *The Home Song Stories* (Ayres 2007) and *Donkey in Lahore* (K-Rahber 2007), exploring the complexities of cross-cultural romantic love as the reflection of a confidently pluralistic society. At the same time, however, government support for the policy of multiculturalism, initiated in the 1970s, was in retreat. No events showed this more starkly than those surrounding 'boat people' during the late 1990s and early 2000s, when the asylum seekers' 'difference' was used to illuminate their unsuitability to be given succour. The term 'boat people' has been used to refer to asylum-seekers who arrived on Australia's shores seeking refuge since the first boatload from Vietnam arrived in 1976; in this chapter, it refers specifically to the wave of 'boat people' from 1998–2003, and who were mostly from Afghanistan, Iran and Iraq. Their arrival has usually caused great alarm in the Australian community and produced much public debate. The official retreat from multiculturalism, however, began much earlier. A key moment was Pauline Hanson's maiden speech in federal parliament in 1996 when, as the Independent Member for Oxley, she called for a reduction in Asian immigration and denounced the provision of state benefits to Indigenous peoples. These sentiments were to reverberate through the newly elected government of John Howard (1996–2007) and become officially sanctioned through various policies and practices.

Australia's responses to strangers have a problematic history, reflected in the corresponding filmic output. The use of love in films to represent the transgression and crossing of cultural borders has also had an equally problematic trajectory. Early films such as *They're a Weird Mob* (Powell 1966) and *Caddie* (Crombie 1975) depict cross-cultural romances as problematic for Australian society generally. They explore the post-World War II 'populate or perish' cultural terrain which brought many non-English migrants to Australia. Later, cross-cultural films (although not necessarily using romantic love) turn to the next generation of migrants and their hybrid experiences (e.g. *Head On*, Kokkinos 1998; *The Sound of One Hand Clapping*, Flanagan 1999; *Looking for Alibrandi*, Woods 2000; *The Prodigal Son*, Radevski 2005). Over time, the cross-border love story was used variously to represent a failed project (e.g. *The Year of Living Dangerously*, Weir 1982; *Turtle Beach*, Wallace 1991; *The Good Woman of Bangkok*, O'Rourke 1991; *Heaven's Burning*, Lahiff 1997), a site of future yet imperfect possibilities (e.g. *The Piano*, Campion 1992) or triumphant (if too comedic) transgression of boundaries against the odds (e.g. *Strictly Ballroom*, Luhrmann 1992). While the theme of cross-cultural impossibility has continued in more current films (e.g. *Japanese Story*, Brooks 2003; in this case, an impossibility redolent with unfinished promise), many more have recently tended towards an exploration of the existence of cross-cultural love as a taken-for-granted phenomenon, and are usually discussions of the difficulties and intricacies of such entanglements (e.g. *Fish Sauce Breath*, Nguyen 2003 (short film); *Everyone Loves a Wedding*, Hayes 2004 (documentary series); *A Pig, a Chicken, and a Bag of Rice*, Gould 2004 (documentary series); *Donkey in Lahore*, Rahber 2008 (documentary series); *The Home Song Stories*, Ayres 2007 (feature film)).

These latter films may be an instantiation of a culture poised and confident with its pluralist values, expressing through their intimate relationships a deeply felt appropriation and application of the ideals and ethical position espoused by multiculturalism. On the other hand, they may suggest an anxious need to inscribe these ideals with taken-for-granted mundanity, given their ominous disappearance from the cultural landscape. If the latter, then we must consider whether the films are using cross-cultural love to reassert and cement pluralist values in the face of governmental hostility.

Engaging with these questions, and given the significance of the 'boat people' events to multicultural values, I will explore two films produced in 2003 that deal with these events through the theme of cross-cultural love. *Molly and Mobarak* (Zubrycki 2003) and *Amanda and Ali* (Hodgkins 2003) are two films that make explicit use of love in the cross-cultural context for political/ethical purposes. 'Boat people' engendered a number of films (e.g. *We Will Be Remembered for This*, Taylor 2007; *Lucky Miles*, Rowland 2007) and an inaugural Refugee Film Festival in Sydney in 2007 (www.triumphant.org.au/filmfestival.html). Yet in both *Molly and Mobarak* and *Amanda and Ali*, the use of love to transgress cultural boundaries becomes the integral vehicle for the merger of the personal and the political/ethical, and no mere peripheral thematic. They portray a type of embodied ethics where love is deployed self-

*Molly and Mobarak* (Tom Zubrycki, 2003). Image courtesy of Tom Zubrycki.

consciously and explicitly as a device for the anxious reassertion of the pluralism embedded in multiculturalism. However, they also implicitly critique multiculturalism as an imposition from above rather than viewing it as erupting from within the popular imaginary and hence seeing its failure to engage with the most intimate and vulnerable spaces of everyday, personal life.

The central position granted to love in these films achieves its significance mostly because the films seek to intersect a cultural order which, it is suggested, has become morally suspect by the dismantling of the ethical position heralded by multiculturalism. That is, ethics as the set of values underwriting a cultural order, where official *and* everyday decisions are made about how we will relate to others, to whom we owe what and to whom we owe nothing, forms an integral part of these films. They effectively raise ethical questions about the interplay between cultural difference and what we owe to those who enter this geopolitical space after us with or without official permission. According to these films, romantic love makes the welcome of the stranger possible in the deepest and riskiest manner. They add to ethics a personal dimension that is usually missing, one which recognizes that ethics is more than mission statements for large organizations, but involves how we behave with others, and what responsibilities we owe others, every day.

Ethics, difference and love form a significant theoretical framework for this chapter, as I propose that romantic love as expressed in the films *Molly and Mobarak* and *Amanda and Ali* suggests to us that there is a space for thinking about romantic love as ethics. In order to consider the questions posed by these films, I will engage with the thinking of Emmanuel Levinas (1998), whose work on ethics and difference and the welcome of the stranger in his/her difference is significant for those engaged with these topics. Levinas makes an explicit distinction between 'love of the neighbour' as 'love without concupiscence' (1998: 103) and Eros, which is not an end in itself in ethics but the journey towards fecundity and futurity; the actualization of the latter then forms part of ethics, but not so the production of its possibility. I will interrogate this demarcation and propose that the romantic encounter – Eros – as shown in these films is the welcoming of the stranger *par excellence* because it welcomes at the most intimate level of engagement. Therefore, it is the riskiest but also the most potentially profound engagement where we can gain and express some of the fullest dimensions of our humanity as adult beings. It is a welcome, therefore, which *is* ethics – although in its most embodied form.

## Love and the refugee film

[O]ur culture doesn't recognize passion because real passion has the power to disrupt boundaries. I want there to be a place in the world where people can engage in one another's differences in a way that is redemptive, full of hope and possibility. (Hooks 1996)

For many within the Australian community, the events which demonstrated the erosion of the values inherent in the principles of multiculturalism were those surrounding 'boat people' during the late 1990s and early 2000s. During this time, a significant increase in of the number of boats arriving in Australia carrying asylum seekers produced an uncompromising governmental response intended to keep boats from arriving, and/or to enable the easy return of refugees to their home countries. This included the introduction of legislation to enable the indefinite detention of asylum seekers, the introduction of temporary protection visas (TPV), the excision of national territories for migration purposes, the active turning away of boats from Australian waters, increasing the threat of return to home country, and provision of limited services for those determined to be refugees and released into the community. Many in the community read these events as related to Australia s anxieties about invasion (Burke 2001), as incompatible with its international obligations (Brennan 2003) and, most significantly for this chapter, as eroding a value position of the welcoming of strangers in diversity (Tascón 2001; Lange, Kamalkhani and Baldassar 2007), which to many had become embedded within narratives of nation-building (Tascón 2008).

The films *Molly and Mobarak* and *Amanda and Ali* were produced as a result of these events. The rejection enacted on the bodies of refugees – as those who represented the unambiguous position of the stranger in need of welcome and hence what multiculturalism as policy was intended to fulfil – was the clearest rejection of this as a narrative imbued with ethical promise. The refugee signifies in these films the most ardent supplicator of our ethical responses. If we hold, as Luce Irigaray (2002) does, that 'the wisdom of love' poses for us the most profound questions of our heterogeneous existences, that it pushes us to transgress 'artificial and authoritarian unity' and form 'a loving encounter, particularly an encounter able to dialogue in difference' (2002: xvi), then we can consider that these films are attempting to begin to represent for us the possibilities inherent in loving encounters across difference. The use of romantic love in these films therefore makes possible the understanding of a loss that can only be conceived of as understood at the space where one and another meet in proximity.

In *Molly and Mobarak*, a film by Tom Zubrycki released in 2003, two Australian women, Lynn and her daughter Molly, a young high school teacher, reach out and welcome into their family a young 22-year-old Hazara (Afghanistan) man, Mobarak, who has arrived in Australia on a boat. He finds work in the local abattoir in the small town of Young, New South Wales, after being released from immigration detention on a TPV. Mobarak, who has not seen or spoken to his family for some years, becomes attached to these women, and they form bonds with him – maternal in relation to Lynn, and romantic with Molly. While the love that Mobarak comes to have for Molly is not fully reciprocated, she is visibly torn between feelings she begins to have towards him and her inability to return the level of love she realizes he needs in order to repair and return all he has lost. Lynn, as a maternal presence, tries to protect both Mobarak and Molly by speaking of 'making boundaries' and emphasizing, very early in the film, that Molly has a boyfriend. Despite this, Molly caresses Mobarak often and their hands entwine tenderly more than once. As the days progress – the film follows a linear temporal sequence – the relationships between Lynn, Molly and Mobarak develop. The depth of emotions that Mobarak is obviously experiencing with regard to Molly becomes untenable, and Molly decides to go overseas for a number of weeks. As her departure date looms Mobarak spirals into utter despair and despondency, and his language increasingly enters into registers of profanity. Molly's ability to flee this intense situation, and Mobarak's mad search for the same intensity in her without return, reaches a poignant turning point as Lynn explains to Mobarak that Molly is fragile and has many things on her mind. Mobarak explains to Lynn that he has 'a lot of problems' too – visa, language, family – but that he still manages to love Molly. Lynn breaks down as she realizes that in the differences between Molly and the damaged Mobarak lies the injustice that whatever love they may give him will never be enough. The unrequited love Mobarak has for Molly is underscored by a situation that is not of Molly's or Mobarak's making, but part of a broader political context over which they have no control and which positions them as unequal partners. All the women can do is love Mobarak as best they are able within the circumstances – and love him they do.

But it cannot be enough for Mobarak, because he is young and also needs parental love; he is alone, he is rejected and misunderstood. These things occur separately to Molly, a young woman with many adventures and possibilities ahead of her. Committing to such a damaged human being - as she eventually realizes he is - is a responsibility she is not yet prepared for. In Mobarak's continuing search for love, which he finds with an Aboriginal girl in Sydney, he recognizes love's redemptive and healing strength. Writing to Lynn after he leaves, he says: 'I am too sad for you and Molly.' He recognizes that they did try, letting him feel his humanity in ways that no other encounter could. Wrenching himself from them in order to seek love elsewhere, a space is created for love to be glimpsed and hoped for. That Mobarak failed in his search for love with Molly does not negate the gift of love that was made possible, and the future possibility of being in love.

*Amanda and Ali* is a much shorter film – just 15 minutes – by Karen Hodgkins, released in the same year as *Molly and Mobarak*. In *Amanda and Ali*, the movement is different from that of *Molly and Mobarak*; the love that is clearly highlighted here as developing between Ali and Amanda is portrayed against the backdrop of a maelstrom of political events surrounding 'boat people'. Amanda meets Ali, an Iraqi asylum-seeker, in Woomera Detention Centre as she is protesting outside and he manages to escape. Ali's face is a smudged presence at the beginning of the film, as Hodgkins films him at night after his escape in a clandestine manner. He is subsequently recaptured, and from that point he becomes a voice on the other end of a phone and a few scribbled words on paper. Some of the phrases from his letters are full of pain and poignancy: 'I am a bird that has no wings to fly', 'I'm grateful that you're always thinking of me'. Later, words of love appear and grow in intensity: after visiting him in detention, Amanda mentions that he told her he loved her and she returned the sentiment. One of his letters declares: 'I looked up at the sky and I found your star beside of my star', and we hear his voice saying to her: 'I'm falling in your love. It's your fault, it's your kindness'. Ali's only presence in the film, as a blurred face, a voice mediated by the phone and words on a page, as Kyle Weise mentions, 'effectively emphasizes the isolation of asylum-seekers, the difficulty of getting their voices heard, as well as the importance of this communication and of the wider community's understanding' (2004).

The love that openly develops between Amanda and Ali, while non-sexual, is nevertheless romantic. Unlike Molly and Mobarak, whose bodies are able to feel each other, Amanda cannot touch Ali physically, and he refers to this in one of his letters. Yet what they feel is deeply intimate, and Amanda reminisces early in the film: 'Never in my life have I been so emotionally affected by someone', later mentioning that his love has deeply transformed her: 'I wouldn't be where I am today if it wasn't for Ali…there were days I couldn't get up if it wasn't for his words'. What transpires between them is clearly romanticized and embodies a personal attempt to correct what is happening politically. Amanda, like Lynn and Molly, reaches out to an['other'] in a welcoming gesture that involves her bodily in providing the possibility that may become politically significant but is also a personal gesture of love and the gift of hope.

## Love as ethics

> Until today what we have found is, at best, to integrate the other: in our country, our culture, our house. That does not yet signify meeting with the other, speaking with the other, loving with the other. (Irigaray 2002: ix)

Can we think through love as ethical? If, as Dayal (2001: para 3) mentions, 'love…is the telos of melodrama' and in films is feminized and privatized, does this then place it outside the purview of public significance? In order for love to suggest a way to be together-in-difference, does it then need to go beyond romance to enter ethics? These are crucial questions because, in order to consider the politico-cultural meanings these films hold, love needs a central place in the analysis; love in these films is not only a private encounter but has significance far beyond the individual stories. Love is not only the sufficient condition for making the political/cultural point in these films, it is the absolutely necessary guiding thread that makes the thinking through of these encounters *possible* in political/ethical terms.

The questions posed by love, ethics and difference are taken up by a number of thinkers (e.g. Levinas 1969; Silverman 1996; hooks 1997; Nussbaum 2001; Irigaray 2000, 2002) in a variety of ways. Here I take up a question posed by Emmanuel Levinas in relation to the role of romantic love in ethics, as his ethics of responsibility in alterity has been seminal for many critics working in the cross-cultural or multicultural arenas. Levinas articulates romantic love, or Eros, as outside the purview of ethics; this has been interrogated by Irigaray (1991, 2001) and others (e.g. de Beauvoir 1971; Downing 2007; Katz 2001). In Levinas's formulations, Eros, or the romantic relationship, is that which provides the conditions for transcendence and therefore ethics; however, it is not ethics itself. This occurs as a result of the distinction between erotic/romantic love and 'love without concupiscence'. The first forms part of the ethical venture only through its performance of 'the caress', which 'consists in seizing upon nothing, in soliciting what ceaselessly escapes its form toward a future never future enough, in soliciting what slips away as though it *were not yet*' (1969: 257–58). That is, by 'soliciting ... toward a future' that is eternally searched for the caress produces the conditions for transcendence, and for ethics, but is not itself ethics. Katz (2001) argues that this movement is clearly gendered and the feminine 'other' merely produces the conditions for transcendence, which hence belongs to the masculine. In this way the feminine performs the utility of the possibility of fecundity and futurity, which is ethics for Levinas, but it is the masculine that enacts the ethical. In Levinasian terms, therefore, romantic love 'remains outside the political, secluded in its intimacy, its dual solitude' (Katz 2001: 154) and outside the regard of ethics. It is the masculine ability to transcend this intimacy that allows the ethical to take place, although it is the feminine that makes masculine transcendence possible.

In Levinasian terms, then, Eros cannot be the site within which ethics is enacted, but is that which can make ethics possible through the caress as futurity and fecundity. In this way, Levinas draws a distinction between the [privatized] romantic encounter – which may be sexualized or not, but is intimate – and the ethics which is [public and] *made possible* by the caress but is beyond it. This distinction may indeed be embedded in the traditional distinction between private and public, and the traditionally gendered way in which this has been constructed. While Levinas, as Katz (2001) argues, may not be disregarding or trivializing the feminine in his account of love as part of ethics, the result is one in which the feminine makes possible fecundity only through the presence of the caress; the ethical importance of such an encounter remains outside of that which the feminine provides. The question this raises for the films being considered here is to what extent the privatized romantic experiences the women – Lynn, Molly and Amanda – are seen to provide for the refugee men as 'other' can then be seen as part of an ethical project. Is what many Australian women did during the 'boat people' crisis – not only give of their time but also form deep and intimate relationships with refugee men – and which are portrayed in these films, not part of an ethical response? Or are their actions, by becoming part of a love that is closer to Eros than to non-concupiscence, outside ethics? Can we see their actions as only existing within that which provides the environment for ethics to be performed, or were their actions directly ethical?

In *Molly and Mobarak* and *Amanda and Ali*, the women's love, as imperfect, incomplete and impregnated with postcolonial power as it is, offers the men, as 'other', an entry into a place that otherwise rejects their presence. They welcome the men in ways that give hope, but also do so in the face of a political climate where love of any kind is denied them. The love they give is not sexual, and so in a sense it is non-concupiscent in Levinasian terms. But it is of a type that cannot be called unromantic – Molly and Mobarak's entwining of hands symbolizes this, as does Amanda and Ali's open declaration of love. It is the act of love in a romantic sense that begins to redeem, not just the men but so much more. The women are acting from a political motive and orient their bodies and emotions towards an 'other' to whom they open themselves in embodied ways. Connected to the political events that surrounded them, and hence the motives that moved them to act as they did, theirs were also acts that worked within a discourse of national redemption. In Levinasian terms, they welcome the stranger and make it possible for this 'other' to transcend their *inhumanity*, through the encounter with another in love. Yet in contradiction to Levinas, they enact the ethical possibilities not simply by being the vessel of fecundity but by being that which directly engenders a future possibility for the men. The actions of these women, arising from political motives but enacted in the personal, must be read as an embodied ethics that does not easily divide the political from the personal.

## Conclusion

> The task here is different. It is a question of making something exist, in the present and even more in the future. It is a matter of staging an encounter between the one and the other – which has not yet occurred, or for which we lacked words, gestures, thus the means of welcoming, celebrating, cultivating it in the present and in the future. (Irigaray 2000: viii)

Love in the shape of romantic love has had an ongoing and persistent presence in Australian films. Its place in narratives of political and ethical significance has been little regarded, although it has been an enduring vehicle for representing personal applications of the political/ethical. Part of the difficulty in seeing narratives of romantic love as contributing or forming part of narratives of political/ethical importance arises from the uncoupling of the private (where romantic love traditionally resides) with the public (where ethics/politics traditionally resides) in modernity, and the gendered dimensions of this (although there has been much feminist literature contesting this). These films begin to suggest that romantic love does have a place within notions of ethics. I would go as far as to suggest that the fecundity that it offers another human being, far from being on the path to futurity, *is* the future, whether biologically or physically reproduced in a third being or not, as Levinas suggests.

If, furthermore, love-across-difference is the welcome of the stranger in his/her strangeness, the development towards a future in the warm regard and safety of another, then I would say that these films clearly point to romantic love as providing that possibility. In contradistinction to Emmanuel Levinas, who in every other regard provides us with a powerful vision for developing an ethics of non-assimilatory response to difference, romantic love has been added here not as the mere road to ethics, but as forming an integral part of the ethical project. The embodied actions of the women in the two films are a welcoming of those who have been constructed as absolute strangers. Their gift of the caress is more than a vehicle towards achieving futurity and ethics; this gift is the direct provision of a fecund future for men who as absolute 'other' could not have had this otherwise.

If multiculturalism as a narrative of the national and the ethical has visibly been threatened by governmental policies and practices, especially evident in their treatment of refugee boat people, then these films attempt to reassert the value of the multicultural in areas where it had most abysmally failed: the private and personal. I would suggest that *Molly and Mobarak* and *Amanda and Ali* attempt to reinforce these values by inserting and developing the most embodied, deepest and most vulnerable aspects of human existence, and turning these intimate spaces into ethical questions about who we are and how we treat strangers. In contrasting the actions of these women to those of their communities, the film-makers redirect attention to the ethical promise of plurality and the welcoming of strangers, injecting it with an everydayness and embodiment that made it an ethics complete in relevance and application. Ethics is not something that happens 'out there', or drafted by experts in dark offices, they seemed to be saying; it is how we behave every day with others, what responsibilities are ours in relation to others, and accordingly the decisions we make behaviourally. By showing how one can be taken into the depths of someone else's intimacy, *Molly and Mobarak* and *Amanda and Ali* show how the ethical/political project is entered into at the riskiest and most fraught area of our existence, and therefore ethics *par excellence*.

# 5

# WHITE ABORIGINES: WOMEN, SPACE, MIMICRY AND MOBILITY

*Anthony Lambert*

[M]imicry is at once resemblance and menace. (Homi Bhabha 1994: 86)

## Introduction: From migration to mimicry

This chapter moves away from discussions of diaspora and representation that focus overtly on the displacement or dispersal of ethnic or 'migrant' communities and the subsequent development and negotiation of cultural practices. It takes advantage of what Astbury, De Smet and Hiddleston (2006: 255) view as diaspora's somewhat problematic 'flexibility of signification', to discuss the appropriation of Aboriginality within the processes of negotiating new or unfamiliar environments in Australian cinema. The cultural and personal diasporas evidenced by 'white feminist' narratives in certain Australian feature films are characterized by movement and transformation. In this way, some foreign white women experience the land as 'real/reel' Australians via the direct physical mimicry of a pan-Aboriginal subjectivity, and its external (bodily) markers of an 'authentic' Australian identity. Little critical attention has been paid to the migrations and transformations of non-Australian white women in the national cinema who attempt to 'become' Aboriginal and, in doing so, Australian.

The movement of British and American women into conceptual and physical spaces of 'the indigenous' is examined here through the films *Journey Among Women* (Tom Cowan 1977) and *Over the Hill* (George Miller 1992). In both films, central female protagonists (British in the former, American in the latter) are seen to mimic Aboriginal women within iconic Australian bush and

Ten Women in a Boat, *Journey Among Women* (Tom Cowan, 1977). Image courtesy of John Weiley.

desert spaces with particular effect: *Journey Among Women* emphasizes mimicry of Aboriginality as the key to survival techniques and female unity, while *Over the Hill* promotes secret women's business as a mystical resolution to universal identity and relationship issues. Finally, both films are placed within the context of spatial transgressions in more recent film-making in order to crystallize some of the ways Anglo-European women in the cinema must bridge the gap between a sense of strangeness and the Australian environment in its most obvious forms.

This exploration of painted white bodies, or 'blacking up', in *Journey Among Women* and *Over the Hill* stages the mimicry of stereotypical female Aboriginality as a product of white women's encounters with Australian/Indigenous space. An explanation of the mimetic impulse in these films is offered through the use of key terms and concepts found in French phenomenologist Roger Caillois's (1984) article 'Mimicry and Legendary Psychasthenia'. At the core of Caillois's exploration is an overlapping between physical mimicry in the insect world and the psychological insecurity of human beings as they attempt to overcome displacement within unfamiliar surroundings. Caillois's invocation of Giard's notions of 'offensive' and 'defensive' mimicry, along with Caillois's own critical framing of homomorphism and anthropomorphism, are used to interrogate survival and fighting strategies in *Journey Among Women*. Callois's psychological state of 'legendary psychasthenia' (a form of surrender and abandonment into one's surroundings) is used to understand the brief indulgence in Indigenous ritual in *Over the Hill*. These two different aspects of Caillois's thesis further amplify the differences between the two interactions and their constructions within the respective films as the (transnational) products of different times, politics and places, as either British (physical, collective, aggressive, convict, historical) or American (emotional, individual, psychological, tourist, contemporary).

In its limited exploration of British and American women in Aboriginal space, this study is situated firmly at the often-unmarked juncture in mainstream Australian cinema between white feminism, neo-colonialism, mimicry and mobility. This is not to imply that eastern and non-white women generally do not have interactions with Indigenous characters or the land in Australian cinema independently of settler-colonial history. Nor is it to say that non-white women, in spite of marginalization and colonial racism, do not benefit from the ongoing effects of (post)colonialism. Rather than using diasporic subjectivity to account for the 'unrecognized implications' of colonialism for multiculturalism (Curthoys 2000: 36), this critique attests to colonialism's continuing power and salience through two specific instances of cross-cultural contact and spatiality within identifiably feminist narratives of self-actualization. In this way, the connection between diaspora and white feminism in the cinema begins to reveal itself as simultaneously transcultural and neo-colonial. Both *Journey Among Women* and *Over the Hill* possess images of contact which mark the female 'white Aborigine' (McLean 1998) as a moment (however ephemeral) of diasporic production. The explicit focus of this discussion is necessarily on the mechanics and politics of this very production.

The movement into Aboriginal space by non-Australian white women and the subsequent impersonation of stereotypically 'traditional' Aboriginality represent 'a correlate of one's ability to locate oneself as the point of origin or reference of space' (Grosz 1995: 90). The brutal, almost sacrificial deaths of migrating or travelling American and British females in the Australian landscape in films such as *Razorback* (1984), *Dallas Doll* (1994), *Lantana* (2001) and *Wolf Creek* (2005) seem to stem precisely from the lack of ability to 'locate' effectively. The required mimicry in Caillois's (1984: 30) sense is thus a 'process of depersonalisation by assimilation to space' in which non-Aboriginal female figures *regress* in order to *progress*; they surrender 'feeling and life' in order to 'take a step backwards'. Such women in the cinema can thus identify with the imagined origins of Australian space, becoming 'white Aborigines'. As the journeys of these non-Aboriginal women take them into the unfamiliar and towards a more complete sense of self, Aboriginal women take on the roles of assistants, merely reduced to the level of useful, albeit somewhat mystical, features of their cinematic environments. The potential of such performative mimicry for liberation and the recreation of identities (both white feminist and postcolonial) necessarily possesses the capacity for a rudimentary reassertion of white belongings. The 'double vision' of mimicry, which colonizes *and* disrupts, extends to a feminist double vision which cannot avoid at least 'partial recognition' of its 'colonial object' (Bhabha 1994: 88).

## Mimicry and strategy in *Journey Among Women*

The 1977 feature *Journey Among Women* is the fragmented and somewhat surreal story of British female convicts deported to early Australia. They escape captivity and British colonial culture by learning from an Aboriginal woman how to survive in the Australian bush. With the exception of

Elizabeth (Jeune Pritchard), the well-to-do companion of a British captain, the women are errant civilians ('whores', criminals and lower class women) who become 'good savages'.

Set in the late eighteenth century, *Journey Among Women* is a rich tapestry of images drawn together within a larger narrative of white women moving into, occupying and defending both the space and the role of an essentialized and imagined Aboriginality. Within its own contentious and contradictory postcolonialism, the film essays a litany of abuses on the part of the male soldiers which prompts the women's mass breakout and exodus deep into the bush of the Hawkesbury River region. Elizabeth (or 'Miss Lizzy', as she is known to the women) seizes this moment to join the women and break free of her own constrictive world. After some initial clashes within the group, the women encounter, and take their lead from, Kameragul (Lillian Crombie), a lone wandering Aborigine. From her they learn techniques of survival, ritual, camouflage and defence. They find personal and collective freedom through *becoming* more like Kameragul.

It is at this stage of the film that the behaviour of the women, with respect to their newfound Australian environment and to Kameragul, can be seen to mirror the phenomenon of mimicry in the biological world of animals, plants and insects. Such an observation, to quote Caillois (1984: 23), is 'not so gratuitous as it sounds', as 'there seem to exist in man (sic) the psychological potentialities' which correlate to the conditions of the biological mimetic process. Grosz (1995: 88) states:

> Mimesis is particularly significant in outlining the ways in which the relations between an organism and its environment are blurred and confused – the way in which its environment is not clearly distinct from the organism, but is an active component of its identity.

The group in *Journey* has found an effective means by which its members are able to function in the harsh, foreign space, to identify with it and to belong in it. The notion of functioning, psychologically and physically, is central to the women's experience of the unforgiving bush. This aspect of the women's mimicry can be explained in the first instance with a general application of Alfred Giard's (1888) categories. As recounted by Caillois (1984: 18), these are as follows: 'offensive mimicry' (designed to surprise) and 'defensive mimicry' (to escape the aggressor or to frighten it away), further classified as 'direct' (when it is in the immediate interests of the imitating animal) and 'indirect' (when animals belonging to different species become similar in appearance).

Caillois briefly recounts Giard's types and dispenses with them in favour of the more broadly effective terms 'anthropomorphism' (1984: 19), transforming in appearance from species to species, and 'homomorphy', 'the adaptation of form to form' (1984: 20). These terms will be deployed specifically with respect to the themes of postcoloniality and feminism in the film, but for the moment Giard's classifications serve to outline the physical requirements, the psychological need and the strategic intent behind the mimesis in *Journey Among Women*.

The women 'become' Aborigines primarily through the offensive, defensive and direct forms of mimicry. Offensive and defensive mimicry is made obvious through the women painting their bodies in preparation for the final battle with the colonial soldiers. As 'Aborigines', they have learnt the art of camouflage using ochre and dyes so that when they fight off the soldiers they are able to blend into the environment and emerge from it at will. The contrast of colours in the film highlights the success of the women in this endeavour. As Jennings points out, 'the soldiers who wear bright uniforms seem out of place in the bush. In the sequences where they pursue the women their conspicuous clothing contrasts with the women's camouflage.' (1993: 25) Although they suffer some casualties (there is a visual link between the red of the men's coats and the blood of a dead woman in the watering hole), the women are more than able to 'surprise their prey' and to 'escape the sight of their aggressors' through a 'mimicry of dissimulation' (Giard, in Caillois 1984: 18).

It is therefore in the immediate interests of the women to take on the appearance and the habits of Kameragul. They are able to survive and to fight back. This 'direct mimicry' grants them access to fire and water. They emulate Kameragul's techniques of hunting and cooking wallaby. They take on the tribal rhythms of her 'stick music', and this shift is another means by which the film indicates that the women have become 'tribalized'. As the women frolic in the waterhole, and later dance and scream frenetically around the fire, they transform their world into the Aboriginal 'promised land' they had imagined while incarcerated, the 'place over the mountains where people there are as free as a bird'. And it is a freedom which their mimesis of Aboriginality has equipped them to defend.

Both *Journey Among Women* and scholarly discussions of the film in the years following its release reflect a somewhat dated feminist logic/ethic which possesses little capacity for self-reflexivity. The former suggests a victimization that positions deported women solely as the unwitting target of colonial processes, and the latter suggest a representational affiliation with nature that eliminates any possibility of power or responsibility for the women. Susan Dermody's (1977, 1980) interpretation of *Journey* is that 'the overriding myth of the film is the frequently reactionary one that sees women as mysterious creatures who are close to nature' (1980: 84). Such thinking excludes the women from rationality; they are not logical but intuitive, and it is this critical organization of the film along the lines of reactionary patriarchal logic that is in need of revision. Attention to the discursive implications of mimicry within phenomenological and postcolonial contexts enables a deeper understanding of female action throughout. In the world of the film, the women are among the first white Australians placed within a very specific setting at a very specific time. When mimicry is understood in terms of intent, the strategies deployed by the women first to gain their freedom, and then to defend it, contrast their own decision-making power with the machismo and brutality of the soldiers and the colonial camp. The women, once transformed, have access not only to logic and strategy, but also to a sense of belonging unavailable to the uninformed and inexperienced men. In this, the postcolonial is tied to the feminist (because it is supposedly non-colonizing) and as such is exalted above the colonial senselessness to which patriarchy is unproblematically attached.

It is not the criticism of patriarchal ideology which the film's 'persistent lyricism' of the environment seeks to hide, as Jennings (1993: 26), in response to Dermody, suggests. It is the exaltation of a feminist aesthetic masking the cultural ordering of a postcolonial vision. Caillois's classifications of the homomorphic and the anthropomorphic are useful in gauging the ordering of the postcolonial new world the women have created. When Meg (Nell Campbell) plays at being a Kangaroo with Kameragul, she is seemingly mimicking another species, as the butterfly does the wasp, or the caterpillar the snake's head in Caillois's (1984: 18) examples of anthropomorphism. As the women paint themselves the colours of the bush, attaching leaves and skins to their bodies, they become the features of the bush, like homomorphic examples of the box crab imitating the pebble, or the octopus curling to resemble a stone (20). In both cases, they are imitating *the Aboriginal woman's interaction with the Australian bush*; they are not necessarily imitators of the bush or creatures themselves. In order to do this effectively, they must negotiate 'the Aboriginal' as form and 'species'. Kameragul must be viewed as a different form and a different species, an essential image, if the women's transformations are to be successful. In effect, she is reduced to the level of non-human representation, as they previously have been by the colonial forces. Jennings (1993: 26) adds that: '*Journey Among Women's* essentialist representation of the Aboriginal woman further problematizes its oppositional construction of gender and class relations, adding a conservative dimension of race as well.'

The stereotypical treatment of race in *Journey Among Women* is an even stronger force than either Dermody or Jennings suggests. Within the chaos of the women's new world, there is an order which is illuminated by their painted white bodies. Their liberation comes at the essentializing of a racially differing female. 'We are thus dealing with a *luxury*, and even a dangerous luxury,' writes Caillois (1984: 23), as mimicry is 'a real temptation by space' (1984: 26). This tempting luxury is dangerous to the women of *Journey* whose lives are lost in the bush, but for the most part it is dangerous in its curious leaning toward a restatement of the colonial mindset the film so desperately seeks to challenge.

### *Over the Hill* and 'temporary psychasthenia'
The Anglo-centric luxury of mimicry (as mobility and rebellion) calls the positioning of Aboriginal women in both Australian film and diaspora studies into question. The 'new Australian' white women of *Journey* achieve in life an anti-colonial escape that cinematic women such as Jedda (the Aboriginal female from Chauvel's 1955 film of the same name) can only achieve in death. The notion of Aboriginal 'memory' (Brewster 1995: 4) is appropriated and rendered a viable and potent visual fantasy, via white women, for non-Aboriginal identity at large – one that assimilates the threat of Aboriginality into its experiential domain.

*Journey Among Women* illustrates the functional and intentional ends of mimicry in the Australian bush, posing problems for the feminist and postcolonial themes in the film. There is another dimension to the diasporic transformation that mimicry represents: that of the insecurity of identity, which will now be explored through the Aboriginal experience of American grandmother Alma Harris (Olympia Dukakis) in *Over the Hill*. In Alma's search for belonging, she must pass through a moment of 'primitive' incantation in the desert landscape before she can resolve her own crisis of identity – which involves a spiritual, ritualistic experience of Aboriginality with a group of women around a fire in the middle of the night.

In cases such as Alma's, where mimicry within a foreign space has little or nothing to do with physical survival, other questions come into play. When Caillois (1984: 23) begins to argue that mimicry is a 'luxury', and a 'temptation to space' (1984: 26), the direction of his thesis necessarily changes. As Grosz (1995: 88) writes, 'he abandons neurological and naturalistic interpretations and seeks some kind of answer in psychology'. This is because 'predators are not at all fooled by homomorphy' and 'one finds many remains of mimetic insects in the stomachs of predators ... Conversely, some species that are inedible, and would thus have nothing to fear, are also mimetic.' (Caillois 1984: 22–23) The answer for Caillois is an instance of 'legendary psychasthenia' – that is, a state brought on by 'a disturbance in the perception of space ... from the moment when it can no longer be a process of defence, mimicry can be nothing else but this' (1984: 28).

The perception of space and the displacement of identity are the twin narrative engines of *Over the Hill*, and the film is about a loss of connection between the two. Exploring damaged emotional and genealogical female connections *vis-à-vis* a spiritual engagement with Australian 'nature', the narrative revolves around a dysfunctional relationship between American widow Alma and her daughter Elizabeth (Sigrid Thornton). After many unsuccessful attempts at contacting her daughter (who is the wife of a prominent Australian politician), Alma decides to surprise Elizabeth with a visit and in doing so embarks on a stereotypically 'Australian' adventure. Elizabeth is cold and dismissive; she has no place for her mother in her busy life. The dejected Alma buys a 1959 Chevrolet Bel-Aire from her granddaughter's boyfriend and heads south towards Melbourne. She is attempting to 'loop the loop' (to drive a circular stretch of inland desert and bush roads which eventually lead south), but is distracted by a sign which reads 'Elizabeth's lookout'. As she moves further toward the arid centre of Australia, she comes ever closer to the secrets of Elizabeth's lost happiness, the possibility of her own independence, and romance on her own terms.

A resolution between mother and daughter is only possible after Alma's ephemeral abandonment of, and subsequent return to, her American identity. The pivotal moment of the film, based on Gladys Taylor's (1987) book *Alone in the Australian Outback*, hinges on Alma's encounter with the Aboriginal women of the Red Heart area, where she momentarily takes up residence as a garage attendant and part-time cook. Late one night, Alma is restless in bed and hears a noise outside her cabin. Through her window she sees an Aboriginal woman standing and staring at her, dressed in skins and full body paint. Drawn to her, Alma follows her to a desert clearing where a tribe of women is gathered in a circle around a fire. They take her among them, removing her clothes and painting her breasts and face. They attach headbands and armbands. Chanting becomes louder as the fire's flames reach higher. The camera cuts back and forth between the fire, the women and Alma's face. Transfixed, Alma begins to chant and mumble, and in her trance-like state she shakes profusely, as sweat beads form across her forehead. The fire rages and within the flames she sees a dolphin caught in a net. The dolphin morphs into her daughter Elizabeth, who is wailing and desperately trying to free herself. Alma rushes back to the garage and begins packing her car. The garage owner begs her to stay, telling her 'they've done something to you ...' Her only response is: 'I have to go. I have to see my daughter.'

The similarity, in feel and visual execution, between Alma's surrendering to the seductive strangeness of Aboriginality and Jedda's hypnotic response to Marbuk (the 'savage' and 'pure' Aboriginal) in Chauvel's film is remarkable. Alma, too, is lost and dispossessed in the wide-open spaces of Australia. However, she is engaged in a crisis of represented space in which the connection between self and spatial placement, between consciousness and surroundings are 'dispossessed of its privilege', where one then 'enters into the psychology of ... legendary psychasthenia' (Caillois 1984: 30). Alma surrenders to 'the magical hold' of 'dark space' because it is 'filled' and 'touches the individual directly' (1984: 30). With her Aboriginal 'spiritual guides', Alma is able to fill some 'darker need of the hungry spirit' in the manner of White's novel *Voss* and Burstall's (1976) film *Eliza Fraser* (Poppenbeek 1994: 36). This is a kind of psychosis that takes Alma into the realms of mimicry where she can be fully depersonalized, and momentarily assimilated into space. The void between identity and location is overcome psychologically by an abandonment of her civilized (American) self, and a sense of openness to the power of the environment in which she does not belong in an originary sense.

Alma's psychasthenia is not so much legendary as it is temporary. Her mimicry and morphology are constructed as steps backwards into 'the primitive' in order to move forward. There remains in the primitive (or at least white constructions of it) 'an overwhelming tendency to imitate, combined with a belief in the efficacy of this imitation' (Caillois 1984: 27). Potent in its psychological impact on the characters and its effect on the narrative, Alma's brief moment in Aboriginal space and activity is a fundamental stepping-stone toward the reconciliation of her confused sense of self with unfamiliar personal and geographical terrain. Her engagement with the Aboriginal 'magic' at Australia's heart space allows her to discover a 'universal' truth (of 'common ground', of similarity) and move on. For Caillois (1984: 27), this kind of search 'would seem to be a means, if not an intermediate stage. Indeed the end would seem to be assimilation to the surroundings.'

Alma's mimicry is therefore a means to an end. Her temporary psychasthenia is the intermediate stage on the way to a simultaneous mastery of the self and nature. Aboriginality is reduced to the realms of the mysterious and the primitive, so that Alma has no problem finding her way back through the desert to Elizabeth and to the city. In the film's final moments, Alma and her daughter confront the lingering issues from Elizabeth's childhood, and attend to the developing gulf between Elizabeth and her own daughter. Caillois (1984: 32) argues that his proposition of psychasthenia should not arouse suspicions of dogmatism, as 'it merely suggests that alongside the instinct of self preservation, which in some way orients the creature toward life, there is generally speaking a sort of instinct of renunciation that orients it toward a mode of reduced existence'. However temporarily, it is the 'reduced' existence of Aboriginal women which provides access to life here (as in *Journey Among Women*). Once she has been reduced, Alma's Aboriginality is discarded, and she uses the power and focus found within her momentary process of mimesis and depersonalization.

## Conclusion: When the paint washes off

As a diasporic 'embodied politics of mobility' (Blunt 2007: 691), an alignment of the existential experiences of white women with stereotypical versions of Aboriginal corporeality and culture is a familiar preoccupation in Australian film. The focus on feminist and postcolonial aspects of white female identity in Australian films like *Journey Among Women* and *Over the Hill* masks an ordering of Aboriginality, and female Aboriginality in particular, against the Australian land. And, just as the path to self-actualization of the female 'white Aborigine' is told through migration, mobility and mimicry in those films, the political intricacies of white female incursions into Aboriginal space has since been investigated in a small number of contemporary films, such as *Dead Heart* (Nick Parsons 1996) and *Jindabyne* (Ray Lawrence 2006).

In *Dead Heart*, the temporary 'blacking up' of the white female problematizes the construction of both black and white identities and their relationships to Australian spaces. Kate's (Angie Milliken) physical and symbolic transgressions in the central Australian desert area of the Walla Walla tribe reveal her ignorance of local cultural norms and set off a chain of events which destroy the Aboriginal and non-Aboriginal communal structures in the area. In one very brief scene, Kate enters a space covered with traditional Aboriginal drawings reserved for male initiation rituals by the Aboriginal tribe. Here an Aboriginal male undresses her and she allows him to cover her with sand and clay before they make love. A local Aboriginal woman witnesses their union and the subsequent exacting of 'blackfella law' against the male results in his death. The position of white 'assistance' is irrevocably compromised, as neither 'learning from' nor 'living together' is now possible. Mimicry in this case is not a solvent to displacement in the environment. When the paint washes off, the figures of the white mission are unable to adequately resolve the confusion and clash between different ways of being. The complexities of cultural interaction are foregrounded, and it is this aspect of 'Australianness' which the cinema now seems to be exploring.

In *Jindabyne*, Claire (Laura Linney), an American wife and mother, becomes the agent of reconciliation between Aboriginal and non-Aboriginal communities after a group of men discover the murdered body of an Aboriginal woman while on a fishing trip. Claire's Irish-born husband secures the body to keep it in place until the weekend is over. A fetishistic relationship between foreign white man and naked Aboriginal corpse develops. In *Jindabyne*, as Guy Rundle (2007) observes, 'the particular complexities of Aboriginal life and politics became obscured by the uses to which they were being put, as a sort of "fund" of meaning that could give an instant charge to texts…it also obscured the way in which Aboriginal politics was becoming trapped in a role of victimhood'.

Although in Carver's (1977) original short story (*So Much Water So Close to Home*) the dead body is white, an Aboriginal corpse is required in Lawrence's film version as the trigger for crisis and panic in an Australia after native title, the 'stolen generation' and the war on terror. This insecurity, Collins and Davis (2004: 7) argue in *Australian Cinema After Mabo*, spawned a wave of films that 'backtracked' as a response to such 'aftershocks' which made 'being at home in Australia' ever more uncertain. It is an environment, as described in Bradshaw's (2007) review for *The Guardian*, 'in which one may so easily lose one's bearings of Anglo-Saxon normality, and in which violence or loss are so terrifyingly possible'. The movement of a foreign non-Aboriginal woman into Aboriginal space intertextually reanimates the processes of 'settlement', resolution and environmental assimilation for its still 'unsettled' white protagonists. Still fragile from a post-natal breakdown years before, and isolated from her own relatives and

Jindabyne life, Claire attempts an apology to the woman's family and the Aboriginal community – in an Australia before Kevin Rudd where official apologies for the travesties of Australian/colonial history had not been forthcoming. The cinematic white woman has a history of moving between cultural spaces, and her movement towards reconciliation here is reflective of the 'moral failure' of a disconnection from Aboriginal history – 'the fact that many Australians, living their lives in the increasingly non-specific suburban space of the globalized West, did not feel a strong relationship, either negative or positive, to this history' (Rundle 2007).

While white women in the cinema are now moving into traditional spaces (the initiation space in *Dead Heart*, the funeral in *Jindabyne*) without engaging in the mimetic practices of their cinematic predecessors, there are also those such as Sandy (Toni Collette) in *Japanese Story* (2003) moving through the desert landscape with little or no need for Indigenous contact. Taking a Japanese businessman off road, the Australian-born woman effectively plays the role of 'white tracker'. Simpson (2006) uses Morris's notions of 'phobic narrative' and 'cultural trespass' to point out that while the film possesses a post-*Mabo* consciousness, 'the issue of ownership and protocol is realized through the expertise of the white woman guide and is not directly represented by an indigenous person'.

Whether British, American or Anglo-Australian, all of these women draw on a representational tradition which produces the available subject positions of Aboriginal and non-Aboriginal women with respect to each other and to Australian space. The women of *Journey Among Women* are imitating the artificial markers of Aboriginal female bodies, hence creating a meaningful place for themselves in a harsh foreign landscape. In *Over the Hill*, the painted white body in search of herself (and the Australian centre) goes beyond hunting and tree climbing, and makes a direct incursion into the space of Aboriginal female ritual. She is exposed to the 'true' secrets at the heart of Australia and finds there the possible conditions for self-actualization and healing, for both herself and her family.

The transformations examined within this chapter represent some of the 'processes-in-tension' which constitute 'subjective' and 'group' identities (Willemen 1994: 217). Through mobility, physical transformation and ephemeral abandonment, non-Aboriginal women are often able to transgress the spaces between settler anxiety and a mysterious, timeless Aboriginality. This aspect of diasporic movement problematizes the textual structure of feminism and postcoloniality in Australian cinema, which can then be seen as a basis for recent cinematic discussions of conflicting and competing elements of Australian culture. The movement into Aboriginal spaces represents a larger psychasthenia in the trajectory of the national cinema, continuing compulsions towards feminized journeys and moments of contact that produce and reproduce highly politicized identities and environments.

# PART TWO: REPRESENTATIONS

# 6

# Wogboy Comedies and the Australian National Type

*Felicity Collins*

Popular Australian film comedy since the early 1970s has been dominated by reinventions of the national type. These reinventions involve transformations of the urban larrikin and the bush battler, first established in silent film classics such as *The Sentimental Bloke* (Raymond Longford 1919) and in Cinesound Studio's Rudd family comedies of the 1930s, directed by Ken G. Hall. These comic types continue to surface in popular film and television as the larrikin, ocker or decent Aussie bloke, exemplified in the 1970s by Bazza McKenzie, in the 1980s by Crocodile Dundee, in the 1990s by Darryl Kerrigan in *The Castle*, and most recently by cable TV showman Steve Irwin until his untimely death in 2006. Yet, despite decades of multiculturalism, little attention has been paid to the impact of post-war, non-British immigration on Australian comic types. This chapter examines three popular comedies which champion ethnically marked characters as either 'New Australians' (*They're a Weird Mob*, Michael Powell 1966), 'wogboys' (*The Wog Boy*, Alexsi Vellis 2000) or 'chockos' (*Fat Pizza*, Paul Fenech 2003). It asks whether 'wogboys' and 'chockos' – as diasporic, multicultural or new world comic types – have trumped the larrikins and ockers of Australian screen comedy, or whether 'wogsploitation' films are popular with Australian film and television audiences precisely because they tap into a long-standing national type without disturbing its key characteristics.

In an article on 'wogsploitation' comedies, Lesley Speed argues that ethnic protagonists simultaneously 'assert their ethnic identities and reconfigure the Australian stereotype of the "ocker"' (2005: 138). The celebration in recent times of the 'ocker-wogboy' as a transgressive,

A local (Jack Allen) teaches Nino (Walter Chiari) the meaning of 'a shout' with the barmaid (Anne Haddy) looking on in *They're a Weird Mob* (Michael Powell, 1966). Image courtesy of Williamson Powell International.

hybrid figure marks a shift in the cultural meaning of the 'wog' epithet. Initially, in the 1950s and 1960s, 'wog' was used in Australia as a derogatory slur directed at the influx of non-British immigrants of Mediterranean, North African or Arab extraction. Subsequent appropriations of the insult (along with 'Dago' and 'I-tye') by those it was meant to ostracize are evident in the three films under discussion here. In *They're a Weird Mob*, the Italian protagonist, Nino, informs his future (Irish-Catholic) father-in-law that if he is a 'Dago', so is the Pope. In *The Wog Boy*, the Greek-Australian protagonist, Steve Karamitsis, adopts the playground taunt, 'wog boy, wog boy, wog boy' as a brash, self-protective measure, going so far as to brandish it in the 'WOG*BOY' number plate of his car. In *Fat Pizza*, the 'one hundred percent dinkus-di Australian man' of Maltese extraction, Pauly Falzoni, explains the term 'chocko' to Aussie Davo Dinkum, who lacks the ethnic distinctiveness of Pauly's cohort of pizza delivery mates, Sleek, Habib and Rocky: 'chockoness man, it's like the opposite of Anglicized. Like you would be Anglicized, I would be chocko.'

As landmark Australian comedies, *They're a Weird Mob*, *The Wog Boy* and *Fat Pizza* have each turned the comic spotlight on 'Australian ethnicity' as a work-in-progress. But rather than accept too readily the supposed transgressiveness of 'wogboy' or 'chocko' figures, I want to reconsider each film in terms of Ghassan Hage's (1998) deconstruction of 'the tolerant society' as a 'White nation fantasy' (1998: 79–104). I also want to reconsider the hybrid figure of the 'ocker-wogboy' in light of Tom O'Regan's insistence that European-derived and diasporic constructions of Australian identity are more exclusive, and by implication more problematic for an open national cinema, than either multicultural diversity or the convergence of multiple ethnicities in a 'new world' melting-pot (1996: 331–32).

## The national type

The Australian national type derives from an Anglo-Celtic and bohemian social imaginary forged in the 1890s during a period of radical nationalism that preceded Federation in 1901 and underpinned the new nation's adoption of the 'White Australia' policy, enshrined in *The Immigration Restriction Act* 1901. The urban-based radical nationalism of the 1890s glorified the Australian bush worker as the source of a distinctive national culture, and as 'the coming man' who combined the best of old and new worlds. According to Richard White (1981), the Australian national type developed in three phases. Initially tainted by convictism, the type was seen as degenerate stock transplanted in poor soil. In the second phase, the colonial type emerged on the battlefields of empire as the wholesome product of antipodal space, soil and sunlight. In the third phase, this superior colonial type was transformed into 'the common man', coming of age as the egalitarian digger at Gallipoli. Later, as the population became more urbanized, the moral and physical superiority of the digger were transferred to the iconic Bondi Beach lifesaver (White 1981: 79–82). However, despite these historical transformations, the convict taint was never fully removed from the national type, and it is this degenerate taint that has been so productive for Australian comedy, especially in its 'ocker' mode. As White argues, the digger was 'portrayed as an ideal type on the one hand and, with self-mocking humour, as an unkempt larrikin on the other' (1981: 136). The unkempt larrikin, together with his narrative transformation into a decent Aussie bloke, has enjoyed an extraordinary longevity in Australian culture and has been the lynchpin of Australia's most popular film, most recently in the 2006 mockumentary *Kenny* (Collins 2007). How, then, have diasporic, multicultural or wogsploitation comedies engaged with this well-entrenched national type?

## Ocker-wogboys

There is a consistent theme in the scant literature on wogboy comedies which celebrates the films and related television series, *Acropolis Now* (7 Network 1989–92) and *Pizza* (SBS 2000–07) as an extension of the ocker spirit of 1970s Australian culture. As Tom O'Regan (1989) points out, the ocker films of 1970–74 – notably *The Adventures of Barry McKenzie* (Bruce Beresford 1972), *Alvin Purple* (Tim Burstall 1973) and *Barry McKenzie Holds His Own* (Bruce Beresford 1974) – belong to a broader cultural moment of ockerism which aggressively celebrated the hedonistic Australian urban ocker 'in an inventive, usually male, anti-language for bodily functions, sex, drinking and women' (1989: 76). This aggressively ocker moment was closely tied to a revival of cultural nationalism in theatre, film and television in the 1970s. Cultural nationalism underpinned state-sponsored film production and shored up the position of the Anglo-Celtic male as the embodiment of Australian nationhood in a highly acclaimed cycle of period films, notably *Sunday Too Far Away* (Ken Hannam 1975), *Breaker Morant* (Bruce Beresford 1980) and *Gallipoli* (Peter Weir 1981). The clean-cut larrikin shearers and soldiers in these films conformed to the 'ideal type' of the nineteenth-century bushman and the twentieth-century digger, eclipsing the 'unkempt larrikin' of the popular ocker comedies and helping to establish a prestige or quality cinema in the late 1970s. However, the consolidation of official multiculturalism and the commercial turn in film funding policies in the 1980s opened up spaces for different 'accents' and a broader range of comic types and genres in Australian film and television programs. The revival, since 2000, of the 'larrikin carnivalesque' in *The Wog Boy* (and in the popular television series *Kath and Kim* and *Pizza*), has been described by Tony Moore as a response to 'the pious censoriousness of the Howard years' (2005: 71). Earlier suburban comedies foregrounding ethnicity, such as *The Heartbreak Kid* (Michael Jenkins 1993) and *Death in Brunswick* (John Ruane 1991), proved popular with critics and audiences, but as Speed (2005) points out, 'wogsploitation' films 'differ from previous comic depictions of Australian ethnic minorities' (Moore 2005: 138) in their affinity with the 'vulgarity, uncouthness, bigotry and male chauvinism' relished by ocker comedies (2005: 141). Moore posits a continuity between ocker and wog humour, ending his study of the Barry McKenzie films by claiming that 'the Anglo-Celts lost their monopoly on larrikinism in the '90s when "wog humour" emerged from the suburbs with the stage show *Wogs out of Work* followed by film and TV spin-offs' (2005: 71). For Moore, the ocker spirit remains in good hands with the 'vulgar, sexually explicit, hip-hopping homeboys of Mediterranean or Middle Eastern appearance' outraging middle-brow critics and offending good taste in the high-rating series *Pizza* (2000–07), commissioned by SBS Television (the state-funded, multicultural broadcasting service with a nationwide audience).

### 'We're all blokes here'

If the Australian national type continues to thrive in the form of the 'decent Aussie bloke' (embodied particularly by Paul Hogan as Crocodile Dundee, Steve Irwin as the Crocodile Hunter, and most recently Shane Jacobson as Kenny), on what terms have non-Anglo, diasporic or wogboy characters achieved popular recognition by Australian audiences? In *They're a Weird Mob*, Australia (or more accurately Sydney and its 'weird mob' of Australian working-class and upwardly mobile types) is seen through the bemused eyes of newly arrived Italian sports journalist Nino Culotta (Walter Chiari). The film was a British-Australian production, directed by Michael Powell (at a time when his career in British cinema had stalled), adapted by Powell's long-time collaborator Emeric Pressburger (under the pseudonym of Richard Imrie) from John O'Grady's popular novel (published in 1957 under the pseudonym of its narrator-protagonist, Nino Culotta). As the only feature film produced in Australia in 1966, *They're a Weird Mob* won instant success with audiences and attracted a great deal of commentary (much of it negative) from lobbyists for a revival of feature film production in Australia (Hoorn 2005; Caputo and Danks 2007). Although routinely dismissed as the 'apotheosis of the repressive assimilationist policy' by earlier critics (O'Regan, quoted in Caputo and Danks 2007: 94), more recently the film has been reprised as a harbinger of the inclusive multiculturalism which replaced the notorious 'White Australia' policy in the 1970s. Caputo and Danks (2007), for instance, argue that: 'Nino's impending marriage to the Irish-Catholic in origin, Kay, is both an assimilationist's dream and presents the possibility of an increased, encouraged and rather benign multicultural tolerance…glimpsed inside the insular "ocker" world that dominates the film.' (2007: 99) The most famous scene in the film (frequently shown in documentary histories of Australian cinema) epitomizes both assimilation and benign (if not multicultural) tolerance.

In this scene, set in Sydney's famous Marble Bar, the urbane Nino is initiated into Australian drinking rituals by a typical 'Aussie bloke' who translates vernacular terms such as 'a schooner' and 'your shout' to the bewildered Nino under the wry gaze of a friendly barmaid, herself an outsider in this 'ocker world'. At the end of the scene, the decent Aussie attempts to explain what 'a bloke' is to Nino, whose impeccably proper English is no match for the Australian vernacular: 'You're a bloke, I'm a bloke, we're all blokes here.'

This too-easy inclusion – some would say 'assimilation' – of the newly arrived migrant (or 'New Australian' in 1960s parlance) into the tolerant ethos of Australian mateship clearly owes more to comedy's prodigious capacity for wish-fulfilment than to social reality. Writing in a different context – addressing racial violence rather than diasporic comedy – Hage proposes that 'liberal tolerance' sustains the 'White nation fantasy' in the face of multi-ethnic reality. He argues that liberal practices of tolerance, 'although … perceived as morally "good" … are structurally similar to the "evil" nationalist practices of exclusion [namely, racial violence] that they are supposedly negating' (Hage 1998: 79). This is because liberal practitioners of tolerance, '"good" as they are, share and inhabit along with White "evil" nationalists the same imaginary position of power within a nation imagined as "theirs"' (Hage 1998: 79). In light of this deconstruction of Australian practices of tolerance, when the 'decent Aussie' buys Nino a beer and declares him 'a bloke' on his first day in Australia, the film could be accused of skating far too lightly over the nation's history of intolerance – enshrined in the 'White Australia' policy in 1901 and still practised at times under successive state policies of assimilation, integration and multiculturalism (Hage 1998: 81). Whether this charge can be made to stick in the case of comedy is another issue. Nino's attempt to moderate the local norm, by buying the Aussie bloke a beer but not having one himself, is firmly defeated – but the tone of the defeat is comic and inclusive, allowing Nino to preserve a modicum of difference in the face of insistent hospitality.

## The 'Australian' wogboy

While Australian audiences were flocking to see They're a Weird Mob in 1966, the policy of assimilation – which tried to maintain a dominant Anglo-Celtic heritage in the face of increased European migration after World War II – was undergoing a shift towards a policy of integration. This new policy, which gave way to multiculturalism in the 1970s, acknowledged that 'Australianization' was a gradual process that would find its fulfilment in the second generation (Hage 1998: 82–83). As I argue elsewhere, They're a Weird Mob straddles the shift from assimilation to integration through Nino's fish-out-of-water adventures in the workplaces and playgrounds of Sydney, implying that it takes time to learn a new culture and take up a place within it (Collins 2007). Similarly, The Wog Boy, three decades later, straddles the ongoing tension between 'Australianization' of the second generation and the assertion of cultural difference under the aegis of multiculturalism. But Hage argues that the suppression of difference in the era of multiculturalism is evident in 'outbreaks of exclusionary nationalism' exemplified by the social security raids on Greek households in the 1970s, and the emergence of the right-wing One Nation political party in the 1990s (Hage 1998: 84). If both Weird Mob and Wog Boy promote the utopian belief that enlightened tolerance rather than racial prejudice is the norm in multi-ethnic Australia, they do so in the certain knowledge that Australia's post-war immigration history has been marked by 'the suppression as well as the elevation of what one tolerates' (Lyotard, quoted in Hage 1998: 85).

As a comedy of evasion (of the combined powers of the police, the bureaucracy, the media and the state to control and integrate wayward ethnic types), *The Wog Boy* is knowingly attuned to, if not a participant in, the suppression and elevation of the hybrid figure of 'the Australian wogboy'. Building on his ground-breaking stage show, *Wogs Out of Work*, Melbourne-based writer/producer/performer Nick Giannopoulos created Australian wogboy Steve Karamitsis, whose stated aim is to become 'the best wog I could be'. Steve's charmed life as a hip 'dole bludger' at the service of his demanding multi-ethnic community comes under the spotlight of national television when he crashes into the car of the lascivious Minister for Employment, Raelene Beagle-Thorpe (Geraldine Turner). After a series of mishaps which take him into the administrative heartland of WASP Australia, Steve – like Nino in *Weird Mob* – ends up with a classy, upwardly mobile career woman, Celia O'Brien (Lucy Bell), who initially uses her advisory position in politics to suppress and discipline the work-shy wogboy. But in order to embrace Steve at the end of the film, she has to shed not only the inhibitions and prejudices of her Anglo-Celtic world but also her position of power within that world. He, in turn, has to moderate his brash elevation of the wogboy identity, originally conferred on him as a schoolboy by his jeering classmates but since then affirmed and elevated by his admiring multi-ethnic community – nowhere more so than in the John Travolta disco-dance sequence.

But does *The Wog Boy* endorse a 'benign multicultural tolerance', as Caputo and Danks (2007) claim, for the ending of *Weird Mob*? In the Marble Bar scene discussed above, *Weird Mob*'s fantasy of tolerance empowers, in Hage's words, 'the White Australian as a manager of national space' (1998: 91) – insofar as the decent Aussie has the unchallenged power to end the scene by declaring: 'We're all blokes here.' There is an early scene in *The Wog Boy* which reprises key elements of the Marble Bar scene; however, rather than assimilating the 'New Australian' into mateship, it plays on the simultaneous suppression and elevation of the wogboy as a new Australian type. The scene begins, as Hage might put it (1998: 96), with two white Australian police 'cast in the role of governing subjects' and the wogboy cast in the role of 'passive object' – that is, pulled over for a bit of idle police harassment for driving a gleaming black Valiant. But it ends with the wogboy stealing the scene, or managing the space. Initially, what is curious about this roadside scene is that it involves the same three social types present in the Marble Bar: a tolerant but authoritative Aussie bloke, a smartly dressed wogboy and a friendly blonde woman with a wry sense of humour. It also involves a translation between proper English and the vernacular, but this time it is the friendly blonde cop (Shazza) who translates the pedantic male cop's officious English into an everyday idiom which Steve, as an ordinary Australian, can understand. Here, translation aligns the viewer with Shazza and Steve as insiders, while the male cop Bazza (though a decent enough bloke) becomes the outsider. But the film goes further than reversing the original elements of the Marble Bar scene. It ends by allowing Steve to take over the space: he whips out his photo album and narrates the restoration of his 'baby' Valiant to an admiring Shazza and a bemused Bazza, each looking over Steve's shoulder while he moves to the centre of the frame.

As Hage argues, 'the White Nation fantasy is dependent on the staging of the ethnic other as an object' (1998: 101), but *The Wog Boy* goes some way towards undermining this fantasy by enacting what Hage calls 'an *Australian* ethnic will' (1998: 103). Throughout the film, Steve's main form of action is to take over public spaces that attempt to control him as 'the ethnic other' – on current affairs television, at a fundraising dinner and at the policy launch that removes Minister Raelene Beagle from the political stage. By taking over these public spaces, Steve punctures the fantasy that the Australian wogboy can be brought under the control of those who wish to administer multiculturalism in the interests of maintaining Anglo-Celtic dominance.

### 'Fully sick' national space

*Fat Pizza*, advertising itself as a 'fully sick' spin-off from the multicultural television series *Pizza*, goes much further than *The Wog Boy* in taking over, or managing, national space. It does this by eliminating from the scene the imaginary position of power embodied by the decent Aussie bloke (as ideal national type) in previous ethnic and ocker comedies. Featuring writer, producer and director Paul Fenech in the lead 'chocko' role of Pauly Falzoni, *Fat Pizza* literally takes over Australian media space by imposing 'fully sick' misreadings of the true-blue 'Strayan' popular culture that One Nation's leader, Pauline Hanson, tried to promote as an antidote to multiculturalism. While *The Wog Boy* attempts a takeover of media space with Steve's inept-but-triumphant appearances on Derryn Hinch's tabloid current affairs show, *Fat Pizza* eliminates the pontificating host (as the voice of white Australia) and puts Pauly Falzoni in his place. This imposition of 'an *Australian* ethnic will' is exemplified in *Fat Pizza* by the rapid-fire montage sequence (featuring the Woomera Detention Centre, Azaria Chamberlain (the baby taken by a dingo) and backpacker killer Ivan Milat) set in the sacrosanct Australian landscape of the desert. In quick succession, Pauly, direct to camera, sets the viewer straight on rioting asylum-seekers, baby-snatching dingoes and outback psycho-killers dispatching ditzy hitchhikers. In *Fat Pizza*, Paul Fenech's on-screen *alter ego*, Pauly Falzoni, takes over the interpretation of both national and media space, commandeering Australian popular culture as a 'new world' or 'melting pot' space of convergence. Melting pot cinema, in O'Regan's (1996) words, 'places emphasis on the cultural diversity of the audience becoming in however a transitory way, a unity around a common story-space – a myth of convergence' (1996: 319).

### We're all 'yobbos' here

Hage's (1998) unmasking of 'tolerance' as a way of controlling ethnic or diasporic integration in Australian national space helps pinpoint how three wogboy comedies might serve *and* attack the fantasy of control which underpins assimilation, integration and multicultural policies. But this critique itself suppresses the wild inclusiveness of hybrid, diasporic and melting pot *comedy* – and it overlooks the assimilation of *ockerness* by wogboys. The DVD release of *Fat Pizza* claims on the cover that the film 'unites "strayans from all ethnic, social, sexual and religious backgrounds – even Lebs and Fat Chicks"'. Here, Australianness is no longer a gift to be conferred by the decent Aussie bloke who, beneath the tolerant mask, is 'worried that migrants might become Australians ... *regardless of his will*, and then remove him from the national centre stage he wishes to occupy' (Hage 1998: 104, my emphasis). Fenech openly declares the wogboy's occupation of the national story-space, arguing that 'Muhammed from Lakemba, Joe

Bloggs from Fairfield and Phung Quoc from Blacktown' are 'the real Australia, the true Australia, not some latte-sipping white nerdy boys in Paddington' (Fenech, quoted in Guilliatt 2003). White nerdy boys, in their role as television critics, have attempted to deal with their elimination from Fenech's Australian story-space in two main ways: by dismissing *Pizza* as a show for 'deadbeat, Commodore-driving outer-suburban hoons' (Warneke 2001); and by coopting the *Pizza* series as 'a televisual essay in praise of assimilation' (Lane 2001). Indeed, Lane goes so far as to champion *Pizza's* 'politically incorrect' jokes (supposedly aimed at the 'pompous cant of multiculturalism') in order to restore 'insouciant ockers' to centre stage in the role of 'multicultural resistors'. Here, Lane seamlessly coopts the ocker-wogboy in order to redeem the Australian national type for a conservative agenda. In the process, he elevates and suppresses the *Pizza* crew for being just as 'crude, sexist, racist, bigoted, stupid, vulgar...as are other yobbos' (Lane 2001).

## Principles of diversity in national space

Writing about 1970s ocker comedy, O'Regan (1989) argues that critics, by condemning 1970s ocker culture for 'elevating the lout, the boor, the coarse, the crass, the anti-intellectual and the vulgar', missed the camp turn taken by the Australian type – as well as the genre's 'avant-garde and experimental dimension' (1989: 77–78). Addressing the problem of nationhood and cinema in 1996, O'Regan suggests that a popular new world or 'melting-pot' cinema, addressing an ethnically diverse audience (as Hollywood cinema did in its formative years), draws on and develops a common vernacular that includes recognizable social types. In Australian cinema, the most popular films at the box office have proved to be vernacular comedies featuring the decent bloke and his larrikin mates in the 1920s, hayseed families from the rural backblocks in the 1920s and 1930s, urban ockers in the 1970s and wogboy-ockers in film and television in 2000–07.

If the broader cultural moment of ockerism in the 1970s can be seen retrospectively as an experiment with an 'Australian voice' emerging from diversity, the wogboy moment of 2000–07 might be seen as a similar experiment with creating an 'Australian' ethnicity out of a hybrid of Anglo-Celtic and diasporic identities. A clear expression of this occurs in *The Wog Boy* photo-shoot when Steve models several hybrid identities, including 'Zorba Dundee'. In contrast to the principle of exclusion at work in Hage's whiteness paradigm, there is an argument to be made that the broad church of comedy operates from more than one paradigm of nationhood. Whiteness might be at stake in European and diasporic paradigms, but for O'Regan multicultural critique and melting-pot populism, based on different principles of diversity, contest these exclusive paradigms (1996: 322). Multicultural film and television affirm cultural diversity, cross-cultural hybrids and post-national identities, 'disposing of tired discourses of traditional Australian nationalism' (O'Regan 1996: 326–27). But a melting-pot, new world cinema affirms cultural convergence rather than cultural plurality. This convergence principle is based on 'an immigrant's readiness to take on new identities and the assumption that native-born identities would be open to change' (O'Regan 1996: 317). This readiness and openness 'produces a dominant ethnicity over time' and 'emphasizes commonality rather than difference, consensus rather than plurality' (O'Regan 1996: 330). But the emergence of a singular identity in a melting-pot society need not be condemned as assimilationist or mistaken for the triumph of white tolerance. Rather, 'the right to assimilate, integrate and contribute to the making of the broader culture' in a consumer market is based on a commercial need for a distinctive Australian identity that, far from being monocultural or 'white', is 'working from different principles of diversity – ones defined in a new world fashion' (O'Regan 1996: 322).

What principle of diversity, then, is at work in the three films under scrutiny here? One way to tease this out might be to remember comedy's utopian or providential endings. Rather than look to the hybrid, diasporic figure of the ocker-wogboy or the melting-pot figure of the Australian wogboy, we might look to the formation of a new cross-cultural couple whose function in these comedies is to reconcile two worlds. The happy ending – celebrating the emergence of the hero and his bride, typical of romantic comedy – is clearly parodied in the disrupted wedding scenes which end *The Wog Boy* and *Fat Pizza*, and in the backyard barbecue that rescues men and women alike from the stultifying atmosphere of a formal afternoon tea party, marking Kay and Nino's engagement at the end of *They're a Weird Mob*. But there is a different principle at work in each of these providential endings. In *Weird Mob*, the backyard barbecue, lubricated by vast quantities of 'bloody beer', is a liminal place of convergence – of men and women, old and new Australians, the boss's daughter and the builder's labourer. But, as lamingtons and meringues are cast aside in favour of a nice cold beer, the male chorus assures us that it's still 'a man's country, sweetheart', despite the evidence that change is in the air. In *The Wog Boy*, the church wedding of Steve's mate to Celia's sister provides an occasion to bring Steve together with his love interest, Celia, so that they can resume their interrupted battle. Here, the church is not so much a liminal place of convergence as a cross-cultural meeting ground where a congenial battle over difference on several fronts (including class, gender and ethnicity) can continue unabated. In stark contrast, the church in *Fat Pizza* is a riotously unreconciled battlefield, where one wedding party after another lays claim to the space, creating a cacophonic convergence of social types, each vying for centre stage with no real hope of triumphing over the others.

## Conclusion

To return to the initial question: How do wogboys 'assert their ethnic identities and reconfigure the Australian stereotype of the "ocker"', as Speed (2005) claims, if they are routinely *excluded* from, or at best controlled, assimilated and contained by, the national type? Speed's analysis of wogsploitation comedy makes clear the continuity and discontinuity between national types and comic types, revealing not only resistance to assimilation, but a degree of complicity between Australian wogboys and regressive ockers. Both revel in the degenerate, regressive or unkempt aspects of the Australian national type: 'These films present the wog stereotype as a hybrid of traits associated with European immigrants and those of another suppressed entity, the vulgar proletariat in the form of the ocker.' (Speed 2005: 143) The outcome of this complicity between wogboys and ockers, in Speed's view, is the 'ultimate banality' of a hybrid type composed of 'migrant shiftlessness' and 'Australian vulgarity' (2005: 143).

Hage (1998) argues that multicultural 'tolerance' of ethnic or diasporic difference contains within it an intransigent whiteness, or Anglo-Celtic hegemony, that seeks to control an emerging

'Australian' ethnicity. However, as Nino Culotta, Steve Karamatsis and Pauly Falzoni show – politely in *They're a Weird Mob*, brashly in *The Wog Boy* and pugnaciously in *Fat Pizza* – Australianization of ethnic or diasporic difference takes place in a melting-pot, consumer market in which the ethnic other evades and even upstages bureaucratic and political attempts to define, contain and control Australian identity. In this process, the wogboy is an active agent rather than a passive object, assimilating the ocker and appropriating the vernacular story-space. Understood from the perspective of the national type, wogboys and chockos – as diasporic, multicultural or 'new world' comic types – have indeed trumped the larrikins and ockers of Australian screen comedy. The fact that women, Indigenous people and Asian-Australians remain, at best, bit players in wogboy-ocker comedies is usually seen as further evidence that 'wogsploitation' films are popular precisely because they tap into a long-standing national type without disturbing its key characteristic: aggressively hedonistic masculinity. Two points could be made here. Aligning recent wogboy comedies with 1970s ocker culture erases the convergence between wogboys and a broader range of comic types which, between them, might have the capacity to remove the anachronistic ideal of a *male* national type permanently from the centre stage of Australian nationhood. What would happen to the national type if, for instance, wogboys were viewed in light of the brazen brides, grotesque daughters, treacherous mothers and old hags featured in women's film comedies (Collins 2003a) and currently enjoying top billing in the long-running television series *Kath and Kim*? It is a measure, perhaps, of the strength of the male national type that this would be a novel, even deeply transgressive, way of looking at the place of wogboy comedies in Australian film and television history. We might see then not only the anachronistic fantasy of *white* supremacy underlying multicultural tolerance, but an equally anachronistic fantasy of *male* supremacy underlying the new hybrid of melting pot, ocker-wogboy comedies.

# 7

# Excess in Oz: The Crazy Russian and the Quiet Australian

## Greg Dolgopolov

How are Russians portrayed in Australian cinema? In contrast to their proportionally small population and minor, non-cohesive multicultural grouping, there have been numerous representations of Russians in Australian films and television serials. These are exoticized images that use Russians as catalysts of narrative conflict and cultural excess. Russia occupies an ambivalent space in the Australian cinematic imagination: romantic, mysterious, dangerous, emotional and dramatic. It is imagery informed by literary classics, especially the psychological lavishness of Leo Tolstoy and the spiritual inordinateness of Fyodor Dostoyevsky. While there is a long history of Russian migration, there is a relatively recent record of the representation of Russians on Australian screens. Russians are not cast as villains in the same way that we came to expect from American cinema during the Cold War, nor are Russians portrayed as 'normal', assimilated members of a broad multi-ethnic nation. They are more often cast as exotic, passionate and radical, dangerous and excessive.

In this chapter, I survey a number of Australian films with Russian themes (*Russian Doll*, Kazantzidis 2001; *Children of the Revolution*, Duncan 1996; *Salvation*, Cox 2007; and the min-series *The Petrov Affair*, Carson 1986), examining representational trends, their cultural functions and cultural significance. I argue that Russians are characterized and represented by a narrative quality of 'excess' that acts as a functional strategy of textual alienation, a management of migrant identity that constructs a narrative of ethnic socialization. Unlike other multicultural film portrayals, Russians are not depicted as migrants or as a community, but as

*Salvation* (Paul Cox, 2007). Image courtesy of Paul Cox.

individual outsiders seeking permanent residency. Traditional clichéd descriptions of Russians as 'radical' (Govor 1997: 223) and 'mad' (Holmgren 2005: 249) converge in Australian representations of sexual, performative and spiritual excess. In exploring excess, I combine the sociological perspective of Georges Bataille with Kristin Thompson's cinematic approach, to make sense of how Australian cinema 'uses' Russian performative excess in defining an Australian identity.

### Russian-themed Australian films

There is a tendency in critical writing about ethnic representations to claim some racist or figurative injustice – often with good reason. Russians have endured negative, politicized typecasting and concomitant portrayals as mad and excessive. Clichéd descriptions of Russians as 'nihilists', 'anarchists' and terrorists', as well as 'dirty and greasy' had constantly been employed by the Australian press since the second half of the nineteenth century. After the Revolution and at various times until the end of the Cold War, Russians were cast in the mould of 'barbarous Bolsheviks', and suffered a permanent lack of status and cultural confidence (Govor 1997: 219–28). Since their cinematic emergence in the 1980s, they have been recast predominately as criminals, bedraggled refugees, spies and prostitutes in a number of screen representations. When I asked Australia's most prominent Russian actor, Alex Menglet, whether he thought that Australian representations of Russians (many of which he had performed) were racist or discriminatory, he was taken aback. He argued emphatically that 'Australian film representations of Russians are not racist, it's just that writers and producers do not have enough time to develop material to create complex, engaging characters and are left with stereotypes. It's not racism it a lack of development time.' This is a compelling explanation that hints at representational vagueness, but it does not challenge the established patterns for imagining Russian characters and their prevailing narratives on Australian screens.

Russians have not experienced the benefits of multiculturalism with respect to representational agency. There is no accented, hybrid and hyphenated Russian-Australian cinema. There are some Russian film-makers working in Australia, but none of them is producing material that engages, even tangentially, with the diasporic condition and a hybrid Russian Australian identity.

In addition to the cinematic adaptation of classic Russian literature (Chekhov in *Country Life* (Michael Blakemore 1994) and Dostoyevsky in *The Prisoner of St Petersburg* (Ian Pringle 1990)), there are a number of original, Australian-made feature films with substantial Russian themes: *The Diaries of Vaslav Nijinsky, Russian Doll, Children of the Revolution* and *Salvation*. Additionally, there are a number of films with minor Russian characters or themes (*The Jammed, A Man's Gotta Do, The Howling III, My First Wife*). However, it is in television serials and mini-series that Russian characters are most prominent in myriad minor roles, offering a touch of exoticism, danger and unassimilable foreignness as prostitutes and criminals. The traditional clichés abound in inverse proportion to the length of time the characters appear on screen – a Russian crime boss in *Fat Pizza*, a jealous husband called Igor in *Neighbours* and an asylum-seeking tennis champion in the 1980s serial *Skyways*. There are numerous long-running serials where Russian characters appear briefly (sometimes performed by non-Russian actors) as guests in a single episode to add a dash of ethnic flavour to an otherwise homogenous Anglo community (*Neighbours, Water Rats* and *MDA* with the Polish actor Jacek Koman playing an anarchic and unqualified Russian doctor). These minor roles present the full extent of ethnic stereotypes: of Russians as mad, anarchic, stop-at-nothing desperados. In series such as *The Petrov Affair* (mini-series), *Palace of Dreams* (mini-series), *Fireflies* (ABC series) and *Kick* (SBS series), Russian characters create the essential sense of dramatic conflict, not as some other East European migrants but specifically as 'Russians', with all the cultural flaws, passions, madness, problems and resonances that this encapsulates in the minds of television audiences.

While most of these films and serials deal with Russian immigrants of some sort, neither migrant experiences nor diasporic connections inform narrative structure. With respect to Russian figures, the focus is on the ideological and covert political activity: communism, revolution and spying (*The Petrov Affair, That Girl from Hong Kong, Children of the Revolution*). The Russian propensity for high art, especially ballet, is frequently a source of humour. In the romantic comedy *Russian Doll*, the lead character Katia plays dumb and pretends not to know *Swan Lake*, undermining the Australian expectation that all Russians are cultured. In the *Howling III* (Mora 1987), absurd werewolf connections between Siberia and Australia are highlighted when a Russian ballerina becomes a werewolf, defects and wreaks havoc in Sydney before joining a werewolf tribe in the bush. Jokes inverting Russians high culture act to neutralize the social distinctions.

Aside from Paul Cox's films (*My First Wife*, *The Diaries of Vaslav Nijinsky*, *Salvation*), which feature wistful Russian creative types, musicians and dancers overcome by extreme passions, the 'high culture' stereotype of Russian seriousness is absent. This is replaced with excessive performances that comply with a comic or sentimental resolution; characters often appear as 'randy Russians' where their difference from Australian characters is highlighted by a voracious sexual appetite. This servicing of fascination and suspicion is unlike the Cold War fantasy of the strict and serious Russian femme fatale, and is not limited to Russian women. Russian men enjoy a rapacious appetite for good times, as attested to by the sexual exploits of Petrov (*The Petrov Affair*), Rudi (the groom in *A Man's Gotta Do*) and Stalin (*Children of the Revolution*).

Extending this pattern of excess and un-Australian difference, the broader range of Russian character types is far from positive. The available positions for Russian men include unreliable (*A Man's Gotta Do*), buffoonish and overly emotional (*Children of the Revolution*), radical (*My First Wife*) and even brutal (*Children of the Revolution*, *Salvation*). Russian women tend to have less scope. They are characterized as driven, highly sexed desiring machines or heart-of-gold whores (*Salvation*, *The Jammed*, *Howling III*, *Russian Doll*) who are always available, especially to unappealing Anglo-Australian men. Portrayals of Russian women share many of the Orientalist projections that Asian women suffer as the 'subservient and sexual' figures of colonialist fantasies. According to Mario Praz, 'a love of the exotic is usually an imaginative projection of a sexual desire, and the Orient symbolized a type of licentious romantic sexual experience that titillated the European imagination' (1951: 207). However, the excessive sexuality and passion of Russian women invariably leads to the salvation of the Australian men who love them. The dénouement of sexual excess translates into the promise of their salvation in the visa economy – where love is traded for the holy grail of Australian migrant films: permanent residency.

## Excess

The Australian approach to representing Russians tends to focus conceptually on excess (physical, sexual, spiritual and performative) that is inclined towards either deep human suffering or the carnivalesque comedy of redemption and inclusion, invoking a variation on the Hollywood 'crazy or mad Russian' (Holmgren 2005: 238) cast dramatically as 'irrational and self-contradictory' (Bulgakowa 2005: 216), but defined in distinction to the rational, relaxed and normal Anglo-Australians.

In order to make sense of this excess of meaning and performance, I draw on the work of Georges Bataille and Kristin Thompson. Bataille (1985) felt that social taboos and their transgression were wholly interdependent and that excess was an essential process for building social cohesiveness (1985: 137–60). Bataille argues that, by transgressing taboos, we simultaneously contrive to endorse or modify them. Each is dependent on the other: 'organised transgressions together with the taboo make social life what it is' (Bataille 1991: 65). Bataille argues that the transgression of law is what he calls an accursed yet ineluctable part of our lives. In this way, Australian social norms are made in the name of prohibiting acts of violence or etiquette crimes, while social and cultural health requires behaviour that violates the cherished rules in order to reaffirm them, through the power of narrative. The fantasy of Russian excess reinvigorates Australian social norms, allowing for what Jennifer Rutherford (2000: 69) calls a 'symbolic expansion' of meaning to challenge an otherwise stultifying ordinariness. Following the logic of Bataille, I argue that Russians, more so than other ethnic minorities, have been constructed in Australian cinema as a heterogeneous energy, unassimilable, charged with an unknown and dangerous force with innate taboos separating them from the ordinary world.

Another way to think of excess is in the cinematic terms identified by Kristin Thompson (1986), developed from a critical approach based on Russian formalism. Thompson argues that the importance of excess is that it renews 'the perceptual freshness of the work' and 'suggests a different way of watching and listening to a film' (1986: 140–41). She describes excess as an intermittent textual phenomenon, a brief moment of self-conscious materiality that interrupts an otherwise conventional, 'non-excessive' film and that excess forms no specific patterns which are characteristic of the work (1986: 132). It is an Australian narrative mode in which the figure of the Russian stands as textual excess. For example, the threat spat out in a heavy accent by Nik 'the Russian' Radev (actually Bulgarian) in the television crime epic *Underbelly* (2008) is more excessively 'real' (perhaps because of the vicious image of Russian criminals in recent mafia films) than any other scene of violence in this casually brutal series. In contrast, the queue of Russian tourists desperate to use the outback toilet and seemingly happy with one sheet of toilet paper doled out to them by their ocker guide in *The Genie from Downunder* (1995) drives the introductory scene into the absurd and characterizes Russians as an interruption to acceptable standards of business and hospitality.

Stylistic excess is featured in the genre-confused *Children of the Revolution* (Duncan 1996), in Vaudeville scenes set in the Kremlin. In this mock-historical comedy, an Australian communist revolutionary, Joan, goes to Russia in 1953 and has a brief affair with Joseph Stalin. Their love child, Young Joe, brings Australia to the brink of civil war. Against the style of a realist family drama, the excessive staging of the Kremlin moments provides a fantastical freedom from the constraints of representing social reality in a realistic form. The staid, serious and dark image of the Kremlin is subverted by high farce. Stalin's Politburo henchmen kick up their heels singing 'I Get a Kick Out of You' as the Father of the Nation shows what it means to party, evoking a mixture of *eros* and *thanatos* within the overwhelmed Joan.

In Australian drama, Russian characters perform these excessive functions, overturning otherwise 'realistic' narratives with their irrational, mad desire, emphasizing what Tom O'Regan identifies as a 'negotiation of political weakness' (235: 1996) with the 'little Aussie battler' unexpectedly thrust on to the world stage. In *Children of the Revolution*, Stalin is now a lonely melancholic in a postmodern reconstruction that points to excess as self-conscious materiality, and the realization that his genetic heritage may underpin the zeal of the Australian union movement. The Russians, in contrast to the Australians, are more passionate, more exuberant and more intense: hardened

KGB officers weep uncontrollably over Joan's letters to Stalin, while Politburo chiefs are party animals and Stalin a Casanova. Aside from revolutionary Joan Fraser and her son Young Joe, Australian characters are presented as compliant, passive, dull, emotionally restrained and overly 'discreet'. Russian characters in Australian films, whether as dancing politicians, spiritual prostitutes or ballerina werewolves, provide the filmic diegesis – and indeed world history – with a fresh and somewhat defamiliarized perspective.

*The Petrov Affair* covers similar but far more serious ground in its dramatizing of Australia's most spectacular international spy scandal. The mini-series tells how, in 1954, Vladimir Petrov, allegedly head of Soviet espionage in Australia, successfully approached ASIO for asylum in exchange for secret documents. His defection triggered the removal of his wife by MVD agents back to Moscow, but in a dramatic twist she was plucked from the hands of the armed Russian agents at Darwin airport and reunited with her husband. The defection sparked a scandalous Royal Commission, and allegations of political conspiracy that contributed to Labor's loss at the elections and eventually to the split of the Labor Party.

Petrov (in Alex Menglet's potent performance) is interpreted counter-intuitively, not as a dark sneaky spy but as a sleazy party animal, a womanizer, a hard drinker, irresponsible, buffoonish, silly and playful – but not useful. Even his dog is out of control, creating mayhem by biting the Soviet flag during the October Day celebrations at the Russian Embassy. Petrov's amusement is clearly contrasted with the stern embassy officials who are disgusted with his dog's behaviour and dismayed at his response. Petrov is in further contrast to dry Australian intelligence forces and acidic Labor politicians. In this way, the mini-series is more concerned with an episode in the history of the Labor Party than it is about the Petrovs' world.

The construction of the Petrov figure offered a blueprint for future portrayals of Russians as emotionally and sexually excessive. Russian characters appear as more radical than their Australian counterparts, more uneconomical and illogical. Katia in *Russian Doll* (Natalia Novikova) is marked as different to other women: she heaps teaspoons of sugar into her tea, her mood is erratic, and she is an Internet bride focused on love and not on a marriage of convenience. Katia is extremely excessive, exhibiting an out-of-control feminine voraciousness that overpowers the quiet Australians. In a collation of the most vituperative Russian stereotypes, *Russian Doll* focuses on Katia, her romance with Ethan, a happily married Jewish publisher, and his best friend Harvey, a miserable neurotic private investigator. In order to keep Katia in the country, Ethan begs Harvey to marry her 'on paper', and to live with her to make it appear legitimate. When Harvey reluctantly agrees, Katia takes over his life. Ethan's plan comes unstuck when Harvey and Katia start to fall in love.

The film sets up a dramatic conflict between the 'normal', honest but dull Australian bloke, Harvey, and the vibrant, emotional, sexually joyous and 'a bit crazy' Katia. Jake Wilson describes Katia as 'a full-bodied cartoon of over-the-top femininity. From her first appearance, decked out in fur coat, leopard-print dress, bouffant hair and sunglasses, her specific identity as a Russian is less important than her status as a one-woman parade of vibrant folk culture and exotic sex-appeal' (2001). While much of this description is apt, Katia's Russianness is an essential part of the normative transgressions (too many spoons of sugar, too loud, too incongruous, too physical, too much). Her Russianness justifies this cultural excess based on a history of national turmoil and suffering. The only other Russian character, Katia's friend Lisa (Sacha Horler), is equally sexually voracious, if not more so, as she actively seduces Harvey, creating a totalizing impression of Russian excessive desire and of the Australian's commensurate inability to fulfil it. Katia's sexuality is an expression of her native desires, her need to be wanted. Her failures in love in Russia are the cause of her migrant condition and Harvey's failures in Australia are the result of his inability to express his desire, both presenting fantastical or perverse possibilities as problems and solutions. Jake Wilson (2001) summarizes the contrast between the two characters as 'she's slovenly and uninhibited; he's anal and reserved. She's a party animal who's never read a book in her life; he's an aspiring novelist who demands absolute quiet for his work.' The differences between these characters elide a Russian point of view, forming the basis of recuperation for an emotionally crippled Australian man. By highlighting Katia's emotional excess, Harvey is able to let go of the anal behaviour that has obstructed his happiness. He falls in love with excess and the freedom and joy it brings him.

The narrative positions the Russian-Australian economy as one where Katia's sexuality and desire are exchanged for a visa and a moral commitment to truthfulness once the charade of the fake marriage is renounced. Katia runs from the altar of the staged wedding and returns to Russia. Harvey, devastated, goes to Russia to track her down. Katia can only find a place in Australia when her excess is curtailed by recognizing Harvey's genuine love for her. In the final scenes of the film, the 'real' wedding transforms the ethnic excess into a material excess, where a shaky amateur handycam provides a moment of pleasure offering a of 'real' ethnic flavour. It stands out as a kind of reverse material filmic excess that defines a realistic, authentic experience of community and communion. Katia's performance of excess is diminished in the midst of this visual style, as she is symbolically integrated into a diasporic Australian community and her excess is dissipated.

## Paul Cox

Perhaps the most devoted Russophile in Australian cinema, Paul Cox is a prolific independent director. Commonly known to be a Dutch émigré, but of Russian parentage, Cox has made more Russian-themed films in Australia than anyone else (*My First Wife* 1984, *The Diaries of Vaslav Nijinsky* 2001 and *Salvation* 2007). He has worked with Russian cinematographer Yuri Sokol on a number of other projects and has been an avowed fan of Russian film masters, displaying a Russian 'melancholia' across his oeuvre.

Cox moves beyond the stereotypes to the elegiac qualities of Chekhov or the intense relationship dramas that were popular in the Soviet Union in the 1970s and 1980s. *My First Wife* (1984) is an intense examination of a marriage breakdown. John, a second-generation Russian composer whose émigré Russian father is dying in hospital, is going mad trying to figure out where his relationship went wrong. The film is not about Russianness, but cultural positioning does help to explain John s excessive grieving and irrational attempts to regain his wife. His unproductive emotional excess is painfully contrasted with his wife Helen's calm and seemingly disengaged separation.

Cox defines a different mood in *Salvation* (2007, as yet unreleased), a much lighter relationship drama that satirizes commercial Christianity. *Salvation* is the first Australian film to feature extensive subtitled Russian dialogue, with Russian actors performing the leading roles and portraying Russians as complex characters capable of spiritual salvation. The film plays with the classic Russian prostitution-as-evil narrative of Alexander Kuprin's *Yama* (The Pit 1909–15) where a man of means 'saves' a woman of ill-repute. In Cox's version, Barry, an aging biblical scholar and frustrated artist, is saved by Irina, a Russian émigré working as a prostitute in order to support her mother and daughter. Irina offers Barry spiritual and sexual salvation (as well as a way out of his deadly marriage) and he in return offers her love and money, and saves her from her violent pimp, Anton.

In contrast, *The Diaries of Vaslav Nijinsky* (2001) dramatizes Russian ballet star Nijinsky's diaries, which detail his madness as well as his relationship with Ballet Russe impresario Sergei Diaghilev. The film is a modernist exploration of a creative madness that is closely aligned with Njinsky's inner voices and his regular proclamations of his love for Russia:

> I am a madman who loves mankind. My madness is my love towards mankind. I am a dancer. I love Russia. Russia feels more than any other country. (Nijinsky voiceover, *The Diaries of Vaslav Nijinsky*, Paul Cox 2001)

Nijinsky's 'performed' Russianness (he was not actually Russian but an ethnic Pole born in Kiev), his complex relationship and affections for Russia are symbolically linked to his obscure and confused state of mind. The film is stylistically excessive in its essayistic play with memory and texture, and voiceover narration that resists a mainstream storyline with a narrative that is continuously interrupted by obtuse meaning and images that draw attention to themselves.

## The recuperation of the unassimilable migrant

Russian excess is sometimes represented as both desirable and as an object of derision. The audience laughs at the Russian's excessiveness – the spirituality, the obsessiveness and the stinginess of characters such as Russian émigré Svettie Burke (Natasha Novikova), married to a small-town chief fireman in *Fireflies* (ABC TV). Svettie wants nothing to do with an organization that distracts her husband from his financial woes and failing marriage. This sort of character, like the countless minor Russian criminal roles, provides an ambivalent, somewhat uncomfortable excess in order to perform its larger social role of bolstering mainstream values and ultimately assimilating the unassimilable.

What the Australian viewer does with this excess is, in part, a political question. The very concept of excess is a relativistic term that posits an obvious norm and a political-social evaluation of that which is beyond 'normal'. Russians are outside the norm of the good migrant

– they are unassimilable, yet the cinematic narrative allows for a resolution that overcomes this seemingly impossible barrier.

Russian-themed Australian films do not follow the Naficy pattern of an 'accented' cinema, even though the Russian accent is the primary form of denoting Russian otherness. It is not an 'intercultural cinema that is characterized by experimental styles that attempt to represent the experience of living between two or more cultural regimes of knowledge' (Marks 2000: 1). Australian films with Russian themes and characters are not about Russians, their experiences or point of view. They are a manufactured multiculturalism – a mode employed by mainstream cinema to exoticize, exploit, ridicule and control an 'ambivalent' ethnic group. These films are about exploring Australian lives in response to their apprehension and interaction with the excessive, out of control, passionate but illogical Russians. These excessive characteristics become available as the stuff of lifestyle consumption or the fantasy of becoming 'other'. Manufactured multiculturalism is about the centre's fantasy, a consumption-based exoticism that is a form of dramatic tourism. It celebrates the alleged benefits of multiculturalism while exploiting ethnic minorities for dramatic and comic possibilities. The majority of Australian ethnic comedies, outside of *Fat Pizza*, operate in this conservative Anglo-centric economy. As the *Neighbours* episode title 'Fools Russian In' suggests, it is the ethnic who is laughed at and it is the Russian who provides the tension that allows the Anglo community to come together.

Russians are rarely represented as a community of loyal, settled migrants who are worthy members of Australia's seemingly cohesive multicultural community. The Jewish family from Russia which runs the pub in the television serial *Palace of Dreams*, set in the 1930s, is about as close as Russian characters come to being 'settled'. Russians do not appear on the land other than as tourists (*The Genie From Down Under*) or as werewolves (*Howling III*). They are not *that* different from other white European foreigners, but it is their ability to merge, to blend, that makes them dangerous as subversives. Their accent is the primary signifier of cultural difference, but it is their history of suffering and their excessive emotionalism that makes them appear unassimilable. They are always 'other' – even as second-generation migrants (John in *My First Wife*) and Tatiana, the daughter in a Serbo-Russian family in SBS multicultural television serial *Kick* (2007). Russians seldom appear as settled migrants who are part of the multicultural *melange*. Since their first appearances on Australian television screens in the early 1980s, Russian migrants have been cast as desperados, escaping the metaphoric barbed wire. The plot device revisits the Petrov narrative, or at least its dramatic highpoint of defecting and moving to Australia at enormous personal cost. The drama is in the desire for migration, not in the settlement that occurs beyond the epilogue.

Films about the migrant experience often act to naturalize the exotic ethnic group – to make them understandable and unthreatening. The narrative logic of the small number of Russian-themed Australian films is that, even though the Russian characters appear unassimilable, the often comic *dénouement* allows for the happy ending of successful migration. The multiple themes of *Salvation* are boiled down to the love-struck biblical scholar Barry acting completely out of character in tricking the brutal Russian pimp Anton out of the blood money so as to save the heart-of-gold prostitute Irina. The logic that occurs off screen is that Barry saves Irina and allows her safety and permanent residency in Australia. Similarly in *Children of the Revolution*, Russianness – or its excessive extreme – is genetically integrated into the Australian psyche and nearly takes root. The ballerina in *Howling III* is summoned by the call of the wild to join the werewolf community in the bush and thereby become part of the land. The inevitable conclusion of *The Petrov Affair* is that defection allows the Petrovs the opportunity to stay in Australia, protected from the reaches of the KGB. The final scene of *Russian Doll* suggests that only a wedding based on true love will allow Katia to remain in Australia. These films are about symbolic integration and acceptance of the mad, excessive Russian who, after the appropriate rite of passage and the logic of sacrifice, is welcomed into the Australian home.

## Conclusion

Russian representations have not participated in what John Conomos argues is the fundamental value of multicultural films that they typify 'a healthy, sceptical response to orthodoxy and dogma; they represent an incisive critique of the narrow-mindedness of monoculturalism articulated from the site of marginality or contrapuntal existence' (1992: 13). Even in *Russian Doll*, a seemingly ideal multicultural film directed by a Greek-Australian (Stavros Kazantzidis) and written and produced by a Ukrainian Jewish migrant (Allanah Zitserman) about Russian-speaking Jewish migrants, there is an insistence on telling the story from an Anglo-centric perspective, one that ultimately denies the difference of Russian excess as it is consumed by ordinary Australian life. Representing Russians in mainstream films is not about multiculturalism, but about Australian fantasies of excess. When the fun is over, it is about the figurative containment of otherness at the level of narrative.

While cinema mediates the construction of individual and group identity (Russian migrants, Australians and Russian-Australians), it violates as many narratives, images and conceptions as it validates. Yet Russian-themed Australian films are distinct to other national cinemas representations of Russians, and indeed Australian representations of other migrants. There are narrative trends that portray Russian characters not as established communities, but as new, tentative migrants seeking permanent residency. The story arc sees them pass through conflict to a gradual assimilation that extends beyond the *dénouement*. Australian cinema, in its limited representation of Russian characters, has privileged a performative excess that masks a chasm of cultural differences. The source of this designation springs from a complex of cultural, political stereotypes and literary antecedents that determine authorial imaginings and directorial choices. Australian cinema may not 'need' Russian themes and characters, but Russian excess can play an important role in allowing a symbolic expansion into difference and potentially illogical, emotional meaning of all that is excluded from ordinary, quiet Australian life.

# 8

# ANZAC'S 'OTHERS': 'CRUEL HUNS' AND 'NOBLE TURKS'

## Antje Gnida and Catherine Simpson

War films are not an obvious starting point to discuss Australia's diasporic cinema. Nevertheless, portrayals of the enemy draw attention to the nationalizing discourses which serve to maintain an assimilationist model of the nation. While neither German nor Turkish identities figure prominently in Australia's contemporary multicultural cinema, these national 'types' play a more significant role in Australian visual culture produced in the first part of the twentieth century. German, and to a lesser extent Turkish, villains feature in numerous films produced in Australia during both world wars. In this chapter, we argue that in the short term Australian film portrayals of the 'the cruel Hun' and 'noble Turk' encouraged glorification of soldiers in Australian and New Zealand Army Corps (ANZAC), while in the long term these perpetuated a more nationalistic construction of the Anzac legend.

In films made during World War II but about World War I, portrayals of German and Turkish enemies were exploited primarily to get the Australian public behind the lagging early World War II effort. These depictions also fed into racist discourses, which reversed the assimilation process of German migrants in their new homeland. This broader racism towards Germans, at least on an institutional level, ceased a few years after World War II with the increase in German migration to Australia. Where negative depictions of the German enemy were fairly stable, varying from Hun to Nazi across World War I and World War II film productions, there is a distinct shift from the few negative portrayals of the Turkish enemy in Australian films produced during World War I as opposed to those made later but concerning this very same war.

*Forty Thousand Horsemen* (Charles Chauvel, 1940). Image used by arrangement with the Licensor, The Estate of Charles Chauvel c/ Curtis Brown (Aust) Pty Ltd.

In 1967, the RSL actively supported a Turkish migration scheme and Turkey became the first 'non-European' country to sign an assisted migrant agreement with Australia (Basarin and Basarin 1993: 3). This could be explained through the newly developing discourse of the 'noble Turk' (Baker 2006), the seeds of which can be glimpsed in C.E.W. Bean's writings about the Turkish enemy (Kent 1985: 386). However, the turning point came with Charles Chauvel's portrayal of Turkish regard for Australian fighting qualities in *Forty Thousand Horsemen* (1940). The discourse lived on after World War II, but came to the fore again in the 1980s with a newly invigorated form of Australian cultural nationalism, glimpsed in Peter Weir's portrayal of the heroic Anzacs in *Gallipoli* (1981) and successful TV mini-series about the fighting of the Australian Imperial Force (AIF) against the Turks in the Dardanelles, such as *1915* (ABC 1982), which depicted amicable relations between the diggers and the Turks on the battlefield. This came at a time when Australian 'pilgrims' started converging on the Gallipoli battlefields in large numbers. What began merely as respect for the enemy has now morphed into a nationally celebrated friendship between Turkey and Australia. In addition, Turkish veterans – dubbed 'our favourite enemies' (Baker 2006) – have been invited to march by the RSL as part of the annual Anzac Day parade. Of course, the Germans have never been afforded the same opportunity, which reinforces the notion that these seemingly gracious gestures towards the Turks in fact serve to reinscribe a 'hegemonic notion of Australian identity' (Nourry 2005: 365), and have little to do with the relationship with the Turks – or the Germans, for that matter. In this chapter, we explore the figures of the 'Turk' and the 'Hun' in films primarily produced *about* World War I and the role they have played since in producing the Anzac legend and reinforcing conservative myths of nationhood. In Australia, the significance of the German enemy has receded in importance while the Turkish enemy has been embraced and elevated as time passes. The structure of this chapter reflects this change.

## German villains: From Hun to Nazi

World War I film portrayals of German and Turkish villains not only supported the government's recruiting drives but also played a role in the earliest phase of the construction of the Anzac myth on film. *The Hero of the Dardanelles* (Alfred Rolfe 1915), for example, elevates Anzac ideals such as honour and fair play. The central character, an Anzac, is depicted drowning a Turk caught sniping at Red Cross workers (Reynaud 2005: 12). The films reinforced prevalent aspects of Australia's social imaginary at the time. One of these was the nation's invasion anxiety, which comes to the fore in *If the Huns Came to Melbourne* (George Coates 1916) and *Australia's Peril* (Franklyn Barrett 1917). Other prevalent aspects are Australia's complete identification with Britain and the nation's belief in the superiority of the Anglo-Saxon race. The Australian heroes in *For Australia* (Monte Luke 1915), for example, are repeatedly referred to as 'English' while *The Joan of Arc of Loos* (George Willoughby 1916) portrays Germans with ape-like characteristics.

The one noted Turkish portrayal from the post-World War I period was in a feature film released in 1924, *Daughter of East* (Roy Darling). Funded by a Greek-Australian café owner but set in Turkey, it tells the story of an Armenian girl who falls in love with an Englishman, but is kidnapped by an evil Turkish *pasha* (Pike and Cooper 1998: 122). Robert Manne argues that a cultural amnesia *currently* prevails in Australia about the Armenian genocide, which occurred simultaneously with the Dardanelles campaign (Manne 2007). However, during 1915, countless Australian newspaper reports conveyed the enormity of the Armenian atrocities at the hands of the disintegrating Ottoman Empire. This film was set against that background and indicates a readiness to 'tar the unfamiliar Turkish enemy with the same atrocity-committing brush with which propaganda had painted the Germans' (Reynaud 2005: 12), something which changes significantly 15 or so years later in Chauvel's *Forty Thousand Horsemen*.

With the outbreak of World War II, film portrayals of the German gained renewed importance. The lack of enthusiasm for the war in the early war years (Elkin 1941: 10–14) not only demanded the re-establishment of the myth of the heroic Anzac for the purpose of recruiting, but also a clear identification of the old and new enemy, the German, to get the public behind the war effort. World War II then saw an almost seamless transition from the unfavourable Australian World War I film portrayals of the 'Hun' to 'Nazi'. In the World War II films, depictions of the German enemy as *racially* inferior (as utilized in the World War I films) are subordinated to portrayals of Germans as *morally* inferior. However, World War II films – especially those of Chauvel – still represent 'ordinary' German soldiers as barbarians or 'abstraction' – for example, as mindless machines. As Sam Keen (1986) points out, dehumanizing and demonizing depictions of the enemy as beast, vermin, barbarian, rapist or abstraction serve a variety of propaganda purposes and absolve soldiers of any moral responsibility for killing other human beings (1986: 61).

Since there is little honour to be won in the eradication of a sub-human or bestial threat, there is also the depiction of the enemy as 'worthy opponent' (Keen 1986: 67). This portrayal of the enemy as honourable and strong can also be utilized to elevate one's own honour and fighting qualities. The positive portrayal of the Turk as honourable soldier in Charles Chauvel's account of the exploits of the Australian Light Horse in Palestine in World War I, *Forty Thousand Horsemen*, not only serves to distinguish clearly the former Turkish enemy from the old and new German enemy, but also helps to further elevate the moral superiority and fighting qualities of the Anzacs, as will be discussed in more detail later in this chapter.

Australian film-makers opted for two approaches in their portrayal of the German in World War II: the treacherous 'enemy within' (German fifth columnists and spies); and the demonization of the enemy overseas (as cruel military officers and 'ordinary' soldiers). Rupert Kathner's *Wings of Destiny* (1940) was the first film to pick up the German fifth column theme, which had already been popular in Australian World War I films such as *Within Our Gates, or Deeds that Won Gallipoli* (Frank Harvey 1915), *For Australia, Australia's Peril* and *Satan in Sydney* (Beaumont Smith 1918). In Kathner's film – which is, according to a title at the beginning of the film, based on a real incident in 1937 – the German fifth columnist Mark Heinrich becomes aware of a large wolfram field in the outback and attempts to get a hold of the material for his Nazi superiors. Two men are killed and a young woman abducted, but eventually Heinrich is captured by an Australian pilot and sentenced to a long prison term. Noel Monkman's *The Power and the Glory* (1941) goes a step further by including an Australian with a German background among the villains. The film, produced with significant assistance from the Royal Australian Air Force (RAAF), tells the story of a Czech scientist who discovers a poison gas as the side product of one of his experiments. The Nazi occupiers of Czechoslovakia want to get their hands on the formula for the gas but the professor and his daughter manage to escape to Australia with the help of an Australian pilot. A German spy is sent after them. He finds their outback hideout with the help of the German fifth column and a treacherous German-Australian RAAF pilot. The RAAF manages to shoot down the villains' plane and destroy a German submarine off the Australian coast.

The fifth column theme in *The Power and the Glory* served to emotionally involve the home front in the war effort by suggesting that Australia itself was of interest to the German enemy, and hence of strategic importance in the war. Another important function of this film was the glorification of a new, then fairly under-promoted, group of World War II servicemen, the RAAF. The film can also be described as a variation of the myth which portrays the Anzac as protector and defender of Australia. This kind of depiction of the Australian soldier, in conjunction with the portrayal of the German 'within' and overseas as a threat to Australia, ties into Daniel Nourry's (2005) discussion of the Anzac myth in the context of what

Ghassan Hage has identified as Australia's post-9/11 'paranoid nationalism'. Hage (2003) defines this as a 'nationalism obsessed with border politics where worrying becomes the dominant mode of expressing one's attachment to the nation' (Nourry 2003: 47). Nourry argues that this kind of nationalism sees threats everywhere, which revives 'white colonial paranoia' (Nourry 2005: 371). Although marginalized after World War II up until the Howard government came to power in the 1990s, this kind of anxiety has always been part of Australian nationalism (Nourry 2005: 371; Hage 2003: 47). The mythical figure of the Anzac is born out of this anxiety and, as the embodiment of conservative Australian values, guarantees the present state and character of Australian society (Nourry 2005: 374). Anzac Day serves as the vehicle through which the myth annually continues to be revived and reintroduced into Australia's national imaginary (2005: 372–73). Hage (2003) explains that 'defensive national imaginary constitutes the ideological backbone of paranoid nationalism' (2003: 32) and elaborates that 'national threats and viruses' are always 'within reach' – for example, migrants as the peril within or terrorists as a threat from without (Hage 2003: 38). While Hage mainly refers to Australia's post-9/11 society in this context, it also helps to explain the unfavourable portrayal of German migrants in both World War I and World War II. Nourry adds that Australia's perception of the 'other' as a threat can partly be explained via the Australian 'fantasy of persecution' that has its origin in the nation's convict past in which an 'entire class of white British people...had been denied white Western status' (2005: 377–78). Hage (2003) also explains this suspicion of the 'other' with British-Australia's self-perception as normal in conjunction with a 'heightened perception of "minorities", migrants and Indigenous people as a threat to one's own well-being' and a danger to one's self-realization (2003: 64–65). In the first half of the twentieth century, this fear was further infused by concerns about the distance from the motherland and Australia's self-perception as white British colony in a (hostile) Asia-Pacific region (2003: 52).

## Chauvel's World War I and World War II Anzacs

In his portrayal of World War I and World War II Anzacs, Chauvel was inspired by C.E.W. Bean (Cunningham 1991: 117). The film-maker substituted the comical diggers of the inter-war years with the heroic Anzacs of Bean's *The Anzac Book* and *Official History*. The Anzacs' bush connections are also stressed through the portrayal of the main characters as outback workers in Chauvel's second war feature film, *The Rats of Tobruk* (1944). *The Rats of Tobruk* retells the story of the heroic deeds of the Second AIF, who had fought so successfully against Rommel in North Africa. While *Forty Thousand Horsemen*, Chauvel's account of the Light Horse's World War I military exploits in Palestine, does not discuss the bush myth explicitly, bush terminology is used by the enemies and allies who refer to the Australians as 'sheep-herders' or 'mad bushmen'. Given that the film was made with considerable military involvement and with the cooperation of the New South Wales government, which guaranteed half of the film's cost (Pike and Cooper 1980: 252), it is no surprise that Chauvel adhered closely to the official versions of the Anzac myth (Reynaud 1996: 171), while featuring the larrikin element in the first half of the film. It is conceivable that the semi-official nature of *Forty Thousand Horsemen* is also responsible for its propagandist tone, especially in its portrayal of the Germans and the Turkish enemy. In a letter to the Minister for the Army, Chauvel promoted the film's potential use as an 'aid to recruiting', hoping that the Commonwealth government would contribute to the costs of his film. This hope was, however, rejected by the Minister for Information, Sir Henry Gullett, who stated that 'the present is a most inopportune time to recall that during the last war the Australians and the Turks were on opposite sides', considering that the Turks were now 'allies'. This was given as the reason for the rejection in spite of an assurance from backer H.G. Hayward that 'special dialogue will emphasize the Turks were tricked by the Germans into entering the war against the Allies, and reveal the distrust and friction existing between Turkish and German Officers'. The film thus establishes a fundamental difference between the 'noble Turk' and the 'cruel and dishonourable Hun', which reinforces Chauvel's portrayal of the Anzacs as extraordinarily competent and morally superior fighters. The difference becomes most apparent when German 'Kommandant' von Hausen inspects a Turkish weapons factory accompanied by the Turkish Commander, Ismet. When a German lieutenant shows von Hausen an Australian uniform and ammunition belt, the Kommandant mocks it, commenting to Ismet that it is 'worse than your Turkish uniforms'. Ismet responds by saying: 'After Gallipoli we do not underestimate the Australians', and tells von Hausen with obvious admiration for the diggers that when they run out of ammunition, the Australians 'come with cold steel'. It is conceivable that Chauvel got his inspiration for this scene from Bartlett, who describes the Australian fighting qualities in a similar fashion in his 'historical' despatch from Gallipoli and also uses the term 'cold steel' (cited in Fewster 1982: 19). Von Hausen, however, is not impressed and laughs wholeheartedly at the Australian slouch hat with its emu feathers, describing it as 'a woman's hat'. Thus Chauvel establishes the German officer as a contemptuous villain for Australian audiences. Not only is von Hausen arrogant and scornful of the Turks and Australians, but he also calls into question the diggers' masculinity.

Meanwhile, the sympathetic portrayal of the noble Turks as the 'Germanized army' (identified in the film's introductory title), who are not responsible for the war, is continued throughout the film. Ismet is depicted as valuing his soldiers' lives, in particular during the Australian attack on Bersheeba when he tries to keep von Schiller from detonating mines which would cause the complete destruction of Bersheeba and the death of Australian attackers and Turkish defenders alike. Ismet calls the Prussian officer a 'filthy Hun', and refuses to kill his own men and the enemy in such a dishonourable fashion, stating forcefully that: 'Turks and Australians have always fought their battles with clean hands.' Von Schiller consequently shoots his ally at point-blank range, but the Australian hero prevents von Schiller from setting off the explosives. Interestingly, while Sir Henry Gullett's official history of the Light Horse in Palestine mentions the respect German and Australian soldiers had for each other (Gullett 1939: 671), it does not mention any large-scale laying of mines in Bersheeba. This aspect seems to have been added by Chauvel to showcase the difference between the dishonourable Germans and the noble Turks.

In portraying the Turks as admirers of Australian fighting qualities, Chauvel reiterates a notion introduced by Bean in *The Anzac Book*: respect for the enemy, which grew out of the trench fighting in Gallipoli (Kent 1985: 386). Kent writes that, while Bean mostly utilized contributions by the soldiers such as poems or artwork in *The Anzac Book*, 'he was solely responsible for adding a chivalrous regard for the enemy to the list' (Kent 1983: 386). The last line of one of Bean's poem's reads: 'In life, in death, You've played the gentleman' (Manne 2007). In Chauvel's film, both enemy portrayals served a propaganda purpose by helping to further elevate the Anzac to the status of a mythical god-like figure. While the depiction of the German as evil served to establish the Anzac as morally superior, the portrayal of the noble Turk as respectful of Australian fighting qualities put the Anzacs on a pedestal as courageous and heroic fighters, who had to withdraw in Gallipoli because they had encountered a 'worthy opponent'. Anything that would tarnish the image of the Turk as the noble enemy, such as the Armenian genocide which coincided with the Gallipoli campaign, could hence never be part of the image of the Turk in Australia: it would damage the Anzac legend.

## From 'mutual respect for the enemy' to the 'noble Turk'

In contemporary Australian culture, portrayals of German identities are few and far between. Notable exceptions are the positive depiction of a German-Australian Anzac in the TV mini series *Anzacs* (9 Network 1985) and the sympathetic portrayals of German World War I internees in the TV mini series *The Alien Years* (ABC 1988) and *Always Afternoon* (WDR 1988), the latter a German-Australian co-production. It is, however, the discourse of the 'noble Turk' that has become more significant, particularly since the revival in conservative Australian nationalism in the 1980s and then again with the Howard era in the late 1990s/2000s. Robert Manne claims that 'the myth of Johnny Turk is benign' (Manne 2007), but this simplistic response belies the complex workings of the discourses of national identity. To understand how this myth – which Tolga Örnek claims began as nothing more than 'mutual respect for the enemy' (Örnek cited in Simpson 2007: 86) – has evolved, and whose interests it serves, gives us insight into the broader workings of Australian cultural nationalism and Australia's international relations with Turkey. The final section of this paper traces the evolution of this friendship. What is unique about the battle of Gallipoli is not the 'mutual respect for the enemy' at the battlefront (after all, this is a feature of many battles), but rather the fact that we are still talking about the battle today.

With the revival of the Australian film industry in the 1970s, countless films explored white Australia's formative, and often nationalistic, narratives which became known as the 'period film' or 'AFC genre' (Dermody and Jacka 1988b). Of the films dealing with the Gallipoli event, Peter Weir's landmark *Gallipoli* (1982) is the most famous. With David Williamson as scriptwriter, *Gallipoli* was based on C.E.W. Bean's writings (Lohrey 1982: 30). 'Johnny Turk' is referred to frequently in the film as a formidable enemy, but beyond that he receives scant attention. As many critics have maintained, *Gallipoli* is not so much a 'war' or 'anti-war' film, but rather a 'celebration of the national ideology' (Freely, cited in Haltof 1993), and has much more to do with the anti-British discourses existing in Australia at the time of its release. However, as one of the films most extensively seen by Australian audiences, this film was pivotal in breathing new life into the Anzac myth and, by extension, into the 'myth of Johnny Turk' as it has inspired a generation of Australians to travel to Turkey's Gelibolu peninsular. At the Australian government's behest, Anzac Cove (or Anzac Koyu), where the ANZAC troops landed in 1915, was officially named as such by the Turkish government in 1985. The successful TV mini-series *1915* (ABC 1982) also drew on C.E.W. Bean's mythology. A scene in this film depicts the famous temporary armistice for the Turks and Australians early on in the battle to bury their dead. This particular event in the war is frequently cited as an example of a 'friendship' between the two countries. In an amusing portrayal of amicable 'exchange' during this event, a Turkish soldier is shown offering a cigarette to a 'digger', who then offers to light them both. As the Turk wanders out of frame, the digger takes a puff then, shocked at its strength, he splutters, curses and stubs it out – a formidable Turkish cigarette for an equally formidable enemy, perhaps.

Robert Manne has recently underscored the lack of attention paid by Australian historians to the Armenian genocide, an event that occurred at the very same time the Gallipoli campaign was being waged. He says that 'in the Australian collective memory of Gallipoli, the Armenian genocide simply has no role, I suspect it never will' (Manne 2007). Quoting a Turkish academic, Tanek Akçam, Manne argues that in the dying days of the Ottoman Empire, at the crisis point in 1915 when it looked like Constantinople might fall, the Young Turks decided they could no longer afford to retain the subversive element, the Armenians, within their borders: 'The Dardanelle campaign and the Gallipoli landings pushed on and maybe not exactly caused, but at least triggered the final events that led to the genocide.' (Colvin 2007) Manne hints that this current blind spot is a result of the friendship between Australia and Turkey. Australia has a motivation for viewing Turkey as a victim of circumstance (without their own agency, or the 'Germanised army', as Chauvel states in his introduction to *Forty Thousand Horsemen*), like Australia's 'fantasy of persecution' (Hage 2005: 377–78) at the hands of the British, clearly exemplified in Weir's *Gallipoli*. The Armenian genocide tarnishes the carefully constructed image of the 'noble Turk' and the Australian-Turkish friendship; thus it is conveniently left out. Australia has an important need to whitewash Turkey because in doing so it, by association, whitewashes itself and makes its formative national narrative, the ANZAC legend, more simplistic and complete. It is also an extension of the quest to see inherent Australian and Turkish goodness and victimhood in the battle at Gallipoli – as pawns of the British and German imperial quests respectively.

In 2005, on the 90th anniversary of Gallipoli, Turkish film-maker Tolga Örnek internationally released his documentary *Gallipoli: the Frontline*. Using re-dramatizations and letters from ordinary soldiers at the front line, this particular film explores the horror of the battle from the soldiers' perspectives – New Zealanders, Australians, Britons and Turks. For his work on this film, as 'service to Australia', Örnek was presented with an Order of Australia Medal (OAM) (Anonymous 2006) – an award that could only be reserved for an 'honorary Australian', a 'noble Turk' perhaps? In an interview, Örnek stresses that this so-called 'special friendship' between Turks and Australians is a rewriting of history, and at the time it was nothing more than a 'mutual respect for the enemy' (Simpson 2007: 86). In Turkey, Örnek's film has become the highest grossing documentary in history. In Australia, the film did relatively well in art-house cinemas. However, although well promoted within the local Turkish community, it did poorly in cinemas that regularly show Turkish product (Simpson 2007: 88). This might have had something to do with the fact that the Turkish Ambassador to Australia publicly took issue with the fact that Örnek's film did not include Turkey's first president, Mustafa Kemal Atatürk's, famous ode, 'To the mothers of fallen soldiers'. However, Örnek's 'oversight' was not an oversight at all. Rather, his decision was primarily concerned with the desire not to buy into the nationalistic myths, Turkish or Australian, that have become central to discourses about Gallipoli.

The English translation of the ode is widely known in Australia. It is what any 'pilgrim' to Anzac Cove first encounters, and is absolutely pivotal to the discourse of the 'noble Turk'. It is often recited at Anzac Day marches (New South Wales Parliamentary Debates 2003) and also graces the Kemal Atatürk Memorial on Anzac Parade in Canberra. The ode also opens the ABC-produced *Compass* documentary *Embracing our Enemies* (2005). For the millions of Australians who have encountered this ode, 'we' imagine that Atatürk is talking personally to 'us' as a nation. On first glance, emanating from the 'noble leader' who personally led an Ottoman battalion at Gallipoli, the liberal humanist and pacifist rhetoric of Atatürk's ode always appears surprising (Jones 2004: 10–12), especially the way in which it honours the foreign aggressors and 'magnanimously counsels' the mothers of the fallen dead (Baker 2006). Without taking into consideration the political and historical context from which it sprang, the ode appears to be an extraordinarily gracious act of forgiveness and quest for peace on Atatürk's behalf:

> Those heroes who shed their blood and lost their lives are now lying in the soil of a friendly country. Therefore rest in peace. There is no difference between the Mehmets and the Johnnies to us as they lie side by side in this country of ours. You, the mothers, who sent your sons to far away countries, wipe away your tears. Your sons are now lying in our bosom and are in peace. After having lost their lives on this land, they have become our sons as well. (cited in Jones 2004: 10–12)

However, Atatürk's poem, 'To the Mothers of the Fallen Soldiers' was written in 1934, almost 20 years after the 1915 battle. In the Turkish original of the ode they remained unnamed 'honoured' soldiers, while in the English translation they became named 'Johnnies', the British everyman (Jones 2004: 10–14). Contrary to what Australians (and Turks) may *like* to imagine, the fact that Australians were at that battle probably never crossed Atatürk's (or his speechwriter's) mind. As Ottoman historian Adrian Jones (2004) argues, the ode is much more about Atatürk's rewriting the heroic foundations of his newly established Turkish nation-state than any special relationship between Australia and Turkey. Jones also surmises that Atatürk's motivation for this gracious act stems from his realization in the 1930s that the Allied invaders of 1915 had prompted him to shape the kind of nation that 'the Turks came to know that they had wanted' (Jones 2004: 10–14). The fact that Australians now see the ode as written primarily for them, and reiterate it at any opportunity, is a strange twist of fate and poetically reifies the myth of the 'noble Turk', and by extension the Anzac legend.

## Conclusion

The films we have examined here present insights into the social, cultural and political discourses current at the time of these films' release. In *Forty Thousand Horsemen*, the portrayal of the 'noble Turk' helped to demonize the German enemy and reify Australian fighting qualities in order to get the domestic audience behind the lagging World War II effort. Forty years on, in *Gallipoli*, when the AIF suffer heavy casualties at the Nek it is reported back that 'the British are drinking tea on the beach', a historical inaccuracy that resonated with pro-Republican sentiments in audiences at the time. Films and mini-series like *Gallipoli* and *1915* fed into existing nationalistic discourses, which in turn has seen a dramatic increase in the numbers of Australian visitors to Turkey since the 1980s – a kind of cultural exchange that could not have been predicted.

In 2008, Australia celebrated the 40th anniversary of Turkish migration to Australia. Many Turks who were on those first flights from Turkey to Australia in 1968 had no idea of the challenges they would face as 'migrants' upon their arrival and settlement in Australia. Many were under the misapprehension they were only coming for a two-year work visa with a paid passage home (much like the Turkish 'guest workers' in Germany), rather than settling in Australia permanently as migrants (Basarin and Basarin 1993: 6). Little-known films such as Ayten Kuyululu's *The Golden Cage* (1975) and *Handful of Dust* (1974) beautifully convey dystopian early Turkish migrant experiences in Australia. The Gallipoli connection has served the interests of both countries – which would otherwise share little in common – well over the past 50 or so years. It is not our intention to undermine any government rhetoric or interventions that might promote greater cross-cultural understanding between two very different countries. However, it is important to realize that much effort has gone into simplifying and perpetuating a hegemonic, nationalistic interpretation of an event that befits two countries still struggling to escape the shackles of their respective imperial Ottoman and British pasts.

# 9

# 'Now You Blokes Own the Place': Representations of Japanese Culture in Recent Australian Cinema

## Rebecca Coyle

A minor character in the Australian film *Japanese Story* (Sue Brooks 2003) ruminates on the ambivalence of many Australians towards Japanese people:

> In the war we thought you blokes were coming after us – we had stuff stashed away up in the hills, evacuation plans, people tying knives to the end of broomsticks – ridiculous really...Now you blokes own the place. There was a time there when nobody would buy anything made in Japan. Wife, she'd go into the shop and turn the thing over and if it said made in Japan she put it back on the shelf – she wouldn't buy it. Still don't, I guess. Only country to have a trading surplus with you lot. Funny life, isn't it? (DVD transcript)

These observations signal various perceptions of Australia-Japan relations for Anglo-Celtic Australians, and the monologue suggests how these can be articulated in Australian cinema. This chapter offers an overview of historical and contemporary relations between Australia and Japan as a framework for analyzing the diasporic cultures represented in two early millennial Australian films, *Japanese Story* and *Bondi Tsunami* (Rachael Lucas 2004). These depict Japanese visitors to Australia, however the approach (as well as the style) is significantly different in the two films, one concentrating on middle-class Euro-Australian cultural contact and the other on youthful transnational surf culture. In contrast to each other, the films raise issues about the practices deployed to represent Australian perspectives on Japanese culture.

Gunja Man (Nobuhisa Ikeda), Kimiko (Miki Sasaki), Shark (Taki Abe) and Yuto (Keita Abe) with the 1961 EK Holden in *Bondi Tsunami* (Rachael Lucas, 2004). Image courtesy of Rachael Lucas, Anthony Lucas Smith and Naomi Lucas Smith.

Hiromitsu Tachibana (Gotaro Tsunashima) and Sandy Edwards (Toni Collette) in *Japanese Story* (Sue Brooks, 2003). Image courtesy of Palace Films.

The moments of intersection and dialogue between protagonists are taken as Euro-Australian positions on Japanese experiences of Australia, from historical baggage to geographically informed consciousness and a postcolonial imaginary of Australia-Japan relations. *Japanese Story* and *Bondi Tsunami* offer notably different viewpoints on these concerns and, when examined together, provide perspectives on Australian attitudes to cultural difference and belonging, on notions of diasporic cultures and Australian 'identities', and on the role of Australian cinema in grappling with such issues.

## Japanese diasporas, characters and characterizations

Both *Japanese Story* and *Bondi Tsunami* focus on Japanese characters who are in Australia temporarily, as visitors rather than immigrants. In its history of white settlement, Australia has accepted Japanese people primarily on the basis of short-term residence, and this impacts on understandings of Japanese diaspora in the Australian context. Jonathan Dresner (2007) identifies diaspora as 'the development of a population across boundaries over time' rather than a fixed community descended from one country and located for a period of time in the one place. As such, Japanese diaspora is 'the dispersion of Japanese from Japan to other countries and colonial territories, resulting in an expanded sense of Japanese community and ongoing cultural and personal connections' (Dresner 2007). The expansion of the Japanese population in Australia has largely been affected by the racist attitudes that resulted in the 'White Australia' policy restricting non-white immigration to Australia in the period 1901–73. Since the early 1880s, Australian politics has come to view ethnic stability – envisaged as the dominance of Anglo-Saxon migrant culture – as the cornerstone of political and social national development, and such themes have persisted in Australian cultural output. In Raymond Longford's *Australia Calls* (1913) and Phil K. Walsh's *The Birth of White Australia* (1928), the perceived threat posed by 'Asiatics' is overwhelmingly conveyed. Meaghan Morris (1998) has argued that the fear of the exterior and external invasion has persisted alongside fear of the 'vast interior' in Australian cinema. In the 1990s, the One Nation political party's policy of reductions in Asian immigration gained widespread support amongst some sectors of the Australian population and was the subject of international attention (see Tada 2000).

The modern Japanese diaspora dates from 1868 and the dismantling of restrictions on foreign contact during the early Meiji Period (see Clammer 2002). For Euro-Australians, suspicion of and antagonism towards Japanese residents in Australian territories has rarely been absent. Japanese groups migrating to Australia in 1880s were often on short-term arrangements – for example, working on sugar cane plantations, as pearl divers or prostitutes (see Sissons 1977, 1988: 635–37). Population census data for 1901 records over 3,000 Japan-born people living in Australia – although, with the *Immigration Restriction Act* passed in the same year together with a collection of subsequent laws, non-white immigration was severely limited, thereby forcing temporary status. World War II conflicts between Australia and Japan exacerbated these antagonistic attitudes. Most Japanese residents in the early 1940s were deported from Australia by the end of the war, many after being interned (see Nagata 1996). Some Japanese women with 'war bride' status were allowed to enter Australia after 1952 (Sissons 1988), but other migration was held back until the late 1960s. About 27,000 people of Japanese origin currently live in Australia – a modest proportion for the nation's 20 million population, and about 7,000 Australians live in Japan. However, tourism and census data from the 1990s show that most Japanese residence in Australia has been temporary rather than permanent (see McNamara and Couglan 1992; Jayasuriya and Pookong 1999), and the different cohorts of Japanese business visitors and holiday tourists identified in these statistics are depicted in *Japanese Story* and *Bondi Tsunami*.

In the post-war era, Japan-Australia relations focused on mutually complementary trade links and an agreement on commerce was signed in 1957. Since then, the relationship has expanded to other economic activities, politics and cultural practices. Japan is one of Australia's largest trading partners, and the third largest source of direct investment – a factor informing the narrative of *Japanese Story* that has a Japanese businessman visiting a mining operation in which his father has investments. Shortly after the dismantling of the 'White Australia' policy, Japan and Australia signed a cultural agreement, and the Japan International Cooperation Agency started sending professionals and skilled labourers to Australia. In 1997, in response to trade conflicts in the 1990s and to strengthen Australia-Asia links, Prime Minister Paul Keating assisted a Joint Declaration on the Australia-Japan Partnership. These activities have since progressed in response to economic and tourism vicissitudes, including major Japanese investment in mining and real estate and the collapse of the Japanese yen in 1990 (see Clammer 2001). Productive dialogue has been inhibited by Japanese whaling and in 2007 the popular election of a government committed to reducing it, especially in the Southern Ocean, has seen whaling re-emerge as a focal point for Australia-Japan antagonism (see *Australian Story*, ABC-TV, 11 February 2008, www.abc.net.au/austory/content/2007/s2160857.htm). In 2006, cultural interchange was emphasized through the Year of Australia-Japan Exchange that included an Australian Film Festival held in Tokyo at which many films (including *Japanese Story*) were screened in Japan for the first time. In the lead-up to this event, creative industry economist David Throsby observed: 'If you are going to trade with a country then they need to understand you and you need to understand them and the way to do that is through cultural exchanges.' (cited in Cameron 2006).

Over the last 20 years, a collection of feature and short films have examined cultural differences and relations between the two countries, including *Gentle Strangers* (Cecil Holmes 1972), Solran Hoaas's studies of Japanese war brides in *Green Tea and Cherry Ripe* (1989) and *Aya* (1990), and Noriko Sekiguchi's story of a Euro-Australian woman's experience of a visit to Japan in *When Mrs Hegarty Comes to Japan* (1992). Both *Heaven's Burning* (Craig Lahiff 1997) and *The Goddess of 1967* (Clara Law 2001) are road movies that feature Japanese characters who transgress expected roles and Australian stereotypes (see Collins 2000; Haslam 2007), a trope also explored by Cate Shortland in her acclaimed short film *Flowergirl* (1999). In these films, the ethnicity of Japanese people critiques Anglo-centric national identity and historical constructions of Asians as 'other'. However, many of these films 'seem unable to offer any workable vision for the future of Asian-Australian relations, besides a (metaphoric) death that eliminates the figure of difference' (Khoo 2004: 15). The 'other' (including the female) is routinely killed off or subsumed, domesticated and/or contained. Asian textual subjectivity is constructed as a lack in relation to Australian identity or located as outside of it. According to Khoo: 'Asian characters are simply not allowed to "live" in the sense of being fully formed, autonomous characters.' (2004: 15)

Several films and TV series made in Australia have explored both Australian perceptions of Japanese people during the war in the Pacific, including *A Town Like Alice* (1981 TV series, David Stevens), *The Cowra Breakout* (1984 TV mini-series, Phillip Noyce/Chris Noonan, about Japanese prisoners of war in Australia), and POW representations (*Tenko* (1981–84 ABC/BBC TV co-production, Lavinia Warner), *Paradise Road* (Bruce Beresford 1997), *Changi* (2001 TV mini-series, John Doyle/Kate Woods) and *Blood Oath* (Stephen Wallace 2002)). Japanese people are frequently conveyed as caricatures, in a manner consistent with war genre cinema in the West that offers a cathartic national perspective with little empathy for 'the enemy' (an aspect explored in Claude Gonzalez's documentary *Sydney at War* 2005). Nevertheless, Annette Hamilton (1990) contends that Australian war films served the function of distinguishing Japanese antagonists from 'other forms of Asianness' (1990: 24), and both memories of the wartime confrontations (reinforced each Anzac Day) and residual impressions of media depictions of these events continue to haunt Australia-Japan representations in Australian cinema.

The representational reconstruction of the World War II hostilities ignores Japan's long-standing involvement in the Western Pacific and periods when Japan was an ally and supporter of Britain and the monarchy (see Broinowski 1992: 2–5, 7; Hayward and Konishi 2001: 49–50). Australian war and cultural history tends to at best marginalize and at worst deny or ignore the British (and therefore Australian) alliance with Japan in the early 1900s, historically recorded in newsreels. Japanese atrocities in the Pacific War are configured as unprovoked and maliciously aggressive rather than responsive to a series of provocations in trading, security and citizenship on the part of Australia (see Frei 1991: esp. 91–100). As Felicity Collins and Therese Davis (2004) argue, explaining the emphasis on grief and remorse in *Japanese Story*, the post-*Mabo* era 'demands that Eurocentric Australians do the work of mourning entailed in giving up a form of emotional insularity which turns a blind eye to our history and place in the Asia-Pacific region' (2004: 180).

Japanese characters in both films explored in this chapter are still 'unwanted aliens' (Nagata 1996). Hamilton (1990: esp. 14, 24–27) has identified attitudes of 'fear and desire' towards Asian people in Australian cinema, while Audrey Yue posits that, in the 2000s, 'alongside Australia's postcoloniality is a disjunctive modernity that simultaneously accords Australia the status of a notional western country with a degree of superiority over Asia' (2000: 192). Australia at once admires and fears Japanese power, and this is evident in tourism operations that exploit and underestimate the cultural intelligence of their Japanese clients (see March 1997). Relations with Japan are different from those with other Southeast Asian cultural groups, and it is necessary to focus on those special features rather than reinforce Australian cultural biases. Both films construct an 'outsider' view of place, space, location and geography, engaging with familiar themes in Australian settler and diasporic cinema: marginality, cultural conflict and the search for identity. At the same time, however, the two films address the specific, complex and historically fractious Australia-Japan relationship.

## Projecting Australia-Japan relations

*Japanese Story* centres on businessman Hiromitsu (Gotaro Tsunashima) and Sandy (Toni Collette), a geologist who wants to sell him the computer software she has developed. Hiromitsu comes to Western Australia hoping to resolve mid-life career and relationship issues. Sandy's business partner asks her to drive the visitor to an iron ore mine to check on his father's investment. Hiromitsu is overwhelmed by the vastness of the Pilbara desert region and demands that Sandy drive him into more remote areas. After they become bogged in the sand and spend a night in the desert, they become lovers. In a sudden turn of events, Hiromitsu dives into a shallow pool at a watering hole and is killed. Sandy moves the body to the nearest township, and arranges a coroner's examination and transportation of the body back to Perth. The last section of the film follows Sandy as she grieves, meets Hiro's wife (Yukiko, played by Yumiko Tanaka) and oversees the body's dispatch to Japan. *Japanese Story* intentionally and explicitly explores cross-cultural tensions between the two characters (Collins 2003b).

In the second film, *Bondi Tsunami,* the narrative is less straightforward; personal reflections and fleeting character interactions are interspersed with travelogue and extended surfing sequences. The film centres around two main characters: Shark (Taki Abe), a surfer on a working holiday in Australia and employed in a fast food outlet, and his friend Yuto (Keita Abe), in Sydney to surf and 'hang out'. They embark on a tour of famous surfing locations and, on the road, meet Kimiko (Miki Sasaki), who loves soft toys and junk food. Another character, simply called Gunja Man (Nobuhisa Ikeda), appears as a mute, ghostlike figure symbolizing the spiritual aspect (and drug use) sometimes associated with surf culture in Australia.

*Bondi Tsunami* has a plot *outline* but is designed to feature tone, rhythm and mood rather than story, coherent plot and dialogue. In fact, the film has been described as a 'music video motion picture' (http://bonditsunami.com.au, accessed 4 August 2006). It was created for the Japanese and Asian home entertainment market and for projection (like music videos) on sports screens and at nightclubs. Designed for consumption as a road movie story or as moving image background, *Bondi Tsunami* cannot be compared with a linear narrative like *Japanese Story*. It is satirical in its use of Western clichés played out by the Japanese cast, and was inspired by home and karaoke videos, as well as by advertisements – especially for surfwear and surf products. In Australia, surf culture is used to sell a wide range of products from cars to Coca-Cola, so the film in some ways operates like 'a living surfwear catalogue (http://bonditsunami.com.au, accessed 4 August 2006). According to the film's director, Rachael Lucas, *Bondi Tsunami* offers a 'cool image' of the 'individualistic Nintendo generation of Japanese surfers' who congregate around Sydney and the Gold Coast, contrasting sharply with the 'camera clicking, koala hugging Japanese' of the 1980s (http://bonditsunami.com.au, accessed 4 August 2006). The character Shark is given voiceover monologues narrating his self-discovery through surfing and, in a nod to Japanese *manga* and the popularity of *anime* in Australia, segments of comic book-like drawn animation (by comic artist Rob Roldan) are inserted amongst the live-action sequences. The film's condensed narratives and various effects (such as split screen, speeded-up sequences and sampled cutaways) reflect the director's own background in music video and advertising.

The different production approaches employed in the two films inform their view of Australia-Japan relations. *Japanese Story* was made in a conventional style, using professional film-makers, funding for script development and for production, and a budget of A$5.5 million. Distributed via the art-house circuit (with a debut at Cannes 2003), the film was critically acclaimed, widely reviewed and won 19 awards, although its ongoing box office takings were modest and, according to producer Sue Maslin (see Johnson and Poole 2005: 121), the film never gained distribution in Japan. In contrast, Lucas was unable to attract government funding for *Bondi Tsunami* and it was privately funded with a shoestring budget of A$150,000. All of the footage was shot on a digital camera and edited on a PC in a home studio arrangement, and the music was produced by documentary and television composer Jamie Saxe using ProTools music software. None of the crew or cast was a professional, and Lucas found the 'actors' through the Bondi Tsunami Surfing Competition event organized by her brother-in-law. At the invitation of the Department of Foreign Affairs and Trade, *Bondi Tsunami* was first screened in an exclusive 'sneak preview' at the Australian Pavilion at Aichi World Expo, Nagoya in 2005. This was followed by a series of promotional party screenings in Tokyo and Sendai, including a surf film festival in Tokyo. In a direct address to this targeted (and modest) marketing strategy, *Bondi Tsunami* offers both Japanese and (halting) English voiceovers, while *Japanese Story* employs the more conventional subtitled translations.

Where *Bondi Tsunami* closely follows the interactions between its Japanese characters, *Japanese Story* concentrates on Sandy's reaction to cultural difference and her subsequent awakening from self-absorption and complacency. The metaphorical weight of Sandy's responsibility (for Australia-Japan relations) is suggested in an extended scene in which she must move Hiro's body from the water and into the back of her four-wheel drive vehicle. And, while the protagonists in *Bondi Tsunami* are Japanese, the point of view (in terms of cinematography, editing and script) is Euro-Australian. Both films are road movies and character development is linked to geographic mobility, suggesting the fluid/mobile nature of Japanese residence in Australia and of Australian relations with Japan.

Dialogue is sparing in both films, apart from the moments of seemingly drug-induced poetic ramblings in *Bondi Tsunami*. While the sparse dialogue by Japanese characters is interpreted along the lines of stereotypical inscrutability, the Euro-Australian characters are not particularly effusive either. Indeed, Sandy speaks in the masculinized laconic language familiar in outback Australia representations (see Coyle 2001), and the halting communication reflects the tentative and spasmodic cultural connections in Australia-Japan relations. These worthy but misdirected attempts to articulate are further exacerbated in the music tracks. *Japanese Story* uses a high proportion of original music scored by an established Euro-Australian film composer, Elizabeth Drake. Western orchestral arrangements, tonality and harmonics (as well as brief references to Aboriginal music) are interwoven with Japanese instruments and Drake draws on two Okinawan folk songs, 'Asadoya Bushi' and 'Chinsagu No Hana', for significant scenes in which Sandy attempts to confront her cultural ignorance. 'Chinsagu No Hana', which provides a melodic motif used at several intimate points in the narrative, was itself interpreted and repopularized in a rock/Japanese world beat style by Ryuchi Sakamoto in 1989 (see Johnson and Poole 2005: 121). Drawing on elements of Japanese culture via Sandy's Australian perception, the music remediates an existing popular cultural item, marginalizes the song origins and employs Japanese instruments for a kind of exotic (and Orientalist) flavouring. The music speaks for Sandy's perspective on her contact with (syncretic) Japanese culture, while the music most overtly connected with Hiromitsu is the Yothu Yindi song 'Treaty', an ironic reference to his involvement with mining and a scene in which he views explosions conducted as part of the mining operation.

In contrast (and predictably for a youth market product informed by music video genres), the intertextual music track for *Bondi Tsunami* comprises largely prerecorded musical numbers. Clips from over 40 songs are employed, with the majority of the music originating from relatively unknown Australian artists that were either unsigned, unreleased or with small record labels. In the style of the film, additional esoteric items are featured including tracks by 1950s/60s exoticist Martin Denny, highlighting the sense of the Japanese characters' immersion in an 'exotic' experience 'Down Under'. The use of prerecorded music tracks in film soundtracks is not unusual in post-revival Australian cinema (see Coyle 2004), but what is unorthodox is the use of relatively unknown artists to minimize copyright charges and ensure a modest music budget. While some tracks are Japanese influenced, none is Japanese in origin; rather, the characters are sonically located in a western or even syncretically global context. Their 'Japanese culture' is represented in quirky idiosyncrasies and as an international urban consumerist lifestyle rather than through iconic moments or cultural traditions. Lucas claims that:

> Japanese design is modern classic design and Japanese style is everywhere in Australia. People eat sushi rolls, wear clothing with kanji on it, try Japanese natural therapies, drink green tea and watch Japanese movies and *anime* DVDs. (http://bonditsunami.com.au, accessed 4 August 2006)

The fascination with Japanese-influenced cultural forms evidenced in the expansion of sushi cafes and shops specializing in Japanese artefacts in Australia reiterates and extends the Japanois obsessions of the 1880s (see Broinowski 1992), suggesting a generational vogue in cosmopolitan culture. This form of commodification of Asianness, however, may be seen to impede the development of more profound (and culturally 'thick') interactions.

## Representative models

Japan-Australia relations are often configured in terms of contrasts: in land and landscape, in population sizes, in work ethic, in appearance. *Japanese Story* represents such contrasts, as we see Hiromitsu photograph himself against the desert. Later on he says to Sandy: 'In Australia, you have a lot of space – no people. In Japan we have many people – no space … There is nothing – it scares me.' This comment reflects the inequitable volume of cultural and manufactured product entering Australia from Japan compared with the limited reverse supply. Sandy's inability to find words to respond to Hiromitsu's observation suggests that Euro-Australians as yet do not sufficiently understand their own space and place, that this is as scary for them as for visitors. Sandy can only express what is not possible, not traversable, and the defiant colonial gesture of entering Aboriginal lands without a permit results in an enforced pause in which Australia-Japan relations and the role of the 'other' must be reviewed.

While both films define difference in terms of cultural origin and background experience, *Bondi Tsunami* is more concerned with similarities, showing the love of surfing – and perhaps the uncommitted lifestyle – shared by the young Japanese and Euro-Australian characters. Both offer a challenge to cultural identity along the lines of Stuart Hall's 1990 model, at once recognizing similarity and difference, the 'ruptures and discontinuities' (1990: 225). Hall argues that cultural identity 'is a matter of "becoming" as well as of "being". It belongs to the future as much as to the past' and is 'subject to the continuous "play" of history, culture and power' (1990: 225). *Japanese Story* and *Bondi Tsunami* replicate the evolutionary nature of Australia-Japan relations – although as yet, Khoo suggests, the 'Asian is "in" Australia, but Asians are not of Australia' (2004: 15). The films are therefore a study of Australians through the 'other' rather than about the 'other' as such – that is, identification by difference.

Both films represent a particular moment in Australian relations with Japan, although from contrasting generational perspectives. *Japanese Story* approaches this project very carefully, being wary of offence and conscious of the need for reparation. This is suggested in Sandy's embarrassment as the boatman (quoted above) describes negative attitudes to Japanese people in Australia. It refers back to her own ignorance as, prior to meeting Hiro, she rings a friend and asks for tips on dealing with 'the Japs'. Later on, when Sandy explores Hiromitsu's face by touching his features as he sleeps, the scene suggests that Euro-Australians are trying to understand similarities and unifying elements, rather than distinguishing or differentiating markers. Later, Sandy studies her face in the mirror, observing how the experience of cultural contact has changed her. Her achievement of an understanding of grieving suggests the tragedies resulting from hostilities in the past.

*Bondi Tsunami* approaches an exploration of Australia-Japan relations with a less serious (and perhaps less 'politically correct') attitude. Indeed, in this film, style is substance – the look, the image and the attitude are critical. Fashion and pop culture is featured to the point of obsession. Australia is viewed from a fun-loving youthful transnational attitude, and relations between Australia and Japan are explored in terms of mobility, consumerism and hedonism, suggesting Masayo Tada's findings (2000: 178) that, for Japan, Australia in the 1990s represented a national interest focused on individualism. The Japanese riding the 'waves' in this film are thus entering Australia on a very different basis to those of the past. The fetishistic opening sequence is an extended slow-motion portrait of the surfers' toned torsos and, unlike the representation of Hiro's sexual passivity in *Japanese Story* (conveyed in a scene in which Sandy dons Hiro's trousers and straddles his prone body), the Japanese characters in *Bondi Tsunami* actively flaunt their physiques and surfing prowess. The camera flicks over the sea and sand to dwell on the male bodies, the surfboards, the cars and admiring girls lining the boardwalk. Furthermore, in its fascination with Australian tourist locations and iconic sites, *Bondi Tsunami* contrasts kitsch and manufactured elements with sea and surf, eschewing other environmental locations that suggest 'authentic' Australia and the unmapped/non-encroachable territories of *Japanese Story*. Rather than the discourses of Orientalism implied in *Japanese Story*, *Bondi Tsunami* is absorbed in the kind of Occidentalism proposed by Ian Buruma and Avishai Margalit (2004). *Bondi Tsunami*, while still a white woman's story, nevertheless attempts to literally and metaphorically adopt the voices of the Japanese protagonists, thereby suggesting the kind of postcolonial experience proposed by Catherine Simpson in which the 'colonial past is folded into the "postcolonial" present' (2006). In this way, the easy pairing of an iconic Australian beach – Bondi – with the Japanese term 'tsunami' – translated as harbour wave – signals the film's concerns in its title.

## Conclusion

The productions of *Japanese Story* and *Bondi Tsunami* both commenced prior to the World Trade Center and Pentagon attacks in the United States on September 11, 2001, although the films were released in the 2003–04 period. Since then, Australian diplomatic attention (particularly in the 'war on terror' era) has been primarily directed away from the Asia-Pacific region, except where security issues (Islamic practices, terrorist attacks, refugees, government instability in Pacific neighbours) or trade draw Australia back to the region. Despite globalization, national divisions are still clearly apparent in diplomatic relations. Cinema representations can assist an exploration of national history and public/private memory, political relations and social connections. *Japanese Story* and *Bondi Tsunami* show that Japanese culture and inter-cultural relations have informed the Australian social imaginary to a larger extent than would be expected for the modest Japanese migrant populations in Australia. Yet these films' stories suggest that Australia has not resolved its vexed relations with Japan despite such cultural communications. Both films are marked by a gap or absence, despite the gestures to reparation. The cinematic stories are unfinished in the sense that neither of them articulates contemporary consensus over productive connections. This is not so much a problem with Australian film as it is a problem to be addressed more generally in Australian society and culture. As such, the films may well be accurate summations of generalized public perceptions.

*Japanese Story* and *Bondi Tsunami* were made by Euro-Australian writers and directors. Khoo (2004) suggests that counter-representations of Asian peoples in Australia may well come from, amongst others, emerging Japanese-Australian film-makers whose stories can speak for themselves. Audrey Yue (2000) has already noted the phases of Asian film-making in Australia, although these are not directly relevant to understanding of the two films discussed. Euro-Australians need the cathartic process of recuperation and reconciliation from the past in order to progress and fashion a model for the future. Sandy's incursion into metaphorical uncharted territories – the 'body' of the Japanese – suggests a desire to transcend the fractious histories of Australia-Japan relations and propose new ways to forge connections and (perhaps thereby) understand oneself – hence the title of the film as *Japanese* (rather than *Australian*) *Story*. When the stereotypical 'old-style' Japanese man dives recklessly into the waters of Australian culture, he perishes and is unaided by Euro-Australia. Meanwhile, the surfers of *Bondi Tsunami* effortlessly navigate its waves. So the latter film refers to a history of tourism and commodity exchange that loops back to an early nineteenth century Japanese trading interaction with Australia. Yet this shoreline contact effectively bypasses those dangerous deeper waters in which continued whaling ensures that Australia-Japan relations are still contentious. A cross-culturally sensitive reconciliation involves both parties acknowledging and moving beyond the past to strategically build an alternative relationship. Cinematic representations are one way of projecting such a relationship, and Australian cinema in the future can play a valuable role in enabling a revised formulation for a Japanese diasporic profile in Australia.

# 10

# OTHER SHORELINES, OR THE GREEK-AUSTRALIAN CINEMA

*John Conomos*

The Mediterranean speaks with many voices. (Fernand Braudel, quoted in Chambers 2008: 10)

Ithaka gave you the marvellous journey.
Without her you wouldn't have set out.
She has nothing left to give you now.

(Cavafy 1998: 29)

This chapter maps how certain film-makers of Greek-Australian descent have delineated important aesthetic, cultural, exilic, gendered, historical and political complexities over the last several decades. The film-makers I examine here are, to varying degrees, nomadic, decentred, exilic and marginal. They include George Miller, Anna Kannava, Michael Karris, Peter Lyssiotis, Bill Mousoulis and Lex Marinos. I begin by examining features of the aesthetic, cultural and political realities that have influenced these film-makers of bicultural estrangement, loss, belonging and identity. Then my discussion ends on Ana Kokkinos's landmark feature *Head On* (1997). All these film-makers are, to cite the critic George Steiner, 'extraterritorial' wanderers across art, culture, language and society (Steiner 1971: 11). But in no way does this chapter speak of the Greek-Australian cinema in definitive, comprehensive terms. The subject is complex because of its intricate enmeshing with questions of bicultural marginality, class, exilic modernity, identity, masculinity, migrancy, sexism and power.

For the purposes of this chapter, Greek-Australian cinema can be understood as a critical-cultural-production category of film-making anchored in 'everyday life', created by anyone, and the descendants of anyone, who was born in Greece and its vast geographical 'diasporic' contexts (e.g. Egypt, Africa, Russia, Turkey, Romania, Italy, Spain, England, Germany, France, the Americas, and so on) and emigrated to Australia over the last and present century. It in this context, Ferdinand Braudel's words, cited above, signal how the Mediterranean, with its complex fluid culture and history of criss-crossing hybridity, has significantly marked the Greek immigrant's cultural baggage. This emigration first took the form of a dynamic 'chain letter', where established Greeks would endorse their relatives, friends and compatriots to join them in this country, working in oyster salons, country cafes, milkbars, factories, and fish and chip shops. Since World War II, and particularly from the late 1960s onwards, their children became upwardly mobile. Significantly, as Iain Chambers (2008) reminds us, the concept of the 'Mediterranean' entered the European lexicon only in the nineteenth century as a mutable space shaped by many vast linguistic, culinary, literary, intellectual and musical forces salient to Greek, Latin, Arab, Jewish and Turkish cultures. It has had an indelible impact on the overall collage/montage, essayistic, fictional/documentary and avant-garde/experimental tropes of Greek-Australian cinema (Chambers 2008).

Greek-Australians, like other ethnic diasporas in Australia, have been positioned between two conflicting hybrid worlds of languages, values and cultural expectations. This is the archetypal form of 'double-bind' marginality – Robert Park, the American sociologist of the 1920s and 1930s, was responsible for theorizing this bicultural phenomenon – that has been one of the watershed factors shaping Greek-Australian subjectivity. Consequently, Greek-Australians have often grown up in a topsy-turvey 'in-between' world of ambiguity, fragmentation, confusion and vulnerability, an 'exilic' post-colonial sensibility that forces the individual to live a life, in Edward Said's memorable phrase, 'outside habitual order' (2003: 186).

A number of Greek-Australian film-makers use their 'hyphenated' identity and life-world to create what Hamid Naficy (2001) has referred to in his groundbreaking study as an 'accented' cinema of exile and diaspora, a cinema made by displaced individuals in the West, and also the postcolonial Third World. It concerns itself with deterritorialization and is located at the complex interstices of cultures and different cinematic production practices. Naficy's (2001: 8) is a 'category more of criticism rather than one of production', and thus is less programmatic, cohesive and generic in its emphasis. Naficy's 'accented cinema' can be divided into three broad (overlapping) types of film: exilic, diasporic and ethnic (2001: 21). All three kinds share varying degrees of stylistic similarity, aesthetics and notable nostalgic and memory-shaped bi/multilingual narratives. Consequently, these films are not only in dialogue with their home and host societies but also with postcolonial and postmodern audiences who are situated in between and outside different cultures and whose desires, concerns and fears these film-makers address in their works.

This leads to the reading of cultural difference in terms of class, identity, gender, migration, post-coloniality, race and landscape (a vital dimension, and germane to any fundamental examination of post-war migration experience in Greek-Australian cinema). From the beginning of the twentieth century until the 1950s, Greek-Australians who settled in country towns as café owners would often travel between country towns to visit one another. In this sense, Greek-Australians would be aware of a sense of place – landscape as lifescape, soundscape, tastescape and memoryscape (Carter 1992: 9–18).

Adrian Martin's (2003: 68) finely nuanced analysis of the *Mad Max* movies posits that the customary readings of the landscape – particularly in the first two films – are not convincing. Martin's monograph includes a valuable discussion of George Miller's Greek-Australian identity and his related childhood cinephilic memories of watching American B movies, matinee serials, genre films and comics. This is seldom mentioned elsewhere (2003: 66). Martin's perceptive thesis that Miller's global success can be attributed to a cinematic imagination that has presented Australia as an ahistorical *tabula rasa*, and its attendant emphasis that the movies' 'blighted wasteland' is anchored in a 'survival of the fittest' view of life ideally suitable for the 'commercial circuits of world cinema', warrants mention. Watching Miller's (1996) British Film Institute-sponsored documentary *40,000 Years of Dreaming: A Century of Australian Cinema* is a disappointing experience for a number of reasons that Martin has rightly suggested, but for me it was also disappointing in that, though Miller starts his film with his family and their house in a country town, there is no mention at all of his Greek Kytherean background.

## Greek-Australian cinema: There and here, inside and outside
Greek-Australian films, and their often (but not exclusively) low to modest budget and production values, are characterized by a marked degree of hybridization in their thematic interests, performative registers and stylistic visuals. They are frequently trans-generic in their outlook, full of bicultural displacement, black humour, irony (usually a privileged aspect of the colonizer's discourse of containing, labelling and homogenizing the marginal, the plural, in order to assert cultural authority) and heterogeneity.

Common to these Greek-Australian films is their key focus on the cross-cultural tensions incarnated in the post-war migration experience, and on the related idea that the stereotypical beliefs of Anglo-Celtic monoculturalism are structured on the idea (to quote Trinh Minh-ha) that the colonizer 'discovers with much reluctance, [that] he is just another among others' (in Longley 1992: 22).

What we need to grasp here is how Greek-Australians have made sense of their experiences in a foreign country – not only through visual perception, speech (this would include the fractured hybrid language of 'Greek-Australian' as N.O.'s brilliant performance poetry illustrates), and the many searching and suspicious gazes and silences that would (and do) take place between the colonizer and the colonized, but also and most significantly through touching the habitat with your body.

The Greek-Australian film-maker is obliged to create a cinema which both contests the ethnic stereotypes of past Australian cinema and is, at the same time, cinematically self-reflexive. Thus, creating films concerned with the challenging task of finding new ways, new languages to say complex things about identity, class, gender and migration is required because, as expressed by Salman Rushdie (1988: 16), to 'give voice to the voiceless, you've got to find a language … Use the wrong language and you're dumb and blind.'

The essay film is an attractive genre for Greek-Australian film-makers for a variety of intricate reasons (aesthetic, cultural and historical). Associated with this generic and stylistic preference are also what Naficy (2001: 101–51) has termed 'epistolary narratives'. Anna Kannava's impressive oeuvre of essay films is an extraordinary achievement in that she examines her exilic past with an inventive visual and performative wit, endowing her films with a subtle intertextuality that is sensitively autobiographical and exquisitely moving. Her 1986 essay film uses an 'epistolatory narrative' and is appropriately titled *Ten Years After, Ten Years Older*. It is about her grandmother and her life in Cyprus, and what it meant for Anna to leave Cyprus for a new horizon of hope. The film has a poetic 'ethnographic' textuality to it, and the engaging collage scenes of her grandmother working over a sewing machine as she recounts her life to Anna, informing her that her own mother was adopted, are truly vibrant in their striking dramaturgical and visual values.

At other times, her familial landscape is probed with existential acuteness, especially her relationship to her absent father, her mother and her two brothers, George, a wedding photographer, and her younger brother, Nino. Kannava's deftly constructed, critically acclaimed film *The Butler* (1996) characteristically features her narrating voice as it subtly works its way across an open-ended, poetic visual and aural iconography that speaks of the many behavioural, cultural and historical intricacies of her life, especially in terms of Nino – 'the butler' of the film's title.

This film is a vital essayistic document of her ambivalent, ironic and humorous exilic life between her past homeland, Cyprus, and her new host country, Australia. With her brother Nino and her friends, she recreates certain sequences from her cinephilic experiences of seeing Greek movies at the Astor theatre in Melbourne. As a child, she would also recreate iconic *rembetiko* music tunes, like the classic 'Cloudy Sunday'. The frankness of her admission that she is suffering from the onset of the crippling disease scleroderma is a tragic undercurrent to an otherwise optimistic and lyrical take on her new postcolonial life.

One of the enduring touchstones of Greek-Australian cinema is the unprecedented collaborative essay film *The Occupant* (Michael Karris, Peter Lyssiotis and Ettore Siracusa 1984). Before this collaboration, all three film-makers excelled in the essay film form. Michael Karris made one of the first established Greek-Australian films, *A Face of Greekness* (1979), while Peter Lyssiotis is the country's most talented photomonteur and a gifted film artist. Finally, Ettore Siracusa is also a fine avant-garde film-maker of Italian background. Arguably, all three film-makers, like their ethnic film contemporaries, seek poetic, intertextual strategies to critique the monocultural ideology of their host society and its oppressive sociocultural institutions.

*The Occupant* (Peter Lyssiotis, Michael Karris and Ettore Siracusa, 1984). Image courtesy of Peter Lyssiotis.

With its powerfully written voiceover, *The Occupant* invents new textual strategies to say difficult things about the untold stories of the (in)visible marginal subject. It consists of a series of vignettes, abstract dreamscapes and dramatized sequences, including a letter written to Lyssiotis's father about his acclaimed photomontage art. All three film-makers, in their respective ways, are gifted 'diasporic' auteurs of contemporary Australian cinema. They have fashioned their own solo and collaborative oeuvres to tell their own multi-layered resonant narratives about being exilic or diasporic in their bicultural world of ambivalence, alienation, migrancy and silence.

Bill Mousoulis is one of the country's most dedicated, visionary and prolific independent film-makers. His work, though not overtly 'diasporic' in its thematic and stylistic concerns, nevertheless suggests an allegorical and metaphorical engagement with states of bicultural angst, fragility, collage and melancholia, as in his fine 1997 diary film *My Blessings*. Mousoulis, who found the influential film journal *Senses of Cinema* as well as the Melbourne Super-8 Film Group in 1985, is also a highly committed and articulate polemicist/researcher for Greek-Australian cinema (see Mousoulis 1999).

Deb Verhoeven's (2007) stimulating discussion of Mousoulis's two essential speculative essays on Greek-Australian film-makers and the question of a 'Hellenic sensibility' as a category of film production, as well as one of critical reception, ought also to be singled out here (2007: 281). Karris's films are a possible example of this notion, as an expression of 'seeing' as production – rather than film viewing – is noteworthy. Two essential earlier examples of Karris's distinctive filmic sensibility are *A Face of Greekness* and *Two Homelands*, both made in 1979.

Finally, Lex Marinos, who is a nationally acclaimed theatre director, actor, author, arts policy consultant, screenwriter, broadcaster and gifted raconteur, has made several engaging and impressively directed and crafted feature films over the years. Like the films of Mousoulis, Marinos's cinema is not overtly concerned with Greek-Australian identity and cultural themes as such. However, Marinos did make a highly incisive and poignant 'odyssey' documentary, *To the Island* (1988), shadowing prominent Greek-Australian actor George Spartels as he returns to his father's ancestral Greek island of Kastellorizo.

Marinos's film deftly articulates the intricate cultural and political history of the island and its close proximity to Turkey. This island, besides Kythera and Ithaca, was one of the earliest diasporic sources of immigration to Australia. The director interweaves an interesting array of interviews with many diverse inhabitants of Kastellorizo who have emigrated to Australia and have come back to holiday or have returned permanently to this alluring island. Most of the interviewees attest to the magnetic appeal of Australia as a place for their diasporic yearnings (a faraway place of economic and existential hope). It is a subtle and thoughtful work that exemplifies Marinos's questioning of the cultural and ideological problematics of twentieth century globalization, identity and migrancy in the context of Australia's pre- and post-war Greek immigration.

## Ana Kokkinnos's *Head On* and beyond the Greek-Australian hyphen

In the 1990s, a number of significant films endeavoured to speak about Australian identity in multicultural terms. These films display the multifaceted contradictions, tensions and agendas of official 'multiculturalism' policy. Some, like Baz Lurhmann's *Strictly Ballroom* (1992), represent the 'other' in rigid assimilationist terms as 'us', while others, especially Ana Kokkinos's *Head On* (1998), represent a hybrid notion of Australian identity as never being absolutely fixed. In terms of the latter film, 'other' remains 'other' in all its multiplying poststructuralist complexities, defined in terms of various gay and lesbian ethnic minorities and the various challenges they face within a western culture and its 'dual' cultural forces (see Jackson and Sullivan 1998).

James Bennett's (2007: 61–78) detailed analysis of both films is a significant contribution to our theoretical understanding of the socio-cultural, gendered and sexual intricacies of present-day Australia and its multicultural identities. Simply put, Bennett's thesis is that the value of Kokkinos's film, in contrast to Lurhmann's film, is a dialogical one. The latter presents the continuing Anglo-Celtic hegemony of tolerance for a non-critical 'good multiculturalism', while the former deploys cinematic space to articulate a rupture with the more problematic conservative notions of Australian identity. In his fecund Bakhtinian approach to *Head On*, Bennett argues that this important film destabilizes notions of mateship and the Australian national identity as a static logocentric construction, arguing for a continuous form of hybridity in the 'margins of society'.

Based on Christos Tsiolkas's 1995 novel *Loaded*, which depicts 24 hours of Ari's postmodern life of intense drug taking and sex, a life grounded in the multifaceted adventure of questioning his sexuality and ethnic identity, Ana Kokkinnos's adaptation of Tsiolkas's novel is the seminal coming-of-age gay and ethnic teen movie of the 1990s. Kokkinos's honest and brutal movie effectively explores many different aspects of cinema narrative – hand-held camera, slow-motion, graphic juxtaposing of fantasy with nitty-gritty reality, and expressionist visual distortion – to engender a dynamic kinetic *mise-en-scène* that records a poetic, musical, squalid beauty of the abject, dislocation and the Greek-Australian diaspora.

*Head On*, with its Baudelairean lyricism of emotional and sexual anguish, urban alienation and anonymous sexual encounters, polarized many film critics and reviewers. Chris Berry's (1999) main proposition that the movie was too easily categorized as either a teen or a gay movie and that it is much more than both of these things, because on numerous different levels it questions the binaries of identity politics, should be noted (Berry 1999; Freiberg and Damousi 2003). Clearly, as *Head On* unfolds in its inexorable speed, showing the far-ranging complexities of Ari's alienation and relationship with his parents, what is clearly discernible is that a huge cultural and behavioural gap exists between him and his parents (whose arrival to Australia is registered in iconic black and white footage of Greek migrants arriving in Australia in its 'nation-building' epoch of the 1950s in the movie's astonishingly powerful concluding scenes).

Ari's uncompromising status as an outsider who does not belong to his parents' new home of 'milk and honey', an Australia promising the newly arrived immigrant success and prosperity, suggests someone who characteristically lives a 'double life'. He simultaneously belongs to, and is rejected by, his patriarchal Greek community. In other words, Ari is arguably a 'marginal' character, someone whose self-destructive behaviour and hedonistic immediacy abundantly denote the extreme antagonistic forces that are tearing him apart. Self-hate and disgust and a scorching refusal to live by the hypocrisies, limitations and contradictions of the Greek-Australian diaspora construct Ari as an outlawed outcast. He does not know where he belongs, but nevertheless his life is a continuous project of ongoing hybridity, questioning the fundamentals of mainstream culture and society.

Numerous scenes show Ari's loathing of the patriarchal and sexist values represented by his father, who we first see tending his garden – a central motif in accented/multicultural cinema and literature that warrants critical scrutiny. (For many migrants, their garden is emblematic of their former homeland.) The scenes depicting Ari, his father and his brow-beaten, self-sacrificing mother accurately reveal the complexities, tensions and problems that afflict many Greek-Australian homes. At one point, Ari's younger sister begs their mother not to live through her children, but to live her own life. These, and the scenes where his aunt reads the coffee cup (she exclaims: 'The cups don't lie. I saw the face. My God. I don't believe it!'), create a world governed by superstition as much as by familial moral rigidity, a world of conflict between freedom, gender and identity.

Despite many requests to compromise, Ari's refusal to yield to his father's insults (in a Nietzschean sense) makes him stronger in his interaction with his family, relatives and friends. Further, Ari's self-disgust, restlessness and overall rebellion against social conformity and ethnic and sexual identity lead (at times) to a recognition that he sometimes embodies the problematical values of his own familial background, and even his father's patriarchal attitudes – as when he is over-protective towards his sister ('You're worse than Dad,' she informs him).

The reasons for Ari's rebellion against the world, including his angst and self-hate, elude him. As he tells us, he is no scholar or poet when it comes to analyzing his own ambivalence, rage and rebellion – in other words, his own emotions. All Ari knows is that he must do what his emotions tell him to do. He can't accept the values of his Baby Boomer parents, who lack any viable solutions to a world of global capitalism, ethnic and identity confusion, and unemployment. Ari's self-destructive behaviour needs to be seen, as Berry (1999), Collins and Davis (2004: 160–61) and Nikos Papastergiadis (2003: 171–77) indicate, in the context of the local and the global.

Ari's world is Virilian in its contours: he is constantly transgressing many different zones, spaces and borders. His hyper-kinetic and negative interaction with Melbourne's working class ethnic minorities (Greeks, Lebanese, Turks, Vietnamese, etc.), and their various spaces of urban gentrification, destitution, loss and encroachment attest to the way in which Ari's intense mobile lifestyle is an expression of the centrality of globalization's focus on the 'time/space compression' – in Zygmunt Bauman's (1998: 2) words, 'the ongoing transformation of the parameters of the human condition'.

The pragmatic and wiser transvestite friend Johnny/Toula (Paul Capsis) likens Ari to the Greek mythical character Persephone, who spends half the year in Hades with her husband and the other half in the world above with her mother. Ari's turbulent self-defining adventure in Melbourne as a rebellious, non-conciliatory Greek-Australian subject takes place in an expressionist, energetic *mise-en-scène* of two distinct stylistic configurations. Kokkinos employs a finely textured, hyper-realistic style when Ari escapes from home to vibrant, exciting places; for home and related domestic spaces, where his relatives and friends reside, Kokkinos uses stark and cold colours to suggest the radical contrasts in Ari's ambivalent, hallucinatory world.

Ari's world is not only deftly constructed by the movie's graphically dynamic, gestural and fast-paced visuals, which render his uncompromising hybrid world of confusion, rage and tenderness with remarkable directorial assurance. Its ubiquitous pulsating soundtrack of popular music and Greek *rembetiko* music (including the great soulful Sotiria Bellou) also markedly suggests the underlying alienation, schisms, tensions and hedonism of Ari's abject behaviour. The various trance-like dance sequences clearly indicate how well Kokkinos is able to use and at the same time critique visual stereotypes – and also, as Sneja Gunew (in Papastergiadis 2003: 197) reminds us, to use dance as a register for the nuances of the character of Ari and his family and their various emotional investments.

Alex Dimitriades, as Ari, has given us one of the tour de force performances of Australian cinema in the last 20 years. The extraordinarily nuanced performance is notable for Dimitriades' elastic capacity to give complexity, strength and cohesiveness to the characterization of Ari as a man out of control. It is truly a superb performance, unforgettable for its compelling emotional subtlety and power. The supporting performers also provide a great foil for Dimitriades, in particular Paul Capsis as Johnny/Toula, someone who refuses to surrender to reactionary forces. His impassioned plea to Ari not to give in, and to keep on asking questions of mainstream culture, is reminiscent of Cornelius Castoriadis's observation that the trouble with the contemporary condition of our modern society is that it has stopped questioning itself (see Bauman 1998: 5).

## Conclusion

There are many critical, cultural, historical and textual issues that are in need of further amplification when examining Greek-Australian cinema. It is, relatively speaking, an untapped terrain of our past and present cinematic imagination, history and popular memory. More to the point, there appears to be a substantial gap between modern film theory, postcolonial theory and current representations in mainstream Australian cinema of post-war migration, identity and cultural difference. More work is needed in the sphere of reflexive film-making that knows the value of not being 'dumb and blind', as defined by Rushdie.

Finally, there is a moment in *The Occupant* where Lyssiotis's father is seen pruning a tree. The garden motif resurfaces time and again in Greek-Australian cinema and writing. He is frozen for a fleeting second as he looks directly at the camera. The accompanying voiceover informs the spectator that he knows he is dying from cancer. Without sentimentality, Lyssiotis and his collaborators have given us one of the most haunting images in contemporary Australian cinema. The gaze of Lyssiotis's father embodies the aspirations, hurt and poignancy of the migrant's lot in this country, as in any other. It is an image that will search you out in your quieter moments.

# PART THREE: FILM-MAKERS

# 11

## 'A European Heart': Exile, Isolation and Interiority in the Life and Films of Paul Cox

## Marek Haltof

> I live in a country that is not my own. I can't go back to my own country, so I don't know where I am. I have no home. (Paul Cox 1993)

Although they possess 'a European heart', writes director Paul Cox of his films, their roots are firmly in Australia (1998a: 82). In this chapter, I attend to the diasporic aspects of the biography and early films of Paul Cox, exploring well-known works such as *Kostas* (1979), *Lonely Hearts* (1982) and *Man of Flowers* (1983), and paying particular attention to *My First Wife* (1984). This largely historical chapter works to better comprehend how such films, from the 1970s and 1980s, 'construct' Paul Cox as an exilic, 'homeless' Australian film-maker. These films, well received by Australian and international audiences and critics, popularized Cox's name in the art-house world as an Australian *auteur* making subtle films about human relationships, as 'Australia's Ingmar Bergman' (Chipperfield 1989: 12; Rattigan 1991: 224–26). It is through the recurring themes of exile and isolation, the diasporic motifs of memory and migration, and filmic strategies deploying the construction of mental landscapes and 'European' interiors that the personal relationship between Cox the film-maker and his adopted homeland is to be understood.

### Paul Cox: Exile and isolation

Paul Cox (full name Paul Henrique Benedictus Cox) is among the most important Australian New Wave film directors who emerged in the mid-1970s. His independent film-making displays a recognizably personal style. According to David Stratton: 'Cox is probably Australia's only genuine auteur.' (1998, vii) Born in 1940 in Venlo, Holland, Cox came to Australia in 1963 as an exchange student, opening his own photographic studio in Melbourne in 1965. He later participated in several photographic exhibitions and published a number of albums. Cox's successes as a photographer and his work at the Melbourne College of Art (Prahran College) enabled him to finance his first films made with a Super-8 camera. From 1965, the year he made his first short film *Matuta*, to 1976, when he made his first full-length film *Illuminations*, he produced several short films that displayed a number of characteristics of his later style. At an early stage of Cox's career, his films were already intensely personal, abundant with formal experimentation, and featuring protagonists who were artists (*Mirka* 1970), schizophrenics (*Phyllis* 1971), sensitive introverts (*Time Past* 1966 and *The Journey* 1972), or lonely and alienated characters (*Marcel* 1969, *Symphony* 1969 and *Skin Deep* 1968).

Many of Cox's early films are unknown to wider audiences. In interviews and in his feature films, Cox consistently refers to his two shorts, *The Journey and Island* (1975). The latter, described by Cox as 'a ten-minute film about homesickness (Cox 1998a: 85), he often considers his best film (Bennetto 1986: 18; Haltof 2005: 211). Frequently discussed as an example of 'homeless film-making', *Island* tells the story of a man who, according to Cox, returns to a place that does not exist (Pulleine 1985: 208). Commenting on his 1989 feature film, also entitled *Island*, Cox noticed that 'it was the only way I could free myself from those obsessive visuals and re-examine the question: "Where is home?"' (1998a: 87).

Cox's own migrant background prompted critics to view his film *Kostas* as an autobiographical picture. Although the Australian Film Institute (AFI) previously honoured Cox's documentary *We Are All Alone My Dear* (1975), he considered himself an underground film-maker until the release of *Kostas*, a work more mainstream than Cox's experimental feature films, *Illuminations* and *Inside Looking Out* (1977) (Pulleine 1985: 208). The first Australian film to open the film festival in Melbourne, *Kostas* tells the story of a Greek journalist (Takis Emmanuel), who immigrated to Australia after the military coup in 1967. The film depicts the loneliness of an educated European trying to move beyond the confines of his 'ethnic Melbourne', the Melbourne Greek diaspora. The film's cinematography clearly favours the perspective of an outsider trying to find his way in an Australian 'reality', a person for whom Australia cannot be home. Cox juxtaposes images of sensitive Europeans (Greeks) with xenophobic 'ocker' Australians who are mercilessly ridiculed in the film. Similarly to several canonical European art films, *Kostas* is a film about alienation: the protagonist has to choose between the system value of his adopted country and that of his original homeland. Mikis Theodorakis's music adds an element of nostalgia for a distant home and also stresses the protagonist's isolation.

Cox's next work, *Lonely Hearts*, the AFI winner in the Best Film category in 1982, became his first film to be critically praised and widely distributed. Reviewers favourably compared this film, featuring Norman Kaye and Wendy Hughes, to Delbert Mann's classic, *Marty* (1955) (Dempsey 1986: 7). Distributed by Samuel Goldwyn, the film also received critical recognition overseas, and was compared to Bruce Beresford's *Tender Mercies* (1983), Robert Redford's

*Ordinary People* (1980), and the films of Woody Allen (Sarris 1983: 43; Boyum 1983: 17). *Lonely Hearts* and two following films, *Man of Flowers* and *My First Wife*, often functioning as a trilogy, established Cox's reputation as a master of intimate psychological urban cinema, able to produce works that are, to use Michael Dempsey's (1986) words, 'mordant, poetic, hilarious, gnomic, and angry' (1986: 2).

Unlike the best-known Australian film-makers of the New Wave period, Cox specialized in urban dramas, set in the easily recognizable scenery of Melbourne. The films' characters shared more similarities with protagonists populating European art films than with typical New Wave characters from the outback who featured prominently in films supported by Australian Film Commission in the late 1970s. Brian McFarlane (1987) rightly points out that Cox's films are 'primarily small-scale studies of somewhat bizarre relationships but they offer, almost incidentally, the spectacle of a director in love with Melbourne's Edwardian suburbia' (1987: 90). Thematically, in *Man of Flowers* and *My First Wife*, Cox once again deals with the alienation of an art connoisseur of European background not wholly understood by his Australian compatriots, who do not necessarily share his values or understand his aspirations.

Some of the subsequent films by Cox also focus on comparable characters: likeable eccentrics isolated from the outside world, unable to move beyond the confines of their own lives in their search for meaningful human relationships. As in *Cactus* (1986), *Golden Braid* (1990) and *A Woman's Tale* (1991), it is not wealth these characters are passionate about amassing (although they seem well to do) but rather art objects. They are fascinated by the world of fine arts and classical music, interested in their own dreams and childhood memories more than in external reality. Two other films, both unconventional documentaries, feature troubled artists, *Vincent: The Life and Death of Vincent Van Gogh* (1987) and *Nijinsky: The Diary of Vaslav Nijinsky* (2002). Stylistically, they also exhibit some of the essence of Cox's early experimental style. Commenting on *Vincent*, David Stratton (1990) fittingly noted that it was 'a portrait of one deeply committed, sometimes misunderstood and neglected, artist by another' (1990: 127).

The overtly intimate nature of Cox's cinema lends justification to the reception of his films as autobiographical pictures. They reflect the director's personal fascinations, obsessions and private life, which he does not separate from his films. For viewers familiar with Cox's films and his biography, it is not difficult to see in his works his own immigrant status (*Kostas* and *My First Wife*), his personal problems (*My First Wife*), childhood memories (*Man of Flowers*), his mother's loss of sight (*Cactus*), an appreciation of Greek culture (*Kostas* and *Island*) and a profound disdain for commercialism (*Man of Flowers* and *Lust and Revenge* 1996). Cox comments frequently upon the relationship between the characters who populate his films and his own life. For example, in his autobiography *Reflections: An Autobiographical Journey*, he remarks that: '*Kostas* dealt with the migrant and my growing love for Greece; *Lonely Hearts* with the shyness of my adolescence; *Man of Flowers* with my childhood and growing obsession with beauty.' (Cox 1998a: 151, 153)

An identifiable deprivation of typical thematic and stylistic features recognized as typically Australian has led to the critical framing of Cox's works as 'interior films', due to their subjective narration and interest in the psychology of their characters (Dermody and Jacka 1988a: 68–70). Australian critics look at Cox's films as being made by a talented outsider, an *auteur* who possesses an individual style that has little in common with the major preoccupations of Australian national cinema. They stress the 'Australianness' and the international character of Cox's films, their affinity with canonical Australian films as well as their 'Europeanness' (e.g. Rattigan 1991: 172–73; O'Regan 1996: 63).

Even a cursory glance at major books on Australian cinema reveals that Cox is often marginalized in his own country. While Tom O'Regan mentions him on several occasions throughout *Australian National Cinema* (1996), there is no entry on him in the *Historical Dictionary of Australian and New Zealand Cinema* (Moran and Vieth 2005). Nor does an analysis of his work feature in Felicity Collins and Therese Davis's *Australian Cinema After Mabo* (2004). In several publications dealing with the Australian New Wave phenomenon, his name appears on the margins of Australian mainstream cinema. For example, Murray's *The New Australian Cinema*, which summarizes the achievements of the pioneering New Wave period, mentions only *Kostas*, Cox's third film, ignoring his earlier accomplishments (1980).

The issue of 'Europeanness' repeatedly returns in interviews with Cox and in the critical appraisal of his films (Haltof 2001: 131–50). Although Cox has been one of several Australian director-immigrants from Europe (others include Rolf de Heer, Carl Schultz and Nadia Tass), Australian critics often emphasize Cox's outsider status, his European sensibility and his affinity with European art cinema. This treatment of Cox positions him as a double outsider within the context of Australian cinema. First, he is a European who is proud of his origins and for whom this milieu is a continuous point of reference. Second, he lives and works in Melbourne – a city rich in film tradition, but not the centre of film production in Australia. Cox operates 'between centres', and such 'in-between spaces', according to Homi Bhabha, 'provide the terrain for elaborating strategies of selfhood – singular or communal – that initiate new signs of identity, and innovative sites of collaboration, and contestation, in the act of defining the idea of society' (Bhabha 2004: 1–2).

In infrequent public appearances, Cox often projects an image of himself as a film-maker without a home, an alienated artist who merely lives in Australia. In an interview appropriately titled 'Paul Cox: Self-Portrait of an Exile', he comments as follows: 'I live in a country that is not my own. I can't go back to my own country, so I don't know where I am. I have no home.' In the same interview, he does not consider himself an Australian film-maker, despite the fact that he is 'very Australian in [his] convictions and in [his] beliefs and in using Australian actors', and 'much more proud of Australia than most Australians', but only 'a film-maker living in Australia' (Caputo and Urban 1993: 7, 9). In a highly critical review of *Cactus*, a film about a young French woman (Isabelle Huppert) losing her sight while visiting her friends in Australia, Liz Jacka (1989) notices that: 'Cox seems to be tailoring his films more and more to this market, self-consciously making "art" films in the worst sense. To me, however, he no longer has an emotional coherence and true sense of place, a reflection perhaps of his own sense of being not quite at home anywhere.' (Jacka 1989: 11)

At the same time, Cox's own biographical 'construction' of himself relies heavily on the romanticized image of a misunderstood artist who is marginalized by Australia's film funding agencies. Numerous times, he has stressed that his work has been ignored by state institutions that have shown continual preference for some shapeless imitations of Hollywood cinema. 'There has never been a retrospective of my work in this country yet the Americans run retrospectives. I've never been asked to be on any (Australian film) board.' (Chipperfield 1989: 12) David Stratton commented in a similar manner in the introduction to Cox's published scripts: 'Despite the fact that his modestly budgeted productions generally recover costs – and reap considerable prestige – he is increasingly neglected by the very government funding bodies which should support such a unique, if at times wayward, talent.' (Cox 1998b: vii) Perhaps as a sign of Cox's growing bitterness, some of his productions in the late 1990s, such as the medium-length IMAX 3-D film *The Hidden Dimension* (aka *Four Million Houseguests*, USA 1997) and *Molokai: The Story of Father Damien* (1999), were made outside Australia. Despite the image of an unwanted, marginalized artist prevalent in interviews with Cox and in writings on his cinema, he has nonetheless been able to raise money for his projects chiefly from Film Victoria in Melbourne, the support of which he also warmly acknowledges in his interviews. Since 1986, with the making of *Cactus*, Cox has been supported by the Australian Film Commission (*Cactus*, *Golden Braid*) and its extension, the Film Finance Corporation (*A Woman's Tale*, *The Nun and the Bandit* and *Exile*). *Lust and Revenge*, a bitter satire on art management bureaucracy, was made with the participation of the South Australian Film Corporation in Adelaide.

As with the setting and content of Cox's films, the process of filming is a private matter. Like several other known film *auteurs*, Cox fully controls every stage of the cinematic process, which he shares with a small company of actors and production crew. The 'Cox group' consists of actor-composer Norman Kay, actors Wendy Hughes and Tony Llewellyn-Jones in early films, Julia Blake, Chris Haywood and, in the 1990s, Gosia Dobrowolska. Cox's frequent collaborators also include co-producer John Ballantyne, editor Tim Lewis, set designer Asher Bilu, co-scriptwriter Bob Ellis and a Russian cinematographer who settled in Melbourne, Yuri Sokol. To maintain full artistic control, Cox makes comparatively low-budget films that are produced by his own production company, Illumination Films, and are regularly co-funded by Film Victoria. The choice of Melbourne suburbs, frequently the actual neighbourhood of Cox's home (Albert Park and Williamstown), and now and then even his actual home (as in *Golden Braid*), certainly helps to lower the production costs. Cox borrowed some of his production strategies from his friend and mentor Werner Herzog (Bristow 1991: 42; Cox 1998a: 153). Taking into account the budget of his films and their box office performance, Cox has proclaimed in the past that he is 'probably the greatest commercial film-maker' in Australia (Chipperfield 1989: 12).

The 'art-house' nature of Cox's films sees them directed at 'sophisticated' international audiences, as they do not share the same thematic fascination with the vastness of the outback landscape that is present in canonical ('AFC genre') Australian films; they are not fixated on the safe and heavily aestheticized version of Australian history; they don't feature images of Aborigines; and they are not preoccupied with Australian mythologies. Some of Cox's films – for example, *My First Wife*, *Golden Braid* and *A Woman's Tale* – could have been made anywhere, and their references to Australia and its uniqueness seem marginal. However, Cox maintains that his films could only be made in Australia because of the unique transnational connections his work represents.

Unlike the majority of well-known Australian film-makers, Cox is interested in urban characters that resemble neither the images of filmic ockers from the 1970s, nor the characters populating the majority of Australian urban dramas. In the settings of Cox's films, a suburb of Melbourne resembles a typical European city: it is deprived of easily recognizable Australian symbols and is populated by eccentric characters with psychological problems, characters alienated and escaping from the present into their childhood memories, personal obsessions and the world of arts.

The theme of alienation, often present in earlier Australian cinema, was previously 'reserved' for films set in the Australian bush, often made by director-outsiders such as Ted Kotcheff (*Wake in Fright* 1971) and Nick Roeg (*Walkabout* 1971). Cox's protagonists, however, have found themselves on the margins of society not because of the colour of their skin, social status or problems with the law, but because of a different, European (not British) sensibility. As portrayed in Cox's cinema, these characters are often marginalized by xenophobic Australians (*Kostas*, *My First Wife*). Cox bitterly comments in one of his interviews:

> Don't forget I'm a migrant. There are only about three million original white Australians and they are pretty much like rednecks and very racist. Look at the people who hold all the so-called important jobs in this country; look at the television presenters, the politicians. They all come from that stock of three million rednecks. They certainly don't come from the wonderful ethnic mixture. (quoted in Urban and Caputo 1993: 60)

The authorial character of Cox's work is also emphasized by his personal appearances in some of his films. He cast himself as a priest in *Golden Braid*, a participant in a funeral procession in *Vincent* and a shop customer in *Lust and Revenge*. His name is also credited as an actor in films made by some icons of contemporary art cinema: Werner Herzog (*Where the Green Ants Dream* 1984) and Guy Maddin (*Careful* 1992; *Waiting for Twilight* 1997). As indicated earlier, in rare interviews and in public appearances Cox creates an image of a sensitive, romantic artist who is determined to fight with the soulless bureaucratic system, whose only chance is total independence to the point of an almost 'internal exile', an aspect stressed by the very subtitle of Cox's interview, 'Self-Portrait of an Exile' (Caputo and Urban 1993: 4). Published in 1998, the director's autobiography also emphasizes this overriding image of Cox (1998a). Like his films, his autobiography is very personal, 'impressionistic', nonlinear and interspersed with enigmatic images from his travels. Cox is aware that his approach to film-making may be perceived as anachronistic in pragmatic times. In one of his interviews, he proclaims: 'In another age, I probably would have been a fool who went from town to town, a troubadour maybe.' (Bristow 1991: 40)

## Mental landscapes: A diasporic strategy

In this section, I examine the use of 'mental landscapes' as a specific device marking the film-making subversions represented by Cox as diasporic figure. The director's cinematic style continues on from the style and themes that originated in his short films. His early works possess episodic structures that define their unconventional protagonists through clashes with equally peculiar secondary characters. At that time, storytelling seemed less important than creating a multi-layered picture of the protagonist's personality through a blurring of reality and dreams, memories and hallucinations. Memories, dreams and love – these were the themes of Cox's early films. Slow-paced action was interrupted by subjective images filmed with a Super-8 camera. In presenting dream sequences and memories, Cox's method resembled that of Werner Herzog, particularly as employed in Herzog's classic film *The Enigma of Kaspar Hauser* (1975). Herzog's own appearance in *Man of Flowers* as a demanding father both references and pays homage to Herzog's cinema, although Cox had already used similar constructions of subjective imagery extensively in his early experimental films.

Over the years, Cox's trademark has become the use of subjective camera to depict the frame of mind of his protagonists. He portrays their 'mental landscapes', usually with the abrupt interruption of the linear narration of his films, forcing audiences to focus on the new film space. These 'mental landscapes' feature disconnected shots, slow panoramas over landscapes that are often exotic and, on the surface, not directly related to the film's main narrative.

Cox uses these signature 'mental landscapes' in the majority of his films. Beginning with *Kostas*, the episodic action of his films is interrupted by non-narrative, expressive shots, apparently far removed from the film's reality. Greek landscapes, fragments from the film *Island*, and violent and distorted memory flashes create a peculiar mood in *Kostas*. Likewise, *Man of Flowers* features landscapes and situations remembered from the protagonist's childhood. In *My First Wife*, Cox is able to deal with the protagonist's psychology by depicting his mental landscape, which is registered through glimpses of memory and through images that create the film's dream-like atmosphere. *Cactus* contains childhood reminiscences and images of Paris belonging to the protagonist Colo (Isabelle Huppert), as well as images that are difficult to decipher belonging to her blind friend Robert (Robert Menzies). Furthermore, the semi-documentary *Vincent* includes non-narrative, 'expressionistic'-in-spirit fragments. The linear narration of two later films, *Golden Braid* and *A Woman's Tale*, is also recurrently interrupted with scenes on Super-8 that emphasize the passing of time, uncertainty and nightmarish dreams.

### *My First Wife*: Interiority

Cox's celebrated *My First Wife* serves as a particularly interesting example of cinema relying on subjective narration. This film, about 'the mysterious, unsettling disappearance of love' (Dempsey 1986: 4), introduces a cultured Australian of European background, John (John Hargreaves), struggling through a marital crisis which is intensified by the infidelity of his wife

Helen (Wendy Hughes). In its narrative, Cox's film employs the strategies of art cinema, its intensity and obsessions. At the centre of his film is a typical art-house protagonist: neurotic, alienated and captured during a deepening crisis in his personal life. The director explores the character's state of mind and his psychology. Michael Dempsey eloquently remarks that 'few of the many movies which have tackled the emotional maelstrom churned up when a marriage explodes can equal its head-on plunge into the embarrassment, the laceration, and the grim comedy of primal emotions suddenly stripped bare and flayed out of all control' (1986: 3).

As in his other films, Cox searches for a new cinematic language in attempting to represent the interior worlds of his protagonists. Several personally interior, 'emotional' shots on Super-8 interrupt the linear narration by introducing images that are removed from the film's reality: images of ships entering a harbour, a child playing with a dog, far-off exotic landscapes. The film employs the expressive motif of night trains and images of trees as seen from the passing train. Those non-linear 'interior shots' are employed by Cox to communicate what is going on inside the diasporic subject, and also his own very personal feelings of displacement and homelessness. To a large degree, the film's atmosphere is created through retrospective images from the character's past: wedding scenes, erotic images of his wife, images of their daughter playing in a park, as well as scenes of her birthday. The director often employs shots from his earlier works – for example, the birth scene in *My First Wife* comes from a documentary *For a Child Called Michael* (1979), also with the participation of Wendy Hughes. Those recurring flashes of memory, often bursting on to the screen unexpectedly, perform an important narrative function. Erupting on their own, they serve as a reminder of a happier past confronted with depressive reality.

Visions from a protagonist's past in Cox's films are not always presented as traditionally retrospective scenes that rely on the character's dreams, thoughts and experiences to make sense. Rather, they function as images marked with emotions, the subjective camera shots reflecting John's 'mindscreen'. Film theorists have often pointed out the type of narration similar to that present in Cox's films. For example, David Bordwell and Kristin Thompson discussed 'perceptual subjectivity' and 'mental subjectivity' (1997: 105). In his classic study, *Mindscreen: Bergman, Godard, and First-Person Film*, Bruce F. Kawin (1978) used the term 'mindscreen'. A similar term, 'mindscreen narration', was employed by Avrom Fleishman in his *Narrated Films: Storytelling Situations in Cinema History* (1992: 173, 232).

*My First Wife*, a film lasting one hour and 40 minutes, employs 13 scenes on Super-8, ranging from three seconds to one minute and 41 seconds, that are deprived of dialogue and voiceover narration. A typical scene, often portrayed in slow motion to achieve a dream-like quality, is accompanied by fragments from Carl Orff's *Carmina Burana* (1937) or the sound of a speeding train. The 'mindscreen' scenes consist of both traditionally understood retrospectives and those that at first glance are unrelated to the narrative. The first group includes images from the protagonist's past: the wedding ceremony and party, erotic images of Helen, the birth of their daughter and playful scenes in a park. The second group includes shots of passing night trains, expressionistic images seen from the passing trains, images of trees reflected on the train's windows, ships entering a port, a girl playing with a dog near the harbour, seagulls, palms in a desert at sunset, exotic scenes (probably from Egypt) and the sun coming through the window.

Cox deliberately attempts to portray John's 'mindscreen', and to represent his mental landscape filled with painful emotions, in purely visual terms. He confesses that for him the greatest challenge is 'expressing feelings without using the language of words' (Cox 1998a: 156). The majority of scenes – particularly those of passing night trains – are not present in the screenplay by Cox and Bob Ellis. The script implies a slightly different film: in the opening sequence, while returning home, John falls asleep on a moving train only to awaken later, visibly disturbed by his marital nightmare. The script ends with a bedroom conversation between John and Helen, suggesting that, in spite of tensions and obvious differences, home is a still lingering possibility, or at least a hope (Cox 1998b).

Analyzing similar directorial attempts by Werner Herzog in *The Enigma of Kaspar Hauser*, Timothy Corrigan remarks that 'the changes in film stock which differentiate these dreams from Kaspar's more socialized visions immediately indicate the alternative status of these visions, the rough film stock correlating to Kaspar's primal imagination' (1983: 139). Corrigan emphasizes that the presence of these strange, still landscapes and the lack of a typical action 'immobilizes the look within its own hypnotic space, a vast and luxurious oasis of unbounded directions' (1983: 140). Such a comparison between Herzog and Cox seems justified. Like Herzog, Cox is not interested in invisible storytelling done with the help of traditional subjective narrative techniques. Instead, he prefers the intrusion of shots from different realms that slow down the narration but introduce new interpretative meanings. Unlike Herzog, however, Cox is not searching for exotic settings, extreme situations or characters who are out of the ordinary. Melbourne serves him well: everyday situations contain enough drama, and his characters – although in many ways eccentric – are part of our reality. In addition, his non-narrative 'mindscreen' images are not as static and painterly as are Herzog's compositions. They testify to his experimental cinema roots, and to the importing of non-Australian traditions, rather than to painterly inspirations.

## Conclusion
Paul Cox has continued to make successful personal films in a world that prefers standard Hollywood narratives. Both his films and his separate (but not marginal) status in the context of Australian cinema certainly deserve more critical scrutiny and recognition, and more than just one book-length study (Haltof 2001). Critics tend to look at Cox's cinema as having an 'alien', 'Dutch/European component', and they often stress the modernist roots of his approach to cinema. It is important, however, to see Cox's films both as influenced by and as part of the international art cinema scene, and also as an integral part of Australian national cinema.

# 12

## SOPHIA TURKIEWICZ: AUSTRALIANIZING POLES, OR 'BLOODY NUTS AND BALTS' IN SILVER CITY (1984)

*Renata Murawska*

Hybridity is a risky notion. It comes without guarantees. (Kraidy 2005: v)

We're a nation of immigrants. As a nation, we've never yet arrived. (Brian Johns in Hessey 1988: 3)

It is 1949. An Australian customs officer examines a photograph dug out from a young male's suitcase. It is of a woman with small children, all shot dead. 'Jesus, what's that?' the Australian official asks with disbelief and disgust. The distressed owner of the suitcase explains in a strange language, 'To moja rodzina, zona'. A young female comes to his rescue to interpret in broken English. The photograph is the only one he has of his family, his wife and children, all perished in the war in far-away Europe. The official grimaces, unimpressed. 'What sort of nuts are we letting into this country?'

The laconic portrayal of the customs officer in one of the first scenes of Sophia Turkiewicz's *Silver City* (1984) is not dissimilar from that of other 'real' (read: Anglo-Celtic) Australians in the film, including nurses who refuse to play darts with the Polish heroine of the film, country boys who want to rape her, and a publican who refers to her and her companion as 'bloody nuts and Balts'.

The women see the camp in daylight for the first time. *Silver City* (Sophia Turkiewicz, 1984). Image courtesy of Tim Long.

Such portrayals belie the fact that *Silver City* is a love story. Two Polish post-war refugees, Nina (Gosia Dobrowolska) and Julian (Ivar Kants), meet in an Australian refugee camp and fall in love. Their relationship is complicated by Julian's marriage to Anna (Anna Jemison). As the story unravels, Nina attempts to escape the pitfalls of their forbidden love and pursues work away from the camp, while Julian's weaknesses and/or his commitment to his family see him oscillate between two women throughout the film.

At the same time, *Silver City* is much more than an 'ethnic love story'. It is the first and thus far the only Australian feature film that focuses exclusively on Polish migrants to Australia. The fictitious film validates a range of immigrant processes and experiences for Polish-Australians of the post-war wave of immigration, as well as of the second refugee immigration wave of the 1980s, after the introduction of martial law in Poland in December 1981. In so doing, *Silver City* addresses a little-known moment of Australian nation-building history, highlighting the complexities of migration and migrant identity formation that occurs through the simultaneous assimilation – or rather integration – and ethnicization of its characters, a phenomenon noted by Jerzy Smolicz and Roger Harris (1984) in their study of Polish immigrants to Australia. With its use of accented English rather than subtitles, *Silver City* also attempts to make an Australian 'ethnic' story accessible to broader audiences. More generally, *Silver City*'s contribution to the overt hybridization of Australian cinema's identity is noteworthy because it wrestles the seat of cultural power, however temporarily, from the concept of Australia built on a dichotomy of non-ethnic (sic!) Anglo-Australians and 'ethnics', a division that still persists in popular circulation in Australia (e.g. Rattigan 1998: 22–26). Most interestingly, at the time of its release it was also one of very few Australian films highlighting the anti-Australian (Rattigan 1991: 273) and anti-European (McFarlane 1987: 60) undercurrents in Australian popular culture, despite that not being Sophia Turkiewicz's intention. In 2008, the director of *Silver City* readily admits that 'with the benefit of a hindsight, [she] wrote Australian characters as types' and she would make them more complex if given another chance (Turkiewicz interview 2008). Nevertheless, many reviewers and commentators did focus on these unwittingly contentious aspects of her film, while their responses were symptomatic of the undercurrents they addressed.

Some reviews welcomed *Silver City* as offering a more honest self-representation of Australia (Dell'Oso 1984: 10) that highlighted the schism between 'New' and 'Old' Australians (*Sunday Press* 1984: 31) and counterbalanced the myth of 'a sunlit WASP paradise, secure in its smug colonial heritage' portrayed in other Australian films (*Ms London* 1985). Others, such as Dermody and Jacka (1988b), took *Silver City* as a righteous counter-reaction to the Australian perception of non-English speaking migrants as 'dense and ludicrous' (1988b: 229), thus granting cultural power in the relationship between Anglo-Australians and non-Anglo immigrants to the latter. Yet others saw the film as a badly disguised political pamphlet (Tivey 1984: 61; Stone 1985: 72), and cultural theorist Meaghan Morris (1984) referred to the customs scene described here at the beginning as 'gross burlesque' (1984: 41). The broad range of opposing and equally emphatic responses to Turkiewicz's film internationally evinces its importance beyond the central love story.

This chapter argues that the significance of *Silver City* is not only its portrayal of an anti-Australian stance, but the fact that Turkiewicz's film meaningfully reflects on the complexities of diasporic hybridization of Polish migrant identities. Turkiewicz's film stresses the malleability and unpredictability of the process of identity hybridization, just as Kraidy does in this chapter's first epigraph. Furthermore, *Silver City* avoids positioning its characters at the extremes of either migrant assimilation or exilic despair. Rather, it points to ethnicization as a viable integrationist migrant strategy, even if such a strategy has varied outcomes and may require an uncomfortable demythologizing of Australia. Evidence supporting this rather complex argument can be found on many levels, as this chapter aims to demonstrate.

First, the schism between the ethnicized, or hybrid, and Anglo Australia finds confirmation in the production context of the film, and the difficult road it travelled from its conception in the late 1970s to its delivery in 1984, which is described below. Second, the historical context of Nina and Julian's story is also a canvas of other similar stories of Polish post-war refugees whose arrival in Australia constitutes *terminus a quo* for the unpredictable process of migrant identity hybridization, also part of Sophia Turkiewicz's personal experience and the basis of her hybrid self-identification (Turkiewicz, in Cremen 1984: 239). The social significance of *Silver City* is enhanced by attention to the historical context of Polish post-war migration to

Australia, a task undertaken in the second part of this chapter. Lastly and most substantially, this chapter focuses on the film itself and the scenes which are most potent in illustrating the argument outlined above.

### Boring migrants in depressing hostels: Producing an ethnic love story

*Silver City* grew out of Turkiewicz's imperative to pay homage to the immigrant experience of her Polish parents (Turkiewicz, in Cremen 1984: 239, 287). Born in Rhodesia, she arrived with her Polish mother in Fremantle in 1950 aged three and a half. Despite having spent practically all her life in Australia, she only recently identified herself as Australian, previously seeing Australian identity in conflict with her 'unusual' outsider status as a migrants' child (Turkiewicz, in Cremen 1984: 239; Turkiewicz, in Pollak 1985: 3), which at that time placed her in the space favoured by a good number of artists and film-makers: that of an existential outsider (Porteous 1985: 118–19). She had also fought off any labelling of 'an ethnic film-maker' who tells exclusively migrant stories (Turkiewicz in Cremen 1984: 237), and in the 1980s was already referring to herself as 'a hybrid in [Australian] culture' (Turkiewicz, in Cremen 1984: 239). This is the type of self-identification with which she feels most comfortable still in 2008, yet without the earlier sense of alienation (Turkiewicz interview 2008).

Turkiewicz's work on *Silver City* started tentatively around 1974, when she prepared a treatment for a film titled *The Refugees*, about a Polish family who arrive in Australia in the early 1950s and by the 1970s show 'all the signs of having assimilated successfully' (Turkiewicz 1974: 4). This remark is in tune with the still-dominant notion that assimilation of sorts is a desirable if not necessary part of a migration process, unlike that of ethnicization which underlies multiculturalism (Johnston 1965: 24; Cohen 1997: x). Before beginning work on the script of *Silver City* in 1978, Turkiewicz had completed *Letters from Poland*, her Australian Film and Television School graduation film. It attracted the attention of Joan Long, an established commercial film producer, who encouraged Turkiewicz to continue the focus on Polish refugees, a challenge that she gladly accepted while away on a film stipend in Poland.

Both women persevered in their efforts to bring Turkiewicz's script to the screen, despite 'a lot of knockbacks from script assessors in the early years because … migrants were [perceived as] boring' (Turkiewicz, in Williamson 1984: 29). Subsequent script assessments from the Australian Film Commission demanded moving the film's action away from the migrant hostel, which was seen as too depressing, and adding more Australian characters; the AFC also urged caution in relation to an 'ethnic love story' which could deem the film commercially problematic, as had been the case with Paul Cox's *Kostas* (1979) a few years earlier. On the fifth draft, Long brought in Tom Keneally who at that time had just returned from Poland, where he was working on *Schindler's Ark*. This was in an attempt to overcome the ethnic stigma of the film and to make a stronger case for funding based on Keneally's literary standing. Finally, the script did get a go-ahead for its 'blockbuster potential' and 'the basis to be quite "epic" and "special"'.

Establishing a strong mix of Australian and migrant acting talent was another significant challenge. With Helen Rowland's casting net spread far and wide, from local migrant hostels all the way to Poland (Stratton 1990: 53), the female lead was eventually given to Gosia Dobrowolska, a Polish migrant actress found in the infamous Villawood Migrant Centre. Ivar Kants, a son of Latvian immigrants, took the male lead role of Julian, while Anna Jemison (aka Anna Maria Monticelli, of Italian, Spanish and French descent), accepted the role of Anna, Julian's wife. Aided by the generous 10BA tax concession scheme (see Dermody and Jacka 1988b: 7–14), the film secured the necessary funding of around A$2 million, and was realized ten drafts and ten years after its conception. In 1984, *Silver City* was delivered in a screening regime that took it to Cannes, the United States, the United Kingdom and all around Australia.

In 2008, Turkiewicz modestly sees the visibility and appeal of *Silver City* as an outcome of the serendipitous tide of cultural interest in migrant issues that came to the public fore in Australia in the early 1980s (Turkiewicz interview 2008), most likely as a delayed reaction to Professor Jerzy Zubrzycki's principles of multiculturalism, adopted by the Australian government in the previous decade. Not only did Turkiewicz's film get made and attract Australian and national interest, but – however arguably – she was also heralded at the time to be the second woman to have directed an Australian feature film for cinematic release (Bunbury 1987: 231). Given her double alienation, being from a migrant and working-class family in the predominantly non-migrant and middle-class milieu of the Australian Film and Television School (Turkiewicz interview 2008), her achievement is a particularly potent example of the Polish immigrant statistics in Australia with, for instance, one 1981 sample showing that only a quarter of first-generation Polish Australians would rise above the manual jobs, but 90 per cent of their children would end up with university education (Pakulski 1985: 172). The fact that, despite their social rise, Turkiewicz and other migrant children of her generation would often resist assimilation and insist on their hybrid identification may be seen as a response to the dominant schism between 'ethnic' and Anglo Australia which preceded and to some extent accompanied Australian multiculturalism.

It is also telling that most assessors' comments would question the commercial viability of the *Silver City* project, based on the 'ethnic' compartmentalization of the film's story. Furthermore, Joan Long also considered briefly bringing in a different Australian director to the project (Turkiewicz interview 2008). Had she proceeded with that idea, most likely the historical veracity of the picture – which validated the Polish immigrant experience of many – would have been lost. In Turkiewicz's words, 'in the '80s, Polish family and friends would not shut up when watching the film. They were interested in all the background detail. Every frame was a trigger for reminding them of their own experience. That's the ultimate impact of a documentary aspect of *Silver City*.' (Turkiewicz interview 2008)

## The promised land: Poles in Australia and *Silver City*

Before 1947, there were only around 5,000 Polish immigrants registered in Australia. An immigration agreement signed that year by Arthur A. Calwell, the Australian Minister of Immigration and Information, opened Australia to over 182 thousand of displaced persons (DPs) of non-British origin, under the scheme of the International Refugee Organization (IRO) and in line with the Australian post-war economic migration policy of 'populate or perish' (Castles and Miller 2003: 76). Over 65,000 Poles settled in Australia between 1947 and 1951, making them the most sizeable group of immigrants to Australia in that period (Johnston 1965: 5; Kaluski 1985: 30–31; Jupp 2001: 623–24). Turkiewicz's film not only remedies the surprising absence of a Polish perspective on this period, but experiences portrayed in it carry uncanny resemblance to many a Polish migrant's experience (cf. Lubelski 2000). That referential effect is clearly illustrated in many stories collected by Achmatowicz-Otok and Otok for their 1985 book on Polish migrant experience in Australia, including the following account:

> We were put on the train to a camp in the bush. For the welcome, we were herded into a huge sheet-metal shed…In the shed…someone was giving a speech. I couldn't understand anything because my English was too poor…The cleverer of us, those who understood bits and pieces, later translated that speech to us: 'Forget Europe. That's a completely different world. Whatever you learned there is worthless. Here you have to start again, anew. Throw your diplomas out. You won't have any use for those here.' Today, after ten years, I have not forgotten that 'speech'. Or Europe. (Szczygielska translated by Murawska, quoted in Achmatowicz-Otok and Otok 1985: 110–11)

The situation described here and in the film was possibly better than the fate experienced by other post-war immigrants. Those recruited by IRO worked in exchange for travel expenses for their whole family's boat trip to Australia. After arrival, men laboured in remote mountain areas, their wives were sent to work on tropical plantations and their children often had to be placed in orphanages. The length of their separation was on average around two years (Achmatowicz-Otok and Otok 1985: 112–13; cf. Jurkiewicz 2003: 23–24). These rather unfavourable settling circumstances in many cases exasperated the production of new diasporic identities in Poles subjected to the IRO scheme 'through transformation and difference' (Hall 2003: 244). Potentially, they would foreground the dichotomy between the freedom of settling in Australia and exilic disappointment of the failed Promised Land (Jones 1995: 253), which resulted in various ways of identity hybridization for Polish and other migrants in Australia.

Part of the Australian socioscape of the 1950s was, after all, 'discrimination in hiring and promotion, non-recognition of skills', 'hostility towards anyone speaking a foreign language in public' and 'resentment towards foreign children at school' (Castles and Miller 2003: 214). In the words of Anna Jemison (Anna in Silver City), as a migrant child in the 1960s, 'you didn't dare let mum put salami on your sandwiches for fear of what they would say at school' (Jemison, in Hanrahan 1983: 29). Some of the common terms for refugees and immigrants of that era were 'rotten reffos, dirty dagos, stinkin' foreigners, flamin' Balts' (Marshall 1984). Interestingly, these epitaphs and Silver City's portrayal of the early migrant moments in Australia reverberated differently for the Polish refugees of the second major intake of over 25,000, who were granted residency in Australia after the introduction of martial law in Poland in December 1981 (Jupp 2001: 624). For them, the experience of Silver City comes through a prism of better education gained in (communist) Poland, greater distance from the events of the film and also, for many, participation as extras in the film, which constituted a welcome respite from the grind of migration centres and allowed at least a temporary involvement with the Australian world outside the dreaded migrant hostels.

What both substantial waves of Polish immigration have in common, however, is their attitude to assimilation, which divides them into enthusiasts (taken with Australia, not interested in maintaining Polish traditions), pacifists (appreciating Australia, but seeing the process of assimilation as a long one that should not be hurried), revolutionists (disliking Australia but giving the appearance of utter assimilation) and neutrals (not interested in assimilating, not disliking Australia and with a strong preference for Polish cultural expression) (Johnston 1965: 145–55). These divisions, together with the dominant myths of multiculturalism, are in circulation in *Silver City*, in which refugees are transformed into Aussie battlers, while their children take the opportunity to advance socially through education as doctors and lawyers (Jones 1995: 259). At the same time, it is only in the opening scene and through one (love) song popular in the pre-war Poland, both described below, that Turkiewicz's film acknowledges a vague possibility of nostalgic longing for (European/Polish) home, itself not a static point of reference (cf. Kalra Kaur and Hutnyk 2005: 18). That lack of fixity in defining and redefining homeland suggests the hybridic malleability of diasporic people who, like the migrants in *Silver City* and their extra-diegetic referents, exhibit an active awareness and agency within the renewal of their own identities. This is best demonstrated in the choices made by the Polish migrants depicted in *Silver City*.

### *Silver City*: Hybridizing Polish Australians and Australian myths
The opening scene of *Silver City* frames the film as an historical (love) epic. The Polish love song 'Milosc ci wszystko wybaczy' ('Love forgives everything'), which dates back to 1933 and was briefly popularized internationally by *Schindler's List* (Spielberg 1993), accompanies a sweeping take of the Australian landscape. The camera then takes the viewer through a depleted congregation of Quonset huts, momentarily focusing on a female silhouette back-lit by the sun at the entrance to an empty hut. This setting is marked as the site of nostalgia. Suggestive of pre-war Poland, the popular love-song becomes indexically connected to the empty hut and its (past) temporality.

The mysterious wistfulness of the opening scenes gives way to the darkness of train corridors. It is 1962, and attractive blonde Nina is visibly disturbed by the sight of Julian, whom she knew when the now-depleted camp was filled with refugees. The couple soon engages in a stilted conversation in English, Nina with a strong Eastern European accent, Julian with a slight, difficult to place foreignness. She is a teacher on her way to a conference in Sydney; he is a factory worker. He comments on her 'looking Australian', to which she answers: 'I'm 100 per cent Australian, I feel Australian.' This juxtaposition of Nina's assured response with her strong accent presents a powerful case for the possibility of a simultaneous assimilation and ethnicization, two processes assumed to be incompatible if not incongruent by most migration writers (cf. Smolicz and Harris 1984: 69). Nina's assertion also exemplifies the fusion of identities inherent in both diasporic experience and being Australian. Julian, on the other hand, although looking less 'foreign' and possessing only a slight accent, does not feel Australian.

It is 'too late' for him, which suggests his greater internal ethnicization beneath the veneer of overt assimilation and, as with Nina, his pacifist rather than enthusiast attitude to the hybridizing process. In neither case is pure, non-hybrid identity an option for the diasporic ontology of these two characters, if such purity may be said to exist at all (Papastergiadis 2000: 208; cf. Gilroy 1994: 54–55). Additionally, the little information given about Julian's son, Daniel, positions Julian's family within a nationalizing migrant mythology, in which the (Australian) land of plenty offers social advancement to (second-generation) new Australians – in Daniel's case, through a medical degree.

One possible, if not alternative, interpretation of that scene, as it is poetically metaphorized by Anna Maria Dell'Oso in her 1984 review of *Silver City*, is that the train travel suspends Nina and Julian 'between departure and arrival', with their conversation reflecting 'an older time in suspension' in the refugee camp (Dell'Oso 1984b: 50). Taken further, such an interpretation implies interstitiality, which is a popular way of conceptualizing various migration processes; this is something which Brian Johns, in the second epigraph to this chapter, suggests is a permanent characteristic of Australia as a nation. However, the process of diasporic – or indeed any – identity hybridization is not clearly marked by finite departures and arrivals, and therefore should be seen as being in a state of perpetual flux. The moments in which we witness that process in Nina and Julian can only be taken as snapshots of their continuously malleable and largely unpredictable existence and identity permutations.

The scenes that follow in the film show the arrival of a ship from Europe with the 100,000 displaced person being given a big toy bear and photo opportunities, in a somewhat farcical attempt to celebrate the new migration policy that contrasts with the much less celebratory fate of the refugees to come. Nina and other Polish and European refugees are loaded on to trucks and taken to their accommodation, a place fashioned on the now non-existent 'Greta' migrant hostel not far from Newcastle (Turkiewicz, interview 2008), which at times housed as many as 14,000 immigrants. On the way, Nina doubts what she and her companions cannot see in the darkness of the night: 'We must be mad.' Her comment is met with: 'Just remember, Poland is a cemetery now.' These few words cut the umbilical cord connecting the refugees with their previous homeland. They also demand that these refugees respond to the identity (re)formation pressures of their new homeland.

Having arrived in the darkness of the night, the refugees are welcomed by the hostel administrator during an evening meal. Neither the meal nor the welcome speech is greeted with any level of gratitude by Polish refugees. The speech is fashioned on Calwell's post-war addresses, and is practically but insensitively translated into German, which is probably assumed to be *lingua franca* for the Balts and other post-war refugees. Polish migrants, supposedly ravished by the experience of the war and then the trip, do not take kindly to Australian bread, since bread is an important and cherished part of the Polish staple. Their comment, 'they even put salt in their butter' is followed by the administrator's insistence that 'the troublemakers' should not complain about the food, especially given that, compared with what they 'left in Europe, this place is a luxury hotel'. Julian dismisses any claim to Australian superiority by saying sarcastically: 'So, welcome to the luxury hotel.' His comment is mirrored by some reviewers, who draw parallels between the living conditions in silver Quonset huts made of steel sheets, most likely impossibly hot in Australian summer, and 'the work camps the immigrant Poles inhabited in their war-torn homeland' (e.g. Kelly 1985). First light of the next day overwrites that cynicism with enthused reactions of women keen to see Australia 'for the first time' and so again opening the possibility of accepting the strange land and 'paper-like' bread with salted butter as part of their life, despite these perceived shortcomings. The contrast of these two scenes disarms the Australian myth of the lucky country, even as it may be internalized as part of diasporic hybridity without the need for mythologizing aspects of nation-building. The ensuing narrative gives prominence to the love affair between Nina and Julian. Their mutual attraction starts before they even reach the hostel. After a while, Julian leaves his family – including a stern mother-in-law – and they move in together. The love story comes to an abrupt end when Anna announces to Nina that she is pregnant with Julian's child.

The other, 'documentary', level of the narrative remains a fragmented telling of refugee lives and stories, and is of greater interest in this chapter, especially in light of Turkiewicz's comment that 'the ultimate impact of [*Silver City*] is as a documentary not as a drama' (Turkiewicz interview 2008). Refugee stories told in the film include that of Nina, categorized – like the majority of IRO refugees – as 'a domestic', a usual designation for post-war female refugees, regardless of their qualifications. On arrival, she harbours hopes that her pen-pal, Mr Roy Jenkins (Tim McKenzie), has romantic potential; however, that potential is dispelled during their first two meetings, also a pattern familiar from other migrant stories. At a dance, 'Mr Roy' awkwardly attempts to explain to Nina's fellow Poles the egalitarian principles at work in Australia by saying that there are 'no Misters in the whole country' and that 'even the Prime Minister is called Ben'. Yet his plea falls on the deaf ears of unmoved Poles. Wiktor (superb Steve Bisley), who is later to become a millionaire, explains that 'Americans choose brains, Australians want muscle' and ironically, given Australia's history: '[Australians] don't need lawyers; there are no criminals here. This is the country where peasants do well; you must learn to think like a peasant.' Again, this sort of comment was not uncommon among educated refugees from Poland. So, in the struggle for social and cultural superiority, it is the Poles who are given the primacy in *Silver City*. However, despite the possible reading of scenes like this and others as anti-Australian, their function is demythologizing rather than iconoclastic. The selection of the most cynical of all Poles depicted here – that is, Wiktor – to be the most impressive financial success of all the characters portrayed in the film suggests the subversive use of myth-making, or even its superfluous nature when it is mismatched with reality.

Another meeting with Mr Roy takes place in his country pub, where Nina is first refused vodka and then cognac, but instead is offered a shandy. Outnumbered by Australians here, she retaliates by rejecting Mr Roy because her and him 'big mistake', even though it is 'not fault for [him]'. In one of the most potent scenes of the film, Nina plays darts by herself in a country hospital where she has secured a position to escape, temporarily, the affair with Julian. Her colleagues, Australian nurses, appear to want to play darts as well but refuse to do so until she vacates the scene. Nina finishes her own game with a bull's eye shot and walks away content, followed by surprised looks from her detractors. These small acts of defiance make room for multi-layered internalization of (at least) two cultures (Smolicz and Harris 1984: 21–22), a condition necessary for construction of integrational (rather than assimilationist) diasporic hybridity. If, in either of the two situations described here – one in a country pub and in a country hospital – Nina were to give into the rules set out exclusively by Anglo-Australians, her character's only choice would be between assimilation and exilic despair. While the latter outcome is utterly undesirable, assimilation is practically impossible – it is unlikely that Nina, or any other adult migrant, would be able to replace her Polish self entirely with a new Anglo-Australian one. Standing her ground when lacking acceptance, she subscribes to an identity hybridity that includes, rather than denies, her diasporic status. For all the notable migrant characters in *Silver City*, regardless of their attitude to being Australian, ethnicization becomes a strategy for their Australianization.

## Conclusion

*Silver City* is a significant film in the history of Australian cinema and Australia's migration history, and one rarely taken up for closer analysis. Its lack of popularity with academic writers could have to do with the very reasons for its seminality: a neglected aspect of Australian history and a focus on the under-represented Polish-Australian population. Unlike the Greek, Italian or Chinese input, the Polish contribution to Australian cinema is rather meagre. However, the visibility of the film at the time of its release, the comments it attracted and its reading as a co-orientation point for Polish and European migrants should not have allowed for such neglect. The migrant experience portrayed in *Silver City* resonates with the veracity that extends beyond Polish-Australians and their offspring.

Dealing with the undercurrents of anti-Europeanism and anti-Australianness, which both reject a less understood culture (cf. McFarlane 1987: 60), however unintentionally, *Silver City* aids in overcoming these undercurrents and gestures towards reconciling the multi-systemic composure of contemporary Australia. It recognizes that, rather than denying the long-standing existence of these two sentiments, film can point to the malleability and unpredictability of migrant trajectories – with Nina's, Julian's and Wiktor's lives evolving differently to the prescriptive possibilities implied by their pre-immigration and pre-war status, as well as their initial attitudes to Australia and Australianization. The demythologizing tendencies of the film, its unwitting insistence on the simultaneous ethnicization and integration, and – at last – its focus on the spaces of migrant/non-migrant interaction, rather than confinement to only one of these spheres, all constitute *Silver City*'s importance to cultural and critical discussions concerning the shape of post-multicultural Australia.

# 13

## LEBANESE MUSLIMS SPEAK BACK: TWO FILMS BY TOM ZUBRYCKI

*Susie Khamis*

It's probably wrong calling it a Lebanese diaspora, that's too generous and not a very useful term. This is a mixture, Australian Lebanese, Islamic – it's a particular community and a particular expression in Australia. The expression has as much to do with the prevailing political climate as anything else. (Zubrycki 2008)

Since his early association with advocacy films in the 1970s, Tom Zubrycki has looked at various permutations of power, influence and accountability (Colbert 1987: 31). Through films like *Friends and Enemies* (1987), *Amongst Equals* (1991), *The Diplomat* (2000) and *Molly and Mobarak* (2003), Zubrycki's storytelling style enlivens over-arching themes like unionism and independence with close and personal accounts. *Billal* (1996) and *Temple of Dreams* (2007), the two films explored in this chapter, are similarly driven, with their focus on young Lebanese Muslims in the suburbs of southwest Sydney, subjects whose identities are split between a war-torn homeland and contemporary Australia. What they underline is the complexity of this community, and its expression in Australia which, as Zubrycki claims above, cannot be adequately described in terms of diaspora. Both films show the slipperiness and subtlety of hybrid identities and the ultimate insufficiency of a sole determining framework. The Lebanese migrants that fled the horror of Civil War (1976–91) share language and heritage, so it is tempting to describe these films in terms of diaspora. However, the unifying starting point for Zubrycki in these films is not the 'old country' but his subjects' experiences of discrimination in the 'new country'. This unfolds in unexpected and often confronting ways, and therefore does not fit within any given template.

*Billal* (Tom Zubrycki, 1996). Image courtesy of Tom Zubrycki.

## An engaged style

Although commentators have likened his style to 'narrative vérité' (Higson 2004: 16; Molitorisz 2004: 3; Armstrong 2005: 96), this term does not adequately describe Zubrycki's approach in these films. The term is in reference to the ambitious (and notoriously contentious) truth-claims of observational documentaries. For the most part, the aesthetics of both *Billal* and *Temple of Dreams* hint at this genre, as the hand-held camera captures events 'on the go' and records a seemingly organic sequence. However, this is the extent of their 'observational' status. In Bill Nichols' classic taxonomy, observational films eschew directorial interventions (like narration, supplementary music, interviews and re-enactments) for an impartial purity that seemingly transcends the film-maker's presence and interests, or at least in ways not possible in more expository, argumentative modes (Nichols 1991: 38). Of course, every attempt to capture a second-order reality stumbles on what Michael Renov calls 'issues of selection' (Renov 1993: 26), as decisions to do with angles, takes and camera stock will frame filming one way and not another. That said, the term 'narrative vérité' is not queried here for this reason. Rather, in both *Billal* and *Temple of Dreams*, Zubrycki's presence might be discreet, but it is far from invisible or inconsequential. There are several ways that Zubrycki cues these narratives. Both films feature voiceover commentary, interviews, inter-titles, soundtrack, archival material and numerous instances where Zubrycki is acknowledged and involved by the subjects as a familiar and trusted friend. These inclusions orient the audience to certain reference points, and structure the narrative within specific parameters. This is not considered here as regrettable interference either, as though there were 'truer' ways these stories could have been told. As Stella Bruzzi (2006) points out, 'the results of this collision between apparatus and subject are what constitutes a documentary – not the utopian vision of what might have transpired if only the camera had not been there' (2006: 10). This 'collision' renders Zubrycki's style more akin to what Nichols termed the 'participatory' mode, where the dynamics of interaction position the film-maker within the 'same historical arena as the film's subjects' (Nichols 2001: 116). In the case of *Billal* and *Temple of Dreams*, and for reasons to be explained, this interaction opens up space for Zubrycki's subjects to speak back to the mainstream, and articulate their hybrid, complex identities. These films therefore prove a powerful counterpoint to a wider cultural tendency: to see Australia's Lebanese Muslims through a narrow and detrimental prism.

## The Lebanese Muslim presence

As portals into one of Australia's most maligned communities, *Billal* and *Temple of Dreams* belong to a growing list of Australian documentaries that deal with the complexity of 'Middle Eastern' identities. Films like *A Wedding in Ramallah* (Sherine Salama 2002), *I Remember 1948* (Fadia Abboud 2004) and *Forbidden Lie$* (Anna Broinowski 2007) cover very different terrain – from romantic love amid bullets and bomb blasts in contemporary Palestine to the heartache of displacement after the first Arab-Israeli War, to the psychology of a transnational scammer across Australia, Jordan, and the United States. As varied as they seem, film-makers Salama, Abboud and Broinowski provide some alternatives to an image of Islam that has taken shape elsewhere, and show the poverty of populist assumptions. *Billal* and *Temple of Dreams* are similarly informed. They spotlight the irreducible variety of the migrant experience, as personal paths divide and fragment in unique and often unpredictable ways.

Zubrycki's focus on the Lebanese Muslim community, particularly its young men, highlights one of the most publicly discussed migrant groups in recent Australian history. Lebanese migrants have been coming to Australia for over a hundred years, yet it is the most recent arrivals, the third wave, whose settlement has caused the most consternation. It is this group (and their children) who feature in both *Billal* and *Temple of Dreams*. For the first and second waves, the move from Lebanon to Australia was relatively smooth (Batrouney 2006c: 32). The first wave that arrived between the 1880s and 1920s primarily comprised hawkers, shopkeepers and textile workers, while the second wave that came during the manufacturing boom after World War II found work relatively easily. In the wake of the Lebanese Civil War, though, and with regard to the third and most recent wave, the Lebanese presence in Australia became larger (doubling between 1976 and 1996) and more varied. Whereas the first two waves mostly consisted of Christians, this third wave has been mostly Muslim. While earlier migrants found economic opportunities quite easily, and could access the support and knowledge of their pioneering (and often familial) antecedents, the more recent arrivals faced not only the trauma of post-war dislocation, but also fewer jobs that required minimal English skills (for example, factory work) (Betts and Healy 2006: 28). Consequently, and from the start, this group was materially disadvantaged, and tended to concentrate in the suburban fringes of Sydney and Melbourne – more so in southwest Sydney, particularly the Canterbury-Bankstown region and suburbs like Lakemba, Punchbowl and Auburn. As many 'clustered with kin who struggled to accommodate them' (Brearley 2002: 12), this third wave soon established a distinct cultural precinct in Sydney's southwest, marked by language (Arabic), religion (Islam) and national background (Lebanese) (ABS 2006).

The timing of this concentration had unfortunate implications. First, since the first Gulf War (1990–91), this group has suffered the most from hate crimes against Arabs and Muslims in Australia (Batrouney 2006c: 33). Second, since Pauline Hanson's electoral success in 1996 and the subsequent attacks on Australian multiculturalism, this group's commitment to Australian culture has repeatedly been questioned (Batrouney 2006b: 11). Even though, as Batrouney points out, '96 per cent of eligible Lebanese take up Australian citizenship – one of the highest of any immigrant group' (Batrouney 2006a: 28), they have been singled out for an apparent *inability* to integrate successfully. Since the early 1990s, anti-discrimination boards have logged numerous cases, including racial slurs, sexualized insults, and the violent removal of women's *hijabs* (Poynting 2002: 45). *Billal* and *Temple of Dreams* track this period of third-wave turmoil, and therefore span a pivotal period in this group's history. Coincidently, Zubrycki's professional interest in Lebanese migrants actually emerged in the 1980s, with an idea of profiling the family of his friend and colleague Stan Corrie. Corrie's parents migrated to Australia from Lebanon in the 1920s, as part of the first wave. Although this project was eventually aborted, it helped Zubrycki to appreciate how much harder settlement had become for subsequent waves of Lebanese migrants. This was brought to Zubrycki's attention in the early 1990s:

> Stan said – 'Listen, I've just been out to Macquarie Fields, researching a story about a group of Lebanese that had settled in the area, and it's a totally different experience to what I went through. It's like a completely different Lebanese community to mine. It's like another world. These people are stuck there on the fringes of society and I think they're experiencing a lot of difficulties settling in, there's a lot of friction, a lack of social cohesion.' I thought that sounded like an interesting film territory to explore.

### *Billal*: A case study of strength and survival

*Billal* is the story of 16-year-old Billal Eter and his slow, partial rehabilitation from a racially motivated hit-and-run accident. The film begins four days after the incident, with Billal in a coma and his family struggling to comprehend the extent of his injuries. From the outset, Zubrycki plots this story from this event, and his commentary and interviews throughout revolve around its effects on Billal and his family. Billal's injury is a shocking climax to what have become ongoing, race-based confrontations in his housing estate. His attacker, Linc Beswick, is just one of the boys from the area, Macquarie Fields in Sydney's southwest, who had been swept into nightly rounds of provocation and violence. It becomes apparent that Billal has suffered serious brain damage, causing permanent changes to his appearance and persona. With this realization, the film becomes a study of adjustment. It is punctuated with 'fly-on-the-wall' glimpses into an otherwise ordinary life (with subjects making coffee, cooking dinner, shopping and smoking), but the chronology (marked by inter-titles) and conversations (with doctors, relatives, and those who took part in the fray) signal Billal's injury as this family's primary concern and constraint.

This family's story could have been about one type of displacement: as refugees from war, the Eters are far removed from their homeland. Billal's father Abdul took part in the third-wave exodus out of Lebanon and into Australia. In the film's only reference to their homeland, and with photos of his young family, Abdul reminisces: 'We came to this country as labourers and we want better for our children.' Sepia toned footage of bustling factories shows that the Eters have travelled far from the wistful longings of a generic, post-war dream. Years of unemployment forced Abdul on to welfare – hence his family's uneasy settlement in Macquarie Fields. In the wake of Billal's injury, though, the family's displacement is not just a question of politics, geography or money – and this is where Billal's story serves something other than a diasporic model. The audience sees home videos filmed before Billal's injury, of the Eters enjoying an otherwise 'normal' birthday party, and this suggests that their suffering now stems from a trauma far more specific than exodus or unemployment. The details of that fateful night are conveyed by Billal's brother (Ahmed), cousin (Walid) and friend (Sawez), who talk and walk Zubrycki through their accounts. An interview with Beswick gives him a chance to explain his actions ('self-defence') but, when Zubrycki scopes Beswick's empathy for the Eters, it is clear how the audience's sympathies have been mobilized.

Billal's injury sees his family call on a range of coping strategies, with varying degrees of success. His brothers Ahmed and Omar, and their mostly male cousins, rely on the machismo and bravado they forge by way of survival. On the outskirts of Australia's most multicultural city, these teenagers take comfort in a camaraderie born of difference. They are both materially disadvantaged and culturally marginalized – their arrival signalled the estate's first encounter with Lebanese Muslims. In them, Zubrycki finds what Poynting, Noble and Tabar (1998) have shown to be a sustained problem in Sydney's southwest: a profound sense of alienation felt by young men, especially Lebanese Muslims (1998: 88). Due to a perceived lack of respect across their social spectrum – in schools, on the street, from the police and in the media – they create an oppositional culture as a form of defence. With their friends and cousins, the Eter boys contrive, like the Anglo-Celtic men of many 1990s feature films, a kind of 'protest' or excessive and violent amplification of masculinity (Butters 1998; Connell 1995). This 'revved-up' masculinity, in spirit and style, owes something to the street gangs of New York and Los Angeles:

> How they felt generally about Australia, their suburb and the people around them was typical of what virtually every Lebanese family felt at the time. With the Eters it went to the extreme, I think the fact they had teenage sons, these kids hung out together, a certain sense of pride and machismo involved – that could be threatening to the Anglo boys. It was sort of pre-gang formation, pre-gang behaviour, with two groups that wanted to claim their turf, tribal and territorial. You couldn't talk about social cohesion in Macquarie Fields; there were little enclaves and people acted in a tribal behaviour.

In the wake of Billal's tragedy, it becomes clear just how much the Eter boys' 'tribal behaviour' springs from feelings of isolation and disconnection. As Zubrycki follows the whirlwind of hospital visits and specialist advice, and as doctors and surgeons talk through Billal's injury, the Eters come undone. Abdul, unemployed and melancholic, withdraws from his family and friends; Billal's brothers vacillate between vengeance and regret; and his mother Amal struggles to comprehend and keep pace with the experts' reports. In her desperation, she relies more and more on Alissar Gazal, whose role in the film begins as Zubrycki's liaison and interpreter, but grows as the family's needs become more urgent. Gazal soon becomes Amal's advocate, confidante and *de facto* counsellor. She deals with the hospital staff on behalf of the family and, as their living arrangements become increasingly strained (especially as hospital visits become more frequent), she lobbies what seems an especially slow Housing Commission.

That Gazal's involvement becomes a matter of moral necessity as well as logistical expedience conveys the family's acute vulnerability, and shows explicitly how some events unfold *because* of the film. Billal's rehabilitation is slow and only slight, and his father and brothers retreat once his behaviour and appearance prove too unsettling. It is left to Amal to at least appear stoic and strong. With Gazal's support, it is a minor miracle that she does.

The Eters' situation is so personalized and specific that *Billal* exceeds any definition of diaspora. The family's suffering has something to do with difficulties experienced by many of Lebanon's war refugees, but their crisis is also (if not more so) due to an extremely atypical event. Although their biography contains elements that are common to the third-wave scenario – war, exodus, unemployment and welfare – this is not 'just' a story of third-wave adjustment because it has not been standardized by these points of commonality. This counters a mainstream tendency to submit such distinct communities to certain parameters, and perceive some link between a given chronology and a subsequent cliché.

That is not to suggest that to view something as diasporic would necessarily produce a hackneyed or tired picture. Rather, it is to broaden the usefulness of this concept to accommodate more than just a one-way or finite journey. This wide-lens approach would be especially edifying in the case of Australia's Lebanese Muslim community. Over the last few years, and at least in Australia, their representation in most media has hardened around several highly unflattering ideas, the most prominent of these to be considered shortly. As it appears in *Billal* (and *Temple of Dreams*, also discussed below), this group's diversity not only disrupts the tidy narratives of mainstream discourse; it also requires analysis that goes beyond the framework of diaspora: the hybridity of a diaspora must be acknowledged and accounted for. In terms of representation, such latitude demands a kind of imagistic generosity – the sort that was seen in *Billal* but was conspicuously absent in the decade or so after its release. In the years between the release of *Billal* (1996) and then *Temple of Dreams* (2007), Australia's Lebanese Muslims were widely discussed in the media, but often in terms of suspicion, fear and dislike. The implications of this, especially for *Temple of Dreams*, deserve closer consideration.

### How Sydney's southwest was branded

From the mid-to-late 1990s, the lesson of *Billal* – that migrants' lives are too richly textured to abide assumptions and expectations – was lost on much of the commercial media. Especially in the daily tabloids and on talkback radio, the issue of Lebanese Muslims in Sydney's southwest was framed primarily as a problem, in that this community differed too drastically from the cultural norm and thus strained any hope for integration. Much of this discussion focused particularly on young men in this community, and their supposed drift into gang activities. This idea gained currency and momentum when the state's (then) premier, Bob Carr, featured it in his 'law and order' agenda of the late 1990s, a strategy backed by police commissioner Peter Ryan. This turned a suburban pressure-point into an electoral, policing and media hotspot, a convergence that was hugely influential in structuring public discourse (Poynting, Noble and Tabar 2001: 67–69, 71–74).

Over the next few years, the impression that Sydney's southwest was replete with race-based gangs became a culturally consonant one (Manning 2003: 59). To understand this resonance, it pays to consider a few of the news stories that, due to the tone of their coverage, galvanized public sentiment against Lebanese Muslims. One of the most high-profile news items in Australia in 2000 and 2001 centred squarely on young Lebanese Muslims in Sydney's southwest. Two young Anglo women in the Bankstown region had been gang-raped, and their aggressors – mostly Lebanese Muslim – had made racist insults during the attacks. Columnists and shock jocks saw this as proof of both flagrant chauvinism and migrant backwardness. These editorials were so inflammatory that even the state's Bureau of Crime Statistics and Research was moved enough to comment and tell Australians that, on the issue of sex crimes in the Bankstown region, and on the cultural identity of the perpetrators, the sensationalist rhetoric was wildly exaggerated. Still, it was too late: an image of violence and misogyny took hold. In the aftermath of September 11, 2001, the Australian media were quick to accommodate a 'signification spiral' (Dreher 2003: 122–23) – that is, the link between Muslims and crime was further normalized. This marked a politically opportunistic time to rethink Australian multiculturalism. The more that Muslims were associated with disloyalty and disorder, the more prepared many were to redefine Australia's 'imagined community' accordingly (Turner 2003: 414). A line was drawn between 'good' migrants and 'bad' migrants – a demarcation based largely on how willing migrants were to exchange old practices for arbitrarily determined new ones (Humphrey 2007: 12).

After September 11, and with Canberra committed to the United States-led 'War on Terror', Sydney's southwest became an even bigger focal point for politicians, intelligence bureaux and journalists. After the Bali bombings of October 2002, in which 88 Australians died at the hands of Jemaah Islamiyah (JI), fears grew that terrorists abroad had Australian empathizers. This prompted a dramatic shift in police protocol: houses were raided, goods confiscated and community leaders questioned, often in the presence of media crews (Poynting and Mason 2006: 378–79). Civil libertarians and members of the judiciary attacked what they saw as a dangerous slide in citizens' rights, but there appeared to be little protest from the Labor opposition (Mason 2004: 235–38). If anything, after the terrorist bombings in Madrid in March 2004 and London in July 2005, both connected to Al Qaeda cells, there was even more fear and distrust. Many worried that, not unlike Spain and the United Kingdom, Australia harboured its own corps of home-grown terrorists. Media reports increasingly assumed a 'dog whistle' quality, with stories coded to concur with a public primed for anxiety and panic (Poynting and Noble 2003: 44). News of halal burgers at Bankstown McDonalds, or women's-only swimming lessons at Auburn Pool, for instance, was explained more in terms of religious intransigence than cultural diversity. By this (unspoken) logic, Sydney's southwest had become a hotbed of religious extremism, a beacon for terrorists and the logical refuge for disaffected youth. A day-long riot in December 2005 on Cronulla Beach became widely symbolic of a hopeless cultural chasm, as locals lashed out against the apparent affront of weekend 'tourists' – specifically, young Lebanese Muslim men who took the short train trip from Sydney's southwest suburbs to the popular beach (Haddad 2005: 24; Nader 2005: 25; Tsavdaridis 2006: 5; Poynting 2007: 2).

### *Temple of Dreams:* **Contesting stereotypes**

After *Billal*, and in light of September 11, gang rape hysteria and the Cronulla riots, the 'problem' of Lebanese Muslims loomed much larger in the Australian imagination. After a decade, Zubrycki found not just a single family in crisis mode, but an entire community. In September 2006, *The Australian* newspaper covered a sermon given at Lakemba mosque by Mufti Sheikh Taj ad-Din al-Hilal, in which the controversial cleric likened scantily clad women to 'uncovered meat', a comparison which, according to outraged detractors, forgave men sexual deviance if faced with such temptation. In the subsequent furore, other Muslim leaders felt compelled to speak out, to distance themselves from al-Hilal and to argue that Islam accommodated a spectrum of principles and practices, one that could easily complement Australian values (Henderson 2007: 9). It was obvious that, in media predisposed to scandal and stereotype, the likes of al-Hilal would overshadow other, more moderate leaders. One of these would-be leaders was a 30-year-old Lebanese man, Fadi Rahman. His attempts to inspire and mentor young Muslims in Sydney's southwest, and contest an overwhelmingly negative and largely misinformed image of Islam, are seen in *Temple of Dreams*. Although the film is not a profile of Fadi, his appearance completely inverts the image of young Lebanese Muslim men in much Australian media. With energy, drive and diplomatic nous, Fadi is a world away from tabloid caricatures – or, for that matter, any of the Eter boys. Even though Fadi's journey to Australia belongs to a larger story of third-wave diaspora, like Billal his individual path diverges too far from this starting point to be his only or even dominant reference. *Temple of Dreams* is the story of a fight – mostly against bureaucracy, but also against prejudice and pigeonholing. The film's opening inter-titles leave little doubt about this:

> The war on terror has meant that Muslims are under the microscope all over the world. The Australian government has done little to dispel a deep anxiety in the wider community. Young Muslim Lebanese feel themselves especially targeted.

The first scenes pose a provocative juxtaposition: the busy streets of Sydney's southwest set to a soundtrack of hostile talkback diatribe. Zubrycki thus pivots this story around the prevailing political mood, something underscored throughout with references (by both Zubrycki and his subjects) to the London bombings and (more so) the Cronulla riots. In a disused Masonic hall in Lidcombe, Fadi establishes the headquarters for the Independent Centre of Research Australia (ICRA), a youth organization that caters to young Muslims in Sydney's southwest and teaches what one of its volunteers calls 'the Australian version of Islam'. This is one of only a few such organizations in Sydney. In the period after the London bombings and the Cronulla riots, Fadi's mission becomes much harder. First, he has to persuade young Muslims that, contrary to popular opinion, their Muslim identity need not inhibit their Australian identity – despite media attempts to dichotomize the two; second, he has to convince Auburn Council that ICRA's use of the building is legitimate, despite the council's claims that it contravenes the lease's conditions and violates zoning regulations. Against the seemingly bellicose al-Hilal, Fadi appears a virtual master of public relations. He also speaks from experience. Having once been involved in organized crime, Fadi credits his turnaround to a religious awakening. In Islam, Fadi finds clarity, conviction and discipline, and this became ICRA's premise. As in *Billal*, this film treats the journey from Lebanon as an important but by no means dominant consideration. It is mentioned only briefly: with photographs of an infant Fadi, and a soundtrack of Arabic *oud* music, Zubrycki notes how the family fled civil war when Fadi was just six. For Fadi (and therefore the film), there is a bigger story of cross-cultural friction, and how his need to reconcile his parents' values with life 'outside' his home proved 'a heavy load for a teenager'.

Inevitably, *Temple of Dreams* draws on and responds to contemporary misconceptions about Islam. For example, one of the most obvious ways that ICRA confounds expectations is through its three main volunteers, Zouhour El-Ghoul, Amna El-Ghoul and Aliyah Assad. In their ambition and assertiveness, these women are not only crucial to ICRA's success, administering events and processing paperwork with disarming efficiency, but they actively refute any notion that young Muslim women lack status or agency, or are somehow less visible by virtue of their *hijab*. They brainstorm ideas to help boost ICRA's profile, scout recruits at festivals and conventions, battle the bureaucracy of Auburn Council, and table proposals for ministers and commissioners – all voluntarily. They share Fadi's conviction and piety but, by his own admission, are far more adept at executing ICRA's plans. Importantly for Zubrycki though, and before filming began, these women were also familiar with his style of film-making and, at a time when Sydney's Muslim communities were wary of most 'Anglo' media, these women trusted Zubrycki to approach ICRA, and therefore their roles, differently. For Zubrycki, this trust is easily explained:

> Making *Billal* made me accepted in the community. The girls in *Temple of Dreams* had seen *Billal*... I was right in [the community] from the start pretty much... The women accepted me immediately and much more easily than the men did, and they were much savvier with what I was trying to do.

The implications here are twofold. First, that these women knew of Zubrycki's style means that their involvement in the film is charged with an implicit knowingness, a readiness to contribute due to some perceived affinity with the film-maker. Second, Zubrycki admits to the contrivance that is necessary of all film-making, documentary or otherwise. That he was 'trying to do' something (anything) suggests that the spaces opened up at Zubrycki's discretion are neither haphazard nor accidental, but linked to a larger project, agenda or philosophy. Given the contemporary political mood, this is seen here as a progressive exercise, as Zubrycki's interventions effectively extend storytelling devices to a group that has been widely represented in Australian media, but rarely on its own terms. Finally able to 'speak back' to the mainstream, these subjects appear so finely graded that any clichés that audiences might expect inevitably crack and crumble.

## Conclusion

In *Billal* and *Temple of Dreams*, Zubrycki finds two very difficult examples of third-wave adjustment. There are, of course, some common denominators. The subjects of both films came to Australia as war refugees, or are children of war refugees, and so suffered an inevitable degree of upheaval in their settlement – emotional, material and psychological. Also in both films, there is the backdrop of discrimination: the Eters struggle with anti-Arab sentiment after the first Gulf War, and ICRA's volunteers struggle with the escalation of this sentiment over the last decade or so. After that, there is an obvious and inevitable splintering. The Eters barely cope with the magnitude of their problems, something which is made heartbreakingly clear in the midst of Billal's tragedy. Already disadvantaged by unemployment, inadequate housing and poor (English) language skills, Billal's brain damage seems the cruellest cap to the family's suffering. In their despair and dysfunction, the Eters are so removed from community support that the film crew ultimately takes some responsibility for their welfare.

*Temple of Dreams* follows a group of Lebanese Muslims who are determined to assume some discursive autonomy. With the benefit of hindsight, self-belief and charisma, Fadi is well placed to make ICRA matter, and ICRA is well placed to get Muslims heard. With their Australian upbringing, ICRA's bilingual volunteers connect with troubled teens in a way that is relevant and empathetic. An ICRA youth conference – undoubtedly the group's most ambitious project (logistically and politically) – is organized around modules specific to the fears and hopes ICRA has identified within their community, issues like police discrimination, media stereotypes and cross-generational conflicts. When the conference proceedings are tabled and presented to an audience that includes members of parliament, police representatives and various community leaders, Fadi claims a significant victory in the recognition of ICRA's work, and in the knowledge that the views of young Muslims in Sydney's southwest have been aired and acknowledged. Fadi effectively plays the politics of recognition.

In this way, and as proof of media's democratic potential, personal stories of suffering and injustice help dissolve reductionist stereotypes of the collective 'other' (Cottle 2007: 42). In their focus on third-wave Lebanese migrants, it is easy to see *Billal* and *Temple of Dreams* as reflective of a Lebanese diaspora. However, as complex portraits of a complex community, they actually highlight just how problematic the concept of diaspora is. All the subjects' journeys include the trauma of civil war; in some way it is a part of each speaker's personal narrative. Thereafter, however, their paths are so fragmented that it is difficult to locate the diasporic content with too much precision or consistency.

The issues at stake in *Billal* and *Temple of Dreams* concern much more than just being Lebanese in Australia, something about which Zubrycki is particularly mindful. As such, these stories might best be viewed in terms of hybridity rather than diaspora – that is, to understand the Eters and ICRA, a prism more elastic than that of diaspora is required. Whereas a diasporic model privileges ancestry and heritage, and largely views identity and experience in terms of 'what has been', the hybrid model is more useful for understanding the here and now, since it is more amenable to inflection, adaptation and therefore 'what has become'.

A major source of ICRA's effectiveness, for instance, is its bilingualism. This suggests that successful integration requires a modicum of assimilation, something that the diasporic template tends to underplay or ignore (Ang 2001b: 19). The diasporic identity rests on closure and sameness; the hybrid one unsettles boundaries – but does not necessarily erase them (Ang 2003: 149). It accommodates the hyphenated and the interstitial, and thus recognizes people 'for whom home is found at the intersection of the global, the diaspora, and the local' (Butcher 2003: 187). This allows all the subjects discussed so far to assert their specific experiences above (or even against) some totalizing historical narrative. As a consequence, this narration might well challenge the diasporic identity (Smaill 2005, 2006: 274). Instead of fixed coordinates and standard markers, there are uneven chronologies and countless variables. At the very least, these stories suggest that there is no such thing as a diasporic endpoint; Australia is not the last stop in these lifelines. These films thus claim for their subjects some autonomous space in what had become a national milieu primed for fear and distrust. They also show lifestyles fashioned from the traditional and the contemporary in ways that defy straightforward categorization.

# 14

# SEJONG PARK'S *BIRTHDAY BOY* AND KOREAN-AUSTRALIAN ENCOUNTERS

## Ben Goldsmith and Brian Yecies

This chapter focuses on some of the flows of film work between Australia and South Korea (hereafter Korea), and some of the roles taken by Australians in the performance (and particularly the sound) of Koreanness in different film contexts. We will explore Korean-Australian collaboration on film, through case studies of Sejong Park's Oscar-nominated short animated film *Birthday Boy* (2004) and two Korean feature films – *Musa* (2001, Kim Sung-su) and *Shadowless Sword* (2005, Kim Young-jun) – for which Australian firms provided sound post-production services. We show how these films instantiate and expand Korean, Australian, diasporic and transnational film-making.

### *Birthday Boy* as Korean-Australian diasporic film-making

The Korean community in Australia is a 'contemporary or late-modern' diaspora (Reis 2004: 41). Most Koreans in Australia are not in exile like the 'classical' Jewish and Armenian diasporas; only a fraction of the 60,000 come from North Korea. None has experienced forced expatriation, and political conflict has not been a motivation for migration. Rather, the diaspora has formed 'as a result of opportunity' (Reis 2004: 49). Around three-quarters of the community have arrived in Australia since 1990, with most living in or around Sydney. The Korean diaspora is not well represented in film in Australia; documentaries about Australian experiences in Korea outnumber those directly depicting the Korean-Australian experience. In recent years, though, several young Korean-Australian film-makers have emerged. Melissa Kyu-jung Lee's documentaries *Secret Women's Business* (2000) and *Soshin: In Your Dreams* (2001) were perhaps the first to depict

*Birthday Boy* (Sejong Park, 2004). Image courtesy of Sejong Park and the Australian Film, Television and Radio School (AFTRS).

aspects of Korean-Australian life (see Lee 2001 for a discussion of their production). And, in addition to Sejong Park's *Birthday Boy*, another Korean-Australian animator, Susan Kim Danta, is winning acclaim for her short film *The Bronze Mirror* (2007), which is adapted from a traditional Korean folk tale. Lee, Park and Danta were all students at the Australian Film Television and Radio School (hereafter AFTRS) when these films were made.

*Birthday Boy* is set in Korea in 1951, during the civil war that pitched the north of the country and its allies, China and the Soviet Union, against the south and a United Nations coalition (including more than 17,000 Australian military personnel) led by the United States. However, the film is not about the Australian experience of this conflict or the contemporary conflict in

Iraq, which began the year before the film was finished. Rather, the film is about the impact of war on those left behind.

*Birthday Boy* exhibits some of the 'accented style' that Hamid Naficy identifies as characteristic of diasporic film-making (Naficy 2001), but it is also in some ways an imperfect example of Naficy's object. The film clearly evidences a 'nostalgic longing' (Naficy 2001: 5) for the homeland; an on-screen title fixes the story-world not as a specific place, but as an entire country – Appadurai's 'imagined world' (2003: 31): 'Korea 1951'. It is then a 'cinematic chronotope' in the sense in which Naficy (2001: 153) adapts Bakhtin's term, placed in time and space, and simultaneously 'interstitial' (Naficy 2001: 4) – between times and places, between home (Korea) and host (Australia) cultures and cinemas. This aspect is not overtly represented in the film, but rather becomes evident gradually as the film unfolds, and in particular at the moment the audience realizes the true meaning of the 'present' the central character Manuk receives. The film is also 'epistolary' (Naficy 2001: 101), in that a postman and a package play key roles. The diasporic subject is evoked rather than directly depicted or addressed, and as Sung-ae Lee (Lee 2004) shows, the significance of the film for the Korean diaspora had to be mediated by the Korean-language print media in Australia. The film was represented in the *Sydney Korean Herald* as an example of diasporic achievement and success, which empowered the Korean-Australian community. Park was also praised for the contribution the film makes to cultural maintenance for diasporic Koreans in its remembrance (rather than celebration) of the war (Lee 2004: 233). Lee observes:

> This collaboration of Australian and Korean creative expertise, a film made in Australia about the Korean War and voiced by a Korean-Australian child who had to be coached in Korean language, redefines the parameters of geography, national identity, and belonging, and, as a result, its foregrounding in the *Sydney Korean Herald* is a significant cultural moment. (Lee 2004: 242)

*Birthday Boy* is 'accented' in the sense that it sounds unlike other Australian films: the only dialogue in the film is in Korean, while sound design (by Megan Wedge) and score (by James K. Lee) utilize digitally produced Korean atmospheres and instruments. Sound design and music are, like the animation, also 'interstitial', with Australian film-makers convincingly evoking the Korean setting. In the absence of English dialogue (Manuk's song, his game, the postman's cries and his mother's greeting are all sung or spoken in Korean, with English subtitles), the work that must be done through sound effects, atmospheres and foley to create the story-world and enable transnational audiences to understand and be moved by the story, is amplified. The film is a journey of homecoming, both narratively for the little boy, Manuk, and metaphorically for the diasporic film-maker, Park. The absence of both parents (at least until the final frames of the film), which Naficy terms 'structured absences' could be seen to be indicative of the absence that shadows the diasporic subject: the loss of home and homeland, although the absent parent is also common to both Australian and Korean cinema.

However, it is more difficult to conceive of the film in Naficy's (2001) terms as contrasting with a 'dominant cinema' that 'is considered universal and without accent' for several reasons. Australian cinema is full of accents, as contributions to this book make plain, but the dominant cinema in terms of box office takings and profile in Australia is American cinema – as it is in the rest of the world, with only a few exceptions, one of which is Korea. To Australian ears, then, the dominant cinema has a clear accent that marks it out from films made in the local vernacular. *Birthday Boy* could be argued as an exemplar of both the artisanal and collective modes of production that for Naficy mark out diasporic film-making. The film was made by a small group of postgraduate students under Park's direction at AFTRS between 2001 and early 2004. Unlike many live-action films, sound designer, editor and composer were involved from the beginning of the project, and revised their work in concert as the drawn-out process of animating and editing the film proceeded.

Precisely because it was made at AFTRS, though, it is as much an Australian as a diasporic film. To underscore this, both Park and the film were clearly identified as Australian by the Academy of Motion Picture Arts and Sciences when *Birthday Boy* was nominated for an Academy Award in 2005. For over 30 years, AFTRS has been one of the core institutions of the Australian media industries and screen culture. The school was established by an Act of federal parliament in 1973 with a brief to train the film-makers who would form the Australian New Wave, and produce 'programs' of high technical and creative merit. It is an Australian Commonwealth government statutory authority, responsible to federal parliament through the Department of Environment, Heritage and the Arts. Unlike the majority of Australian tertiary education institutions, almost all of AFTRS's funding comes directly from the Commonwealth through the federal Arts Department (rather than Education, as for universities). And its postgraduate courses are only open to Australian citizens and permanent residents. The films, documentaries, radio and television programs produced at AFTRS are inevitably, indisputably 'Australian'. They are all enrolled to the national project, as the school retains copyright in its productions. AFTRS is subtly but noticeably credited in publicity for *Birthday Boy* and in the film itself; the school's (then) logo of a stylized map of Australia as a strip of twisted celluloid film above the full name of the institution, which appears on the various DVD releases of the film, inscribes the national upon it. *Birthday Boy* is the poster child of Australian national cinema.

*Birthday Boy* opens up ways of thinking about Australian film and 'national cinema' not as an 'essence' but as 'a relation' (Elsaesser 1994: 25), not as a category with boundaries and limits, but as a mobile and fluid dialogue with film-makers, films, audiences and screen cultures around the world. The film 'weaves in and out' of national and transnational modes of film practice (Choi 2006: 314) in its production, content and reception. Within weeks of completion, *Birthday Boy* was winning prizes at festivals in Australia and overseas. The award of Best Animated Short at the prestigious SIGGRAPH Computer Animation Festival in 2004 qualified the film for the 2005 Academy Awards even before Park and fellow students had graduated from the AFTRS. It was subsequently nominated for the Oscar for Best Animated Short Film, losing to Chris Landreth's tribute to pioneering Canadian animator Ryan Larkin in *Ryan*. To date, *Birthday Boy* has won over 40 awards at festivals around the world, including the Prix Jean-Luc

Xiberras at the Annecy International Animated Film Festival in 2005 and Best Short Animation at the 2005 BAFTA awards. It has screened at over 100 film festivals and is the most awarded film in the almost 40-year history of the AFTRS.

Park came to Australia as a mature-age student, having already worked as an illustrator and commercial artist in Korea (after completing mandatory military service there). He has become nomadic, a transnational migrant – one for whom 'transnational activities are a central part of...life' (Castles and Miller 2003: 30) – navigating back and forth between multiple diasporas, not simply in pursuit of a new place to live or to work, but creating new pathways between the Korean, Australian and US film industries uninhibited by geographical borders and national cultural boundaries.

*Birthday Boy* was provoked by Park's observations of cultural specificity and difference between Korea and Australia. Park, who had migrated to Australia after falling in love with an Australian woman, was struck by the way birthdays were celebrated in his new country:

> Since I moved to Australia I was looking at a lot of Western culture, like for Christmas and birthdays they get a lot of material things, but in Korea when I was growing up, even still now these days, the present really is not that important for birthday...In Korea we have seaweed soup on our birthday. Normally the seaweed soup is for pregnant woman – after somebody who has had baby, they eat seaweed soup all the time for six months to relieve pain. So having seaweed soup on our birthday is thinking of our mother's pain. It's not just 'because I'm great' or 'I deserve this present'. (Sejong Park, quoted in Rankin 2005: 3)

A present – or what appears to be a present – plays a pivotal role in the film. The film looks, sounds and is scored in ways that privilege the perspective of the birthday boy, Manuk. On his tunic he wears the label traditionally worn by Korean children on their birthday. The 'present' turns out to contain the last possessions of Manuk's soldier father. We first encounter Manuk through sound, hearing him rummaging and singing in the wreck of an aeroplane, looking for materials to make a toy soldier. When he eventually reaches home after a number of adventures, Manuk finds a parcel that he (and we) assume has arrived because it is his birthday. Instead, the box contains his father's last possessions: an old leather wallet and photograph of Manuk with his father, dog tags and army boots. While Manuk plays at home, the audience is left to ponder the significance of this discovery and reflect on the box's contents. The film ends as Manuk's mother arrives home. Manuk's discovery of the box and the audience's realization of its true significance are pivotal to the intercultural dialogue performed in and on the film. Taken-for-granted cultural expectations about birthday rituals are challenged in this scene as a space is opened for reflection on cultural values, rituals and cultural difference.

The film clearly speaks to broader audiences than the diasporic Korean community. In its allusions to other films, in the subtlety of its 'camera work', editing, sound and music as well as its use of digital animation, and its narrative structure familiar from mainstream Hollywood cinema (Thompson 1999), the film is a knowing and learned contribution to international screen culture. In particular, the references to the work of French director and comedian Jacques Tati – the comic scene with the postman is reminiscent of Tati's short film *L'École des Facteurs* (1947), and the features *Jour de Fête* (1948) and *Mon Oncle* (1954) – are not simply further exemplification of the intercultural concerns that underpin the film. They also work to position the film in dialogue with the international history of film. Serge Daney once declared that: 'Every Tati film marks simultaneously a moment in the work of Jacques Tati; a moment in the history of French society and French cinema; a moment in film history.' (quoted in Rosenbaum, n.d.) It follows, then, that the allusions to Tati's films in *Birthday Boy* are also moments in film history, which place the film in inter-cinematic as well as inter-cultural dialogue.

*Birthday Boy* was received and celebrated in Korea as an emblem of Korean imagination and achievement. Park himself considered this small, 'personal memory' film to be Korean, which 'rather than having international value, I thought... was more suited to a domestic market as a Korean story' (quoted in O'Dwyer 2005: 73). The film has become one of the most popular and celebrated short animations in Korea. Although specific data are difficult to obtain, illegal copies have spread online throughout Korea. The film was also screened to large domestic and international crowds in the Wide Angle program at the 2004 Pusan International Film Festival. What sets *Birthday Boy* apart is its access to Korean sentiment, history and culture, and the fact that it was produced from within the Australian film industry.

In March 2005, Korean National Assemblywoman Sohn Bong-suk, who is also an Advisory Board member of the Ministry of Culture and Tourism, organized a screening of the film and invited Park to speak before members of the government and film industry as well as several hundred students studying animation. A range of reporters from the Korean press – most notably Arirang TV, a 24-hour satellite broadcaster of English news and programming – covered the event. This screening aimed, among other things, to showcase Park's accomplishment of being the first Korean to be nominated for an Academy Award. Assemblywoman Sohn heralded Park as a national hero and role model for the industry at large by promoting the film as an exemplar of Korea's potential to reach a Hollywood and perhaps global market with thought-provoking stories that capture the imagination of non-Korean audiences. In the audience of this *Birthday Boy* screening was Daniel You, Director General of Media Business in the Gangwon Information and Multimedia Corporation (GIMC), which is located in Chuncheon – 'the City of Culture and Art'. The city's creation and utilization of the International Anitown Festival promotes Korea's national digital animation industry while the GIMC serves as a policy advocate, content producer and investor for the industry – working with Disney and Nickelodeon to produce projects such as the *Danger Rangers* and other family-oriented comedy animation series.

At the *Birthday Boy* presentation, Mr You began envisaging Park as a spokesperson for a new stage in Korea's animation industry. Until recently, the industry was known for its service work on Japanese and American animation. Due to increasing labour costs relative to other countries in Asia, Korea has lost a significant amount of this type of 'original equipment manufacturing'

(OEM) work, which historically has propped up the local animation industry. Producing local content is now a key pursuit of Korea's animation industry. Park's achievements have become particularly meaningful in light of other Korean animations that have attempted to break ground in the global market, such as the highly stylized feature-length animations *My Beautiful Girl, Mari* (Lee Seong-kang 2002), *Wonderful Days* (Kim Moon-saeng 2003) and *Aachi and Ssipak* (Jo Beom-jin 2006).

Mr You and GIMC saw Park as a potential 'aniagent' (our term) who could provide new direction for Korean animators and Korean production to achieve commercial success across the globe. In May 2005, on behalf of GIMC, Mr You advanced Park's status as a 'hero' by offering him a unique support package (including a furnished apartment, office, multi-media lab and regular stipend) to finance Park's future career (You 2008). Park's relationship with the GIMC gave him access to the organization's top animation artists and state-of-the-art equipment. In return, Park simply has to continue doing what he does best – that is, make animations and show the world how the Korean animation industry is advancing. Although Park's activities in Korea were limited in 2007 – due to his work as Digital Effects Artist/ Additional Surfacing on *Shrek The Third* (Chris Miller 2007) – he continues to be supported (at the time of writing) by the GIMC.

Since Park's Academy Award nomination in 2004, the profile and international reputation of animation in both Korea and Australia have risen. Funding in Korea has increased and the number of animation festivals has grown. Production funding remains better in Korea, while production regulations including labour laws are more advanced in Australia. Park's own journey has been extraordinary, with his unprecedented success on the international festival circuit, multiple international awards and being feted in Korea as a national hero. The film has been influential in Korea and Australia, and has been referenced in Korean film and popular culture such as intertextual allusions to it in Park Kwang-hyun's feature film *Welcome to Dongmakgol* (2005).

Park's experience with the reception of the film extends the film's and his own hybrid positioning further. Not only is the film comprehensible as both diasporic and Australian, it is possible to consider it in terms of the transnational, understood as an 'arena connecting differences' in which 'a variety of regional, national, and local specificities impact upon each other in various types of relationships ranging from synergy to contest' (Berry and Farquhar 2006: 5). To that list, we might also add 'diasporic'. Understood in this way, Park and his crew are members of a more intangible diaspora in Australia: the diaspora of transnational film-makers. We understand transnational film-makers to mean those whose work is principally intended for an overseas audience or intended to travel across borders and cultures. It is transnational rather than 'international' because it does not necessarily involve nation-states as 'corporate actors' (Hannerz 1996: 6). It is in the arena of the transnational that we can relate the Korean-Australian film work discussed above, to the work of Australian post-production, digital and visual effects companies on Korean feature films. It is to this work that we now briefly turn, through case studies of *Musa* and *Shadowless Sword*.

### *Musa* and *Shadowless Sword* as Korean/Australian transnational film-making

International or transnational film-making is now a normal feature of the Australian mediascape (Appadurai 2003: 31), just as it is around the world (Goldsmith and O'Regan 2008: 13–44). Australian film-makers have always worked on transnational projects, although this work has not always been valued in the same way as more obviously Australian films (Goldsmith, forthcoming). For the purpose of calculating production activity in Australia, the annual national production survey compiled by the Australian Film Commission defines 'foreign' films as those in which creative control lies with non-Australians, and for which Australian companies provide services during their shoot or post production here. We would describe these films as 'transnational'. American films are most prominent here – *Superman Returns* (Bryan Singer 2006), *Star Wars: Episode 1 – The Phantom Menace* (George Lucas 1999), *Star Wars: Episode II – Attack of the Clones* (George Lucas 2002), *Where the Wild Things Are* (Spike Jonze 2009), for example – but there have been many other transnational collaborations which have been little remarked, in part because it was only in 2007 that foreign films which were shot outside Australia but used the services and creative expertise of Australian post-production, digital and visual effects firms were counted in the national production survey.

Since the early 1990s, collaborations between Australian and Asian film-makers have grown in number and visibility. Films like *Hero* (Zhang Yimou 2002), *Kung Fu Hustle* (Stephen Chow 2004) and *The House of Flying Daggers* (Zhang Yimou 2004) join a long list of Hong Kong and Chinese films to have employed Australian digital effects and post-production companies, dating back to Wong Kar Wai's *Ashes of Time* (1994). Most recently, several Indian films, such as *Salaam Namaste* (Siddharth Anand 2005), *Chak De! India* (Go India, Shimit Amin 2007) and *Heyy Baby* (Sajid Khan 2007), have been produced in Australia. Korean film-makers have also made use of Australian post-production, digital and visual effects firms over a number of years. Notable films include *Chun Tae Il* (A Single Spark, Park Kwang-su 1995), *A Petal* (Jang Sun-Woo 1996), *Wanted* (Howard Hung-Soon Chung 1997) – shot by renowned Geoff Burton – and *Happy Ending* (Jung Ji-woo 1999). Most recently, John Cox's Creature Workshop, the Oscar-winning (*Babe*, Chris Noonan 1995) Gold Coast-based visual effects firm, made the monster for Bong Joon-ho's blockbuster *The Host* (2006), which to date has been the most successful Korean film in Australia (Yecies and Shim 2007).

*Musa* (aka *Musa The Warrior* 2001) and *Shadowless Sword* (2005) are two of 10 known Korean feature films completed by Australian sound post-production firms Audioloc and Soundfirm since 1995. Producers of both films had looked to the Australian film industry because of its preparedness, resourcefulness and record of managing more experienced soundtracks rather than for specific skills. The historical epic *Musa* was brought to Audioloc based on the relationships the firm's managing director, John Dennison, formed with editor Kim Yang-il after they worked together on the *Ginko Tree Bed* (Kang Je-gyu 1996) in Australia in 1995. The sound mix for *Musa* was completed in six weeks by Audioloc in close consultation with the film's visiting Korean post-production support team (Dennison 2008). The film was shot in China and Mongolia over a nine-month period. Massive battle sequences and dialogue recorded in three languages challenged Audioloc not only to create a high production value soundtrack within a limited budget and timeframe, but also to design a soundscape that required appropriate seasonal wildlife and weather conditions. Insights from entomologists, ornithologists and botanists were helpful to the sound designers in constructing a layered mix that was full of dramatic life and natural sound. Next came the overwhelming amount of details in effects, atmospheres and foley for the handmade leather armour, weapons and other costumes. Then there was the question of the actors' intonations and the need to rerecord additional dialogue in multiple languages. Above all, director Kim wanted to maximize the film's appeal to transnational audiences – all while avoiding the types of exaggerated sound designs found in the conventional action scenes in Hollywood films.

Over the years Soundfirm's audio mixers, such as Steve Burgess, have also built close personal relationships with Korean and other Asian film-makers, and have developed a heightened sensitivity for designing Asian sounds in Australian soundscapes. Working on *Shadowless Sword*, Burgess was challenged by director Kim Young-jun's desire to create within the action sequences a different sense of internal combustion or muffled implosion (sounds of air being sucked into a vacuum) as opposed to the more common, outwardly explosive and conventional frenetic sounds heard in Hollywood films. Transnational films such as *Shadowless Sword* and *Musa* require different sights, sounds and most of all a willingness on the part of the sound designer to remain open to cross-cultural forms of expression.

## Conclusion

Transnational film-making, like diasporic film-making, both relies upon and creates new relations between film-makers, films, audiences and screen cultures. Both modes of film practice exceed and expand the national cinema. *Musa* and *Shadowless Sword* are sites of negotiation between the Korean and the Australian. They are a form of transnational collaboration that doesn't obviously or overtly speak to or through the Korean diaspora in Australia (although the finished films may be consumed by the diasporic community). They are not part of the dialogue between the Korean-Australian diaspora and the Korean homeland or the Australian host, nor do they fit within either the imagined world or the statistical boundaries of Australian national cinema. These films do, however, form part of a complex, creative, transnational intercultural dialogue which is little remarked either in Australia or Korea. If we understand a diaspora as a 'scattering of people over space and transnational connections between people and places' (Blunt and Dowling 2006: 199), then we argue we can understand film-makers who work collaboratively on projects that are transnational at the levels of finance, personnel, story and/or setting, or which are intended to find audiences overseas, as collectively forming a diaspora of transnational film. They may not neatly meet William Safran's common features of a diaspora (Safran 1991: 83–84); they are not ethnically linked, they may not have physically migrated although many do temporarily or permanently, and there is no physical 'homeland', although there are many 'imagined worlds' (Appadurai 2003: 25) which film-makers scattered around the world share in common. The dispersal inherent in the term 'diaspora' is a dispersal of film work from one place to perhaps many others. Like some ethnic diasporas, the film diaspora may not be fully accepted in the 'host' society; as in Australia, there may be resistance to transnational film-makers from those groups who see their role as policing and protecting the boundaries of national cinema. This Korean/Australian/transnational/diasporic framework allows us to think these films and the work of film-makers like Dennison and Burgess on a continuum with *Birthday Boy*. It also allows us to re-evaluate what is often dismissively or disparagingly considered service work. Sound editors and mixers, screen composers and orchestrators, digital effects artists and animators are not directors, and do not have total control over the big picture, but they make often substantial creative contributions to the projects they work on. The failure until recently even to count this work as a contribution to production activity in Australia has limited the ways in which it has been possible to think about Australian cinema, film-making in Australia and the Australian creative contribution to transnational films and to international cinema.

Like *Birthday Boy* and the AFTRS films of Melissa Kyu-jung Lee and Susan Danta, the work of Australian firms on Korean feature films performs and exhibits a complex and subtle intercultural dialogue; as forms of collaboration between Korean/Korean-Australian/Australian film-makers, these films give insight into and expand the 'imagined worlds' of film-makers, and of the Korean-Australian diaspora. Here the 'imagined worlds' are both those intended in Appadurai's original use of the term to mean 'the multiple worlds which are constituted by the historically situated imaginations of persons and groups spread around the world' (Appadurai 2003: 31) and the particular imagined world of the film, the story-world, that film-makers seek to realize through image, sound, performance, editing and production design. *Birthday Boy* is simultaneously an exemplar of diasporic or accented film-making, an important component of the Australian national cinema and a transnational film. The film has particular resonance for the Korean community in Australia, and it also resounds as a new way of thinking about and hearing Australian film. *Musa* and *Shadowless Sword* are Korean and transnational films, which made use of Australian creative and technical expertise. They drew on the Australian transnational film diaspora to create distinctive soundscapes. Collectively, these films allow us to think in new ways about the relations between Korean, Australian, diasporic, transnational film-making.

# Diasporic Filmography

## Garry Gillard and Anthony Lambert

**Acropolis Now** (Channel 7 1989–91) TV series; comedy set in the Greek-Australian community.

**Adventures of Priscilla Queen of the Desert, The** (Stephan Elliott, 1994) The Filipina wife character Cynthia (Julia Cortez) has been widely criticized.

**Alexandra's Project** (Rolf de Heer 2003) Writer/director Rolf de Heer is originally from The Netherlands.

**Alien Years, The** (ABC 1988) TV mini-series dealing with the incarceration of German nationals in Australia as World War I breaks out.

**Always a Visitor** (Kuranda Seyit 2000) Short film depicting the personal journey of a Turkish-Australian Muslim growing up in Emu Plains in western Sydney.

**Always Afternoon** (WDR 1988) TV mini-series; romance between a baker's daughter and an incarcerated German violinist during World War I.

**Amanda and Ali** (Karen Hodgkins 2003) Documentary; friendship between an Afghan detainee and a young Australian woman.

**Anzacs** (Pino Amenta, John Dixon and George Miller 1985) TV mini-series; follows a dozen ANZAC soldiers and their loved ones through World War I.

**Aussie Park Boyz** (Nunzio La Bianca 2004) 'An Italian-Australian story' of street gang and prison violence; director/some cast of Sicilian origin.

**Aussie Rules** (Barbara Chobocky 1993) Documentary; director of Czech origin; immigrant teenagers taught the English language and the 'rules' of Australian life.

**Australia's Peril** (Franklyn Barrett 1917) A German raid on the Australian coast sees Sydney under fire.

**Aya** (Solrun Hoaas 1991) Story of a Japanese war bride; director Solrun Hoaas was born in Norway and lived in China and Japan.

**Babe: Pig in the City** (Dr George Miller 1998) Although born in Chinchilla, Queensland, George Miller (born George Miliotis) is of Greek origin.

**Bad Boy Bubby** (Rolf de Heer 1994) Writer/director from The Netherlands.

**Bali Hash** (John Darling 1989) Documentary opposing crass Westerners with spiritual Balinese.

**Bali Triptych** (John Darling 1987) Three films about the history and culture of the Balinese.

**Bangkok Hilton** (Ken Cameron 1989) Mini-series set in Thai prison where an Australian woman is sentenced to death for carrying drugs.

**BeDevil** (Tracey Moffatt 1993) First feature directed by an Indigenous woman; three Aboriginal/non-Aboriginal ghost stories, including one about an American GI who lingers in the quicksand of Bribie Island in southeast Queensland.

**Beneath Clouds** (Ivan Sen 2003) The father of director Ivan Sen was German-Hungarian, his mother Aboriginal.

**Beware of Greeks Bearing Guns** (John Tatoulis 2000) Director is of Greek origin; a Greek school teacher is sent to Australia to settle a score.

**Billal** (Tom Zubrycki 1996) Documentary; young Lebanese Muslims in the suburbs of southwest Sydney.

**Billion Dollar Crop, The** (Barbara Chobocky 1994) Documentary; director of Czech origin; this 'history of hemp' travels from Australia to the United States and Europe.

**Birth of White Australia, The** (Philip Walsh 1928) Dramatization/celebration of Australian (white) racial history, which culminates in clashes between Anglo-Celtics and the 'tide of Asiatics' on the goldfields in the 1860s.

**Birthday Boy** (Saejong Park 2004) Academy Award-nominated animated short; director is an AFTRS graduate from South Korea; the film was influenced by the film-maker's Korean-Australian childhood.

**Blood Oath** (Stephen Wallace 1990) World War II Japanese-Australian relations.

**Blue Fin** (Carl Schultz 1978) Director born in Budapest.

**Bodyline** (Carl Schultz, George Ogilvie, Lex Marinos and Denny Lawrence 1984) Mini-series; director Carl Schultz was born in Budapest, actor/director Lex Marinos is of Greek origin.

**Bondi Tsunami** (Rachael Lucas 2004) Promoted as 'the first Japanese surfing road movie in Australia'; characters/actors are Japanese.

**Book of Revelation, The** (Ana Kokkinos 2006) Director Ana Kokkinos was born in Australia from Greek origins.

**Boy Serpentine** (Heng Tang 1999) Chinese-Australian boy's fascination with snakes speaks to religious and conservative fundamentalism.

**Boundaries of the Heart** (Lex Marinos 1988) Actor/director Lex Marinos is of Greek origin.

**Bra Boys** (Sunny Abberton 2007) Film about the infamous Maroubra Beach surf-tribe touches on multicultural relations after the 2005 Cronulla race riots.

**Breaker Morant** (Bruce Beresford 1980) Murder trial of three Australian Army officers serving in South Africa during the Second Boer War; title role played by British actor Edward Woodward.

**Brothers, The** (Georgio Mangiamele 1958) Film-maker is Italian (born in Sicily, arrived in Australia 1952); explores different ways of surviving in a new country, while questioning 1950s materialism in Australia.

**Bullseye** (Carl Schultz 1989) Director born in Budapest.

**Butler, The** (Anna Kannava 1996) Documentary; Cypriot-Greek-Australian film-maker; auto-biographical exploration of Greek-Australian family.

**Cactus** (Paul Cox 1986) Writer/director from the Netherlands; A beautiful French woman is involved in a terrible accident in Australia.

**Caddie** (Donald Crombie 1976) Title character (based on autobiography) has relationship with Greek man.

**Capitalist Drive, The** (Barbara Chobocky 2004) Documentary; director of Czech origin.

**Careful He Might Hear You** (Carl Schultz 1983) Director born in Budapest.

**Castle, The** (Rob Sitch 1997) Lawyer Dennis Denuto (Tiriel Mora) is Italian-Australian (the actor is not; his father, Philippe Mora, was born in France).

**Cathy's Child** (Donald Crombie 1979) A mother's attempt to reunite with a daughter taken to Athens illegally by her Greek-born father.

**Children of the Dragon** (Peter Smith 1992) Mini-series; British doctor goes to China to find cancer researcher.

**Children of the Revolution** (Peter Duncan 1996) Comedy about Josef Stalin's fictional Australian child.

**China Dolls** (Tony Ayres 1997) Documentary; director is from Hong Kong; explores the 'double minority' of gay Asian men in Australia.

**Chinese Takeaway** (Mitzi Goldman 2002) Documentary; set in old China and Australia; writer/performer Anna Yen exploring her connections with her mother and grandmother.

**Clay** (Giorgio Mangiamele 1964) Film-maker Italian; film is a visual poem of love and tragedy, work, weather and drink.

**Clubland** (Cherie Nowlan 2007) British star Brenda Blethlyn trades in old jokes on the club stage and manipulates her family in suburban Sydney.

**Coca Cola Kid, The** (Dusan Makaveyev 1985) Director was born in Belgrade, but not an immigrant; major character is American.

**Contract, The** (Georgio Mangiamele 1953) Film-maker Italian; five young Italian men immigrate to Australia on a work contract.

**Cosi** (Mark Joffe 1996) Director Mark Joffe was born in Polotsk, Russia.

**Country Life** (Michael Blakemore 1994) Australian adaptation of Chekhov's play *Uncle Vanya*.

**Cowra Breakout, The** (Phillip Noyce and Chris Noonan 1985) Mini-series; mass breakout of POWs in a small town in central-west New South Wales in August 1944, including many Japanese and Russians.

**Craic, The** (Ted Emery 1999) Immigration comedy featuring Irish comic Jimeoin.

**Crossing, The** (George Ogilvie 1990) Features Italian-Australian Robert Mammome in a love triangle with Russell Crowe and Danielle Spencer.

**Dallas Doll** (Anne Turner 1993) American golfer (Sandra Bernhardt) brings both havoc and liberation to a suburban Sydney home.

**Dance Me to My Song** (Rolf de Heer 1998) Writer/director from The Netherlands.

**Daughter of the East** (Roy Darling 1924) An 'untold episode' in the Gallipoli campaign involving an Englishman born in the Dardanelles.

**Dead Calm** (Phil Noyce 1989) An Australian heroine, a New Zealander husband and a psychotic American villain on a yacht in the Pacific.

**Death in Brunswick** (John Ruane 1991) Anglo-Australian Carl has a relationship with Greek-Australian barmaid Sophie (Zoe Carides); his drug-dealing co-worker Mustafa (Nick Lathouris) is Turkish.

**Delivery Day** (Jane Manning 2001) Written by Khoa Do, Vietnamese director of *The Finished People*; set in the Australian Vietnamese community.

**Diaries of Vaslav Nijinsky, The** (Paul Cox 2002) Writer/director from The Netherlands; Nijinsky was a Russian dancer.

**Dingo** (Rolf de Heer 1992) Writer/director from The Netherlands.

**Diplomat, The** (Tom Zubrycki 2000) documentary; the final stages of Jose Ramos Horta's fight for peace in East Timor and the eventual return to his homeland.

**Dish, The** (Rob Sitch 2001) America comes to the remote town of Parkes, as NASA works with local Australian technicians to rig a satellite to transmit images of the moon landing.

**Dismissal, The** (Dr George Miller, Phillip Noyce, Carl Schultz, George Ogilvie, John Power 1983) Dramatized sacking of the Whitlam government; Schultz was born in Budapest; Miller is of Greek origin.

**Dogs in Space** (Richard Lowenstein 1987) Drugs, music and maniacs in a Melbourne squat; features Saskia Post, an American actress born of Dutch parents who lived in Japan before moving to Australia in 1975.

**Donkey in Lahore** (Faramarz K. Rahber 2007) Documentary; courtship between an Australian Goth puppeteer and a Pakistani Muslim woman.

**Double Trouble** (Tony Ayres 1992) Documentary exploring the lives of Aboriginal gays and lesbians, commissioned by Channel 4 in the United Kingdom; director is Australian from Hong Kong.

**Dr Plonk** (Rolf de Heer 2007) Silent comedy about time travel and the end of the world; writer/director from the Netherlands; starring Magda Szubanski, born in England to a Polish father and Scottish mother.

**Dunera Boys, The** (Ben Lewin 1985) Mini-series; HMT *Dunera* took over 2,000 Jewish refugees and prisoners of war in 1940 from England to New South Wales for internment.

**Eliza Fraser** (Tim Burstall 1976) Comedy based on the shipwreck and capture of British Captain Fraser and his wife Eliza by Aborigines.

**Epsilon** (Rolf de Heer 1995) A digital intergalactic romance with and about planet Earth; writer/director from the Netherlands.

**Everyone Loves a Wedding** (Mika Nishimura et al. 2004) Eight-part series about different wedding days and cultural and ethnic traditions.

**Excursion to the Bridge of Friendship** (Christina Andreef 1992) Short film; writer/director born in New Zealand to a Bulgarian father and Anglo-Irish mother; Bulgarian folk singer seeks sponsorship from a woman living in inner Sydney.

**Exile** (Paul Cox 1993) Writer/director from the Netherlands; a man is exiled to an island after stealing sheep and a woman is compelled to join him.

**Exposed** (Tony Ayres 1997) Short; writer/director from Hong Kong.

**Face of Greekness, A** (Michael Karris 1979) Short; director born in Greece; a Greek family deals with the pain of their daughter's rape.

**Far Country, The** (George Miller 1987) Mini-series; a doctor forced to join the German army during World War II moves to Australia.

**Fat Pizza** (Paul Fenech 2003) Director of Maltese origin; comedy set in immigrant milieu connected to a 'dodgy' Sydney takeaway.

**Fields of Fire** (David Elfick and Rob Marchand 1987–89) Mini-series; features sugar cane-cutter who has migrated from Italy.

**Finished People, The** (Khoa Do 2003) Writer/director is from Vietnam; heroin and homelessness impact on Vietnamese-Australians and they construct a 'Vietnamatta' (Cabramatta) unlike that seen in media reports.

**Fish Sauce Breath** (Thao Nguyen 2003) A Vietnamese male attempts to win over his girlfriend's hard-drinking 'Aussie' father.

**Fistful of Flies** (Monica Pellizzari 1997) Director is Italian-Australian; three generations of a dysfunctional Italian family in rural Australia.

**Floating Life** (Clara Law 1996) Hong Kong couple moves to Australia with two youngest sons; writer/director born in Macao, China.

**Flowergirl** (Cate Shortland 1999) Short; collaboration with Australian-Japanese photographer Jun Tagami; young Japanese living in Bondi.

**Footy Legends** (Khoa Do 2006) Writer/performer Anh Do and director Khoa Do are from Vietnam; film focuses on Vietnamese-Australian family and multicultural cohort in Yagoona, Sydney.

**Footy: The La Perouse Way** (Michael Longbottom 2006) short; documents the area's transformation from an Indigenous to a multicultural area of Sydney through the history of local football.

**Forbidden Lie$** (Anna Broinowski 2007) Documentary; international exploration of the motives of Arab author Norma Khouri after her story of a Jordanian honour killing is exposed as fiction in a Sydney paper.

**Forty Thousand Horsemen** (Charles Chauvel 1940) Australian soldiers join the fight against German-backed Turkish forces in World War I.

**40,000 Years of Dreaming: A Century of Australian Cinema** (Dr George Miller) Documentary; references ethnic migration and influence in Australian cinema, but not the director's own heritage.

**Gallipoli** (Peter Weir 1982) Two young men from Western Australia enlist during World War I, ending up in the onslaught at the Nek, Turkey.

**Gallipoli: the Frontline** (Tolga Örnek 2005) documentary; Turkish director uses diaries and letters from Anzacs, Turks and the British to further understand the Gallipoli campaign.

**Genie from Downunder** (ACTF 1996) and **Genie from Downunder 2** (ACTF 1998) TV series; English girl finds an old opal that houses two Australian genies, Bruce and his son Baz.

**Gift, The** (Paul Cox 1988) Telemovie; writer/director from the Netherlands; Greek-Australian family deal with the environmental politics of land ownership and development.

**Gino** (Jackie McKimmie 1994) Main character is Italian-Australian who wants to become a comic instead of following his father into the construction industry.

**Goddess of 1967, The** (Clara Law 2000) Rikiya Kurokawa is JM, who comes from Japan to Australia to buy a 1967 Citroen; writer/director born in Macao, China.

**Golden Braid** (Paul Cox 1991) Writer/director from The Netherlands.

**Golden Cage, The** (Ayten Kuyululu 1975) Written and directed by Turkish-Australian; depiction of Turkish immigrant experience.

**Good Woman of Bangkok** (Dennis O'Rourke 1992) Documentary about a Thai woman working as a prostitute in the Patpong district.

**Goodbye Paradise** (Carl Schultz 1983) Director born in Budapest.

**Grievous Bodily Harm** (Mark Joffe 1988) Director born in Polotsk, Russia.

**Handful of Dust** (Ayten Kuyululu 1974) Experimental short directed by Turkish-Australian, featuring her husband Ilhan Kuyululu.

**Happy Feet** (Dr George Miller 2006) Director is of Greek origins.

**Hard Knuckle** (Lex Marinos 1988) Director is of Greek origins.

**Head On** (Ana Kokkinos 1998) Greek-Australian actors include Alex Dimitriades, Paul Capsis; director born in Australia of Greek origin; main character is Greek-Australian man finding himself; set in Melbourne's Greek community.

**Healing of Bali** (John Darling 2003) Documentary on Bali one year after the terrorist nightclub bombing.

**Heartbreak High** (dir. Dan Burstall et al. 1994–99) TV series; based on *The Heartbreak Kid*.

**Heartbreak Kid, The** (Michael Jenkins 1993) Alex Dimitriades is a Greek-Australian high school student who has an affair with his teacher.

**Heaven's Burning** (Craig Lahiff 1997) Youki Kudoh plays Japanese woman, Midori, whose honeymoon in Australia sees her transform from bride to outlaw.

**Hercules Returns** (David Parker 1994) The film revoiced to comic effect is an Italian epic.

**Hero of the Dardanelles, The** (Alfred Rolfe 1915) A Sydney man enlists to fight in World War I, dealing with pacifists and winning a lady's heart before he leaves. Most of the film after his arrival in Gallipoli is lost.

**Holy Smoke** (Jane Campion 2000) Director from New Zealand; British star Kate Winslet plays an Australian taken in by a cult, and Harvey Keitel the American exiter brought in by her family to make her see sense.

**Home Song Stories** (Tony Ayres 2007) Writer/director is from Hong Kong; a Shanghai nightclub singer's (Joan Chen) story of survival in Australia.

**Howling 3: The Marsupials** (Philippe Mora 1987) Director was born in France; a minor character is Russian; and Chinese-Australian photographer William Yang is a Siberian peasant.

**Human Touch** (Paul Cox 2004) Writer/director from The Netherlands.

**I Remember 1948** (Faddia Aboud 2005) Arabic film-maker; memories of the events that saw 750,000 Palestinians flee as Zionist terror gangs seized villages.

**If the Huns came to Melbourne** (George Coates 1916) Unpopular propagandist film based on a fictional attack from the Turks.

**Illuminations** (Paul Cox 1976) Writer/director from The Netherlands.

**Illustrated Auschwitz, The** (Jackie Farkas 1992) Documentary short; juxtaposes oral testimony of Hungarian holocaust survivor with images and sounds from *The Wizard of Oz*.

**Incident at Raven's Gate** (Rolf de Heer 1989) writer/director from The Netherlands.

**Indecent Obsession, An** (Lex Marinos 1985) Actor/director of Greek origin.

**Innocence** (Paul Cox 2000) Writer/director from The Netherlands.

**Inside Looking Out** (Paul Cox 1977) Writer/director from The Netherlands.

**Island** (Paul Cox 1989) Writer/director Paul Cox is from The Netherlands; previously wealthy Czech-Australian emigrant moves to a Greek Island.

**Jammed, The** (Dee McLachlan 2007) Drama about human trafficking, prostitution and governmental deportation; one of the central characters is Russian, another is Indonesian, a third is Chinese.

**Japanese Story** (Sue Brooks 2003) An Australian guide falls for Japanese visitor to Australia, Tachibana Hiromitsu, with tragic results.

**Jewboy** (Tony Krawitz 2005) A young man returns from Israel to Sydney's Chasidic community after the death of his father.

**Jindabyne** (Ray Lawrence 2006) A depressed American immigrant mother becomes the agent of reconciliation after a group of non-Aboriginal men mistreat the dead body of a local Indigenous woman.

**Joan of Arc of Loos, The** (George Willoughby 1916) Sydney's Tamarama Beach is used to recreate the village of Loos under German occupation in 1915.

**Journey Among Women** (Tom Cowan 1977) A group of British women convicts escapes into the Australian bush, learning survival skills from an Indigenous woman.

**Just Desserts** (Monica Pellizzari 1993) Short; director is Italian-Australian; explores relationship between girl's sexual maturation and food items.

**Kidnapped!** (Melissa Kyu-Jung Lee 2005) TV documentary; writer/director born in Korea; the effects of North Korea's abduction of 13 Japanese citizens continues to impact on their families.

**Kostas** (Paul Cox 1979) Writer/director from The Netherlands; Takis Emmanuel is Kostas, a Greek immigrant taxi driver who pursues a wealthy divorcee.

**La Spagnola** (Steve Jacobs 2001) Writer Anna Maria Monticelli born in Morocco; Lola Marceli plays the ' the Spanish woman' of the title.

**Lantana** (Ray Lawrence 2001) The dead body of an American-Australian psychotherapist (Barbara Hershey) sends shockwaves through the tangled connections of family, patients and investigators. Features Italian-Australians Anthony LaPaglia and Vince Colosimo.

**Last Chip, The** (Heng Tang 2005) Short; film-maker is Malaysian-Chinese-Australian; story of Chinese women in Australia who gamble together.

**Last Days of Chez Nous** (Gillian Armstrong 1993) Features a French principal character, J-P (played by Swiss Bruno Ganz).

**Last Days of Yasser Arafat, The** (Sherine Salama 2006) Documentary; film-maker is Australian-Palestinian-Egyptian; filmed over a year in the president's compound before his death.

**Learning the Ropes** (Barbara Chobocky 1993) Documentary; director of Czech origin.

**Lempad of Bali** (documentary John Darling 1980) Documentary on the life of Bali's most famous artist.

**Letters from Poland** (Sophia Turkiewicz 1978) Short; director born in Rhodesia and brought to Australia by Polish parents; film explores young Polish migrant woman's experience in the 1950s.

**Letters to Ali** (Clara Law 2004) Documentary; writer/director born in Macao; film explores Afghani refugee's relationship with an Australian family.

**Lilian's Story** (Jerzy Domaradzki 1996) Director from Poland; the taxi-driver character (Bohdan Koca) is also Polish and one of the people Lilian discovers as she reacquaints herself with Sydney after 40 years.

**Little Fish** (Rowan Woods 2005) A heroin addict lives with her mother in 'Little Saigon' (Cabramatta), Sydney's Vietnamese community.

**Lonely Hearts** (Paul Cox 1982) Writer/director from The Netherlands.

**Long Lunch, The** (Antony Redman 2003) Uncle, the owner of Chinese restaurant The Palace, goes to extreme lengths to pay back money he owes to the Triad.

**Looking for Alibrandi** (Kate Woods 2000) A schoolgirl (Pia Miranda) from an Italian-Australian family deals with love, loss and a father she's never met (Anthony LaPaglia).

**Love in Ambush** (Carl Schultz 1997) Writer/director born in Budapest; an Australian woman searches for her soldier brother in Cambodia during a time of civil unrest.

**Love Serenade** (Shirley Barrett 1997) Features a Chinese restaurateur named Albert Lee as the boss of one of the sisters in the film.

**Love's Brother** (Jan Sardi 2004) Italian-Australian man uses a picture of his more attractive brother to entice a woman from Italy to Australia.

**Lucky Miles** (James Michael Rowland 2007) A group of male refugees (Iraqi, Indonesian and Cambodian) are illegally transported to Australia in an Indonesian fishing vessel.

**Lust and Revenge** (Paul Cox 1996) Writer/director from The Netherlands; stars Polish-born Gosia Dobrowolska from *Silver City*.

**Mad Max** (Dr George Miller 1979), **Mad Max 2** (Dr George Miller 1981) Miller (born George Miliotis) is of Greek origin.

**Mad Max 3: Beyond Thunderdome** (Dr George Miller and George Ogilvie 1985) Miller (born George Miliotis) is of Greek origin.

**Mail Order Bride** (Stephen Wallis 1984) Telemovie; Kevin's mail order bride is from the Philippines.

**Man From Hong Kong, The** (Brian Trenchard Smith and Yu Wang 1975) Australian-Hong Kong action film featuring Yu Wang (as Jimmy Wang Yu) and Sammo Hung Kam-Bo.

**Man of Flowers** (Paul Cox 1983) Writer/director from The Netherlands.

**Man Who Sued God, The** (Mark Joffe 2001) Director born in Russia; Scottish comedian Billy Connolly is the immigrant who sues against an 'act of God' that destroys his fishing boat.

**Mandarins of New Gold Mountain, The** (Tony Matthews 1993) Epic story of the arrival and survival of the Chinese in Australia.

**Man's Gotta Do, A** (Chris Kennedy 2004) An Aussie standover man may be responsible for the disappearance of his daughter's Russian fiancé.

**Maria** (Barbara Chobocky 1991) Documentary; director of Czech origin; biography of her mother over 40 years in Australia and Czechoslovakia.

**Memory** (Michelle Blanchard 2005) Short; death, love and mourning and Indigenous communities.

**Menace, The** (Cyril Sharp 1927) One of a batch of films demonizing ethnic (usually Asian) difference.

**Message from Fallujah, A** (Richard Gibson 2005) Short; an American civil engineer is taken hostage on his last day working in Iraq.

**Mike and Stefani** (Ron Maslyn Williams 1952) Documentary; reconstructs the story of two Ukrainian refugees and their journey to Australia, and attempts to satisfy official criteria for entry into the country.

**Modern Marriage, A** (Rebecca Barry 2003) Documentary exploring the place of Hindu arranged marriage in contemporary Australian culture.

**Molly and Mobarak** (Tom Zubrycki 2003) Documentary; Molly and her mother befriend Mobarak, an Afghani refugee.

**Molokai: The Story of Father Damien** (Paul Cox 2000) Writer/director from The Netherlands; true story of nineteenth century Belgian priest who lived amongst the lepers of Molokai.

**Moving Out** (Michael Pattinson 1983) An Italian migrant teenager (played by Vince Colosimo) is trying to fit into his inner Melbourne environment, but ultimately starts to appreciate both his heritage and his new life.

**Mrs Craddock's Complaint** (Tony Ayres 1997) Short; writer/director is from Hong Kong.

**Musa** (Kim Sung-su 2001) Australian sound post-production services were used in this film about the battle to protect a Chinese princess in 1375.

**My Blessings** (Bill Mousoulis 1997) Writer/director Greek-Australian; diary film following film-maker Jane Friedman over six days.

**My First Wife** (Paul Cox 1984) Writer/director from the Netherlands; a minor character is Russian.

**My Mother India** (Safina Uberoi 2001) Documentary; Indian-Australian film-maker. Examines the lives of Uberoi's Indian parents and family, events surrounding anti-Sikh riots in 1984, and their move to Australia.

**My Sister** (Yen Ooi 2004) Short; a young Chinese-Australian girl has difficulty comprehending her cultural heritage.

**My Tiger's Eyes** (Teck Tan 1992) Short; a young Chinese boy growing up in Sydney at the height of anti-communism in the 1950s.

**Ned Kelly** (Gregor Jordan 2003) The story of the best-known Irish-Australian may be part myth but embodies historical tensions between the Irish and the English in early Australia.

**1915** (Di Drew and Chris Thompson 1982) TV mini-series; two young men from a rural community enlist to fight in World War I.

**Nirvana Street Murder** (Aleksi Vellis 1991) Writer/director Greek-Australian; offbeat farce about brothers, 'wogs' and amphetamines featuring Greek-Australian star Mary Coustas (Helen).

**No Worries** (David Elfick 1993) Young central character (Amy Terelinck) forms relationship with girl from Vietnam, Binh (Ngoc Hanh Nguyen).

**Norman Loves Rose** (Henri Safran 1982) Jewish 13-year-old falls in love with his sister-in-law, who falls pregnant.

**Nun and the Bandit, The** (Paul Cox 1992) Writer/director from The Netherlands.

**Occupant, The** (Michael Karris, Peter Lyssiotis and Ettore Siracusa 1984) Short; two directors Greek and one Italian; collaborative essay film considered a 'touchstone' of Greek-Australian cinema.

**Odd Angry Shot, The** (Tom Jeffrey 1979) Australians in Vietnam during the war.

**Old Man Who Read Love Stories, The** (Rolf de Heer 2000) Writer/director from The Netherlands.

**Only the Brave** (Ana Kokkinos 1994) Short; director of Greek origins; two 'wild' Greek-Australian girls share a dream to leave school and travel that goes horribly wrong.

**Oscar and Lucinda** (Gillian Armstrong 1997) En route to Australia, an English clergyman bets an Australian heiress that he can transport a glass church to the outback in return for her inheritance.

**Over the Hill** (George Miller 1992) An American grandmother finds inspiration in the landscape and people of the Australian outback.

**Piano, The** (Jane Campion 1992) Australian French co-production with two Americans, about a silent Scotswoman's marriage to a New Zealander and her relationships with a neighbour and a piano.

**Palace of Dreams** (Denny Lawrence et al 1985) TV mini-series; Sydney in the Great Depression of the 1930s, featuring the Mendels, a family of Russian Jews.

**Paradise Road** (Bruce Beresford 1997) Women of differing ages and nationalities (including American, British and Australian) are imprisoned by Japanese forces in Sumatra in 1942.

**Petrov Affair, The** (Michael Carson 1987) TV mini-series; dramatization of Soviet spy Vladimir Petrov's application for political asylum in Australia in the 1950s.

**Pig, a Chicken, and a Bag of Rice, A** (Mark Gould 2004) Documentary; wedding of Australian groom and Sikkimese bride.

**Pioneers of Love** (Julie Nimmo 2005) Documentary; two-part series about Russian dissident Leandro Illin, Kitty Clarke, an Indigenous woman, and their descendants.

**Power and the Glory, The** (Noel Monkman 1941) The Nazis steal a formula for nerve gas from a Czech scientist working for the Australian Air Force.

**Prisoner of St Petersburg, The** (Ian Pringle 1990) A curious Australian turns up in Berlin speaking only in Russian quotes from Gogol and Dostoyevsky.

**Prodigal Son, The** (Tony Radevski 2005) Short; film-maker of Macedonian heritage; examines father–son relationship between film-maker's Macedonian migrant uncle and gay cousin after years of no contact.

**Projectionist, The** (Michael Bates 2002) Short; cinema projectionist walks through Sydney as images of displacement and despair flash across walls and buildings to the music of Rachmaninov.

**Promised Woman** (Tom Cowan 1975) Writer Thodoros Patrikareas of Greek origin; Greek woman arrives in Australia for an arranged marriage only to be rejected and start life in Australia on her own.

**Quiet Room, The** (Rolf de Heer 1996) Writer/director from The Netherlands.

**Ra Choi** (Michael Frank 2005) Deals with four young Vietnamese Australians' immersion into street life in Sydney.

**Rabbit on the Moon** (Monica Pellizzari 1987) Short; director is Italian-Australian; an Italian girl in 1970s Australia negotiates the values of her classmates with those of her family.

**Raid, The** (Barbara Chobocky 1994) Documentary; director of Czech origin; 11 Iranian Australians are charged with attacking Iran's diplomatic mission in Canberra.

**Rats of Tobruk, The** (Charles Chauvel 1944) Australian defenders hold the Libyan city of Tobruk from attack for 250 days during World War II.

**Razorback** (Russell Mulcahy 1984) When an American TV journalist is killed by a feral pig in the Australian outback, her American husband comes to Australia in search of the wild animal.

**Romper Stomper** (Geoffrey Wright 1992) Contains street fighting between white Australian racists and the Vietnamese community in inner Melbourne.

**Romulus My Father** (dir. Richard Roxburgh 2007) The son of a Romanian father (Romulus) and German mother comes to terms with their estrangement and growing pains in country Victoria.

**Russian Doll** (Stavros Kazantzidis 2000) Director of Greek descent; Natalia Novikova (aka Natasha Novak from Moscow province) plays Katia, a Russian mail-order bride; Sacha Horler plays the daughter of Russians.

**Sadness: A Monologue by William Yang** (Tony Ayres 1999) Documentary; director is from Hong Kong; Yang is an extremely prolific Chinese-Australian photographer and performer working at the intersections of ethnicity, history and sexuality.

**Salvation** (Paul Cox 2007) Writer/director born in the Netherlands; Biblical scholar Barry becomes involved with Russian prostitute Irina.

**Satan in Sydney** (Beaumont Smith 1918) Wartime melodrama about a nasty German and a good girl from the country.

**Serenades** (Mojgan Khadem 2001) Writer and director Mojgan Khadem was born in Iran; significant characters in the film are Afghani.

**Shadowless Sword** (Kim Young-jun 2005) Australian sound post-production services were used in this Korean martial arts epic about the last prince of the Balhai kingdom.

**Shine** (Scott Hicks 1996) Written by Jan Sardi; young pianist David Helfgott is traumatized by his Polish father.

**Silver City** (Sophia Turkiewicz 1984) Director was born in Rhodesia and brought to Australia by her Polish parents; film features Gosia Dobrowolska and Ivar Kants as Polish migrants, telling their romantic story based in a compound (or 'silver city') in flashback.

**Six Pack** (Kay Pavlou, Di Drew, Sue Brooks, Rodney Fisher, Megan Simpson and Karin Altmann 1991) Mini-series; Kay Pavlou is of Greek origin.

**Soft Fruit** (Christina Andreef 2001) Writer/director born in New Zealand to a Bulgarian father and Anglo-Irish mother; father (Linal Halt) of the family who gather to nurse a dying mother is a very angry Russian immigrant.

**Song of Ceylon** (Laleen Jayamanne 1985) Film-maker from Sri Lanka; refers to the 1934 documentary of the same name using classic images to explore colonialism and the female body.

**Sound of One Hand Clapping, The** (Richard Flanagan 1998) Story of a 'haunted' Slovenian migrant family in Tasmania.

**Spag, The** (Giorgio Mangiamele) Film-maker from Italy; an Italian-Australian boy is tormented by youths and run over by an Australian drink driver while trying to escape them.

**Spank!** (Ernie Clark, 1999) Three Italian-Australian men in Adelaide decide to go into business together after years of not taking life or work seriously.

**Spotswood** (Mark Joffe 1993) Director born in Russia; British actor Anthony Hopkins is the efficiency expert out to show the Australians how to improve productivity.

**Stereos, The** (Graham Bond and John Martin 2004) Short, absurd comedy about a multicultural family.

**Street Hero** (Michael Pattinson 1984) Central character (played by Vince Colosimo) is an Italian-Australian teenager who becomes involved with the local mafia (and some scary fashion choices).

**Strictly Ballroom** (Baz Luhrmann 1992) Heroine from a Spanish family, the Spanish father and grandmother giving Paul Mercurio some of his best dance moves in the film.

**Strike Me Lucky** (Ken G. Hall 1934) Vehicle for Roy Rene (Harry Van der Sluice aka Henry van der Sluys) as Mo McMackie; Roy Rene's father was a Dutch Jew and his mother Anglo-Jewish.

**Struck by Lightning** (Jerzy Domaradzki 1990) Director from Poland; includes, predictably, an Italian-Australian who teaches soccer to the handicapped workers.

**Sundowners, The** (Fred Zinnemann 1960) Classic pioneer film about a sheep-droving family in the outback, featuring Scottish-born Deborah Kerr, American Robert Mitchum and British Peter Ustinov.

**Tail of a Tiger** (Rolf de Heer 1985) Writer/director from the Netherlands; stars British actor Gordon Poole as an old man who helps make a young boy's dreams of flying a Tiger Moth bi-plane a reality.

**Temple of Dreams** (Tom Zubrycki 2007) Documentary; young Lebanese Muslim activism in the suburbs of southwest Sydney.

**Ten Canoes** (Rolf de Heer, Peter Djigirr 2006) Writer/director from The Netherlands.

**Ten Years After, Ten Years Older** (Anna Kannava 1986) Documentary; Cypriot-Australian film-maker; explores relationship with grandmother and leaving Cyprus.

**They're a Weird Mob** (Michael Powell 1966) Main character is Nino Culotta, a migrant from Italy who manages to overcome weird Australian ways to build a life for himself.

***To the Island*** (Lex Marinos) Documentary; Greek-Australian film-maker; follows Greek-Australian actor George Spartels' return to the Greek island of Kastellorizo.

***Tracker, The*** (Rolf de Heer 2002) Writer/director from The Netherlands.

***Traps*** (Pauline Chan 1994) Director is Vietnamese-Australian; set in Vietnam in the 1950s.

***Travelling Light*** (Kathryn Millard 2003) Coming-of-age film that features a spiritually free American poet and stars Italian-Australian Pia Miranda from *Looking for Alibrandi*.

***Travelling North*** (Carl Schultz 1987) director born in Budapest.

***Trouble with Merle, The*** (Maree Delofski 2003) Documentary; Merle Oberon was actually from Calcutta, though she claimed Tasmanian birth.

***True Love and Chaos*** (Stavros Andonis Efthymiou 1996) Director born in Cyprus.

***Turtle Beach*** (Stephen Wallace 1992) An Australian reporter travels from Sydney to Malaysia to cover the crisis of Vietnamese boat people.

***Two Homelands*** (Michael Karris 1979) Documentary; Greek-Australian film-maker; footage from a concert by Savvas Christodoulou is interspersed with photographs and images that highlight the event's significance for Greek-Australians.

***Underbelly*** (Peter Andrikidis et al 2008) TV series; drama recounts the 'ten-year war' involving Melbourne underground crime figures and a group known as the 'Carlton Crew', in particular Greek-Australian and Italian-Australian actors, characters and production crew.

***Unfinished Sky*** (Peter Duncan 2007) An outback farmer takes in a refugee Afghani woman, who reinvigorates the homestead.

***Velo Nero*** (Monica Pellizzari 1987) Director is Italian-Australian; a young Italian woman has difficulties adapting to life in Australia.

***Vietnam*** (John Duigan and Chris Noonan 1987) Mini-series; the Vietnam War impacts on all members of an 'average' Australian family.

***Vincent*** (Paul Cox 1987) Writer/director Paul Cox is from The Netherlands; Dutch artist Van Gogh's career recounted through letters to his brother.

***Viva la Diva: Portrait of Yvonne Kenny*** (Barbara Chobocky 2001) Documentary; director of Czech origin.

***Wahori Days*** (Joseph Wong II 2003) A young Japanese man in Australia on a working holiday visa joins a local basketball team.

***Walkabout*** (Nicolas Roeg 1971) British school children encounter a wandering Aborigine in the desert after the suicide of their father.

***Walking on Water*** (Tony Ayres 2002) Writer/director is from Hong Kong; the film stars Italian-Australian Vince Colosimo and Greek-Australian Maria Theodorakis as friends involved in a euthanasia plot gone awry.

***We Will be Remembered for This*** (Jessie Taylor 2007) Documentary; a group of people from a range of ethnic backgrounds visits detainees held in the Baxter Detention Centre.

***Wedding in Ramallah*** (Sherine Salama 2002) Documentary; Australian film-maker of Palestinian and Egyptian parentage follows an arranged wedding at the height of the Ramallah wedding season.

***Weekend of Shadows*** (Tom Jeffrey 1978) A Polish murder suspect, 'the Pole', is killed to save him further torment from a pursuing posse.

***Welcome to the Waks Family*** (Barbara Chobocky 2002) Documentary; director of Czech origin; a Jewish family with 17 children closed off from secular life.

***Wind*** (Ivan Sen 1999) Director of German-Hungarian and Aboriginal descent.

***Wings of Destiny*** (Rupert Kathner 1940) German espionage in Australia in an attempt to control the local production of weaponry.

***Witch Hunt*** (Barbara Chobocky 1986) Documentary; director of Czech origin; Greek-Australians falsely charged with social security fraud.

***Within Our Gates***, or ***Deeds that Won Gallipoli*** (Frank Harvey 1915) Another Gallipoli landing, this time staged at Obelisk Bay.

***Wog Boy, The*** (Aleksi Vellis 2000) Features Nick Giannopoulos, Vince Colosimo; writer/director Aleksi Vellis born in Australia of Greek origin; comedy about Greek-Australian character based on successful television and stage comedies.

***Woman's Tale, A*** (Paul Cox 1991) Director from The Netherlands.

***Year of Living Dangerously, The*** (Peter Weir 1982) An Australian correspondent in Indonesia during the fall of Sukarno in 1965; American woman Linda Hunt plays Billy Kwan, a male Indonesian photographer.

## Other films cited

***Adventures of Barry McKenzie, The*** (Bruce Beresford 1972)

***Alvin Purple*** (Tim Burstall 1973)

***Amongst Equals*** (Tom Zubrycki 1991)

***Back of Beyond, The*** (John Heyer 1954)

***Baran*** (Majid Majidi 2001)

***Barry McKenzie Holds his Own*** (Bruce Beresford 1974)

***Borders*** (Mostafa Djadjam 2001)

***Crocodile Dundee*** (Peter Faiman 1986)

***Crocodile Dundee 2*** (John Cornell 1988)

***Crocodile Dundee in LA*** (Simon Wincer 2001)

***Dead Heart*** (Nick Parsons 1996)

***Dirty Deeds*** (David Caesar 2002)

***Fireflies*** (David Caesar et al. 2004) TV series

***Friends and Enemies*** (Tom Zubrycki 1987)

***Games Gamblers Play*** (Michael Hui 1974)

***Gettin' Square*** (Jonathan Teplitzky 2003)

***God of Gamblers*** (Wong Jing 1989)

***God of Gamblers 2*** (Wong Jing 1990)

***God of Gamblers Part 3: Back to Shanghai*** (Wong Jing 1991)

***God of Gamblers Return*** (Wong Jing 1994)

***High Tide*** (Gillian Armstrong 1987)

***In this World*** (Michael Winterbottom 2002)

***Jedda*** (Charles Chauvel 1955)

***Jour de Fête*** (Jacques Tati 1948)

***Journey of Hope*** (Xavier Koller 1990)

***Kath and Kim*** (Ted Emery 2002–07) TV series

***Kenny*** (Clayton Jacobsen 2007)

*Kick* (Ebsen Storm 2007) TV series
*L'École des Facteurs* (Jacques Tati 1947)
*MDA* (Ray Argall et al 2002–05) TV series
*Mon Oncle* (Jacques Tati 1954)
*My Brilliant Career* (Gillian Armstrong 1979)
*Neighbours* (Grundy Television 1985–85; 1986–present) TV series
*New Gold Mountain* (Ziyin Wang 1987)
*One Night the Moon* (Rachel Perkins 2001)
*Rabbit Proof Fence* (Phillip Noyce 2002)
*Saint of Gamblers, The* (Wong Jing 1995)
*Schindler's List* (Steven Spielberg 1993)
*Sentimental Bloke, The* (Raymond Longford 1919)
*Shame* (Steve Jodrell 1988)
*Shrek The Third* (Chris Miller 2007)
*Sunday Too Far Away* (Ken Hannam 1975)
*Water Rats* (John Hugginson, Tony Morphett et al. 1996–2001) TV series
*Welcome to Dongmakgol* (Park Kwang-hyun 2005)
*Wolf Creek* (Greg Mclean 2005)

# REFERENCES

Abbas, A. (2001), '(H)edge City: A Response to 'Becoming (Postcolonial) Hong Kong', *Cultural Studies*, 15: 3/4, pp. 621–26.

Achmatowicz-Otok, A. and Otok S. (1985), *Polonia australijska*, Lublin: Wydawnictwo Lubelskie.

Advisory Council on Multicultural Affairs (ACMA) (1989), *National Agenda for a Multicultural Australia*, Canberra: Australian Government, http://www.immi.gov.au/media/publications/multicultural/agenda/agenda89/toc.htm. Accessed 21 February 2008.

Ang, I. (2001a), 'Hybrid Life', *Metro Magazine*, 127/128, pp. 14–22.

Ang, I. (2001b), *On Not Speaking Chinese: Living Between Asia and the West*, London: Routledge.

Ang, I. (2003), 'Together-in-difference: Beyond Diaspora, into Hybridity', *Asian Studies Review*, 27: 2, pp. 141–54.

Ang, I., Chalmers, S., Law. L. and Thomas, M. (eds) (2000), *Alter/Asians: Asian Australian Identities in Art, Media and Popular Culture*, Sydney: Pluto Press.

Anonymous (2006), 'Turkish Film-maker Honoured', *The Australian*, 28 April, http://www.theaustralian.news.com.au/story/0,20867,18955928-1702,00.html. Accessed 10 June 2008.

Annan, K. (2003), 'Emma Lazarus Lecture on International Flows of Humanity', 21 November.

Anzac Cove World Heritage Listing (2003), *Hansard*, 1 July, http://www.parliament.nsw.gov.au/prod/parlment/hansart.nsf/V3Key/LA20030701022. Accessed 10 June 2008.

Appadurai, A. (2003), 'Disjuncture and Difference in the Global Cultural Economy', originally published 1990, republished in J. Evans Braziel and A. Mannur (eds), *Theorizing Diaspora*, Malden: Blackwell, pp. 25–48.

Appiah, A. (2005), *The Ethics of Identity*, Princeton: Princeton University Press.

Armstrong, P. (2005), 'Tom Zubrycki on Film-making, History and Other Obsessions', *Metro Magazine*, 142, pp. 96–100.

Astbury, K., De Smet, I. and Hiddleston, J. (2006), 'Introduction', *French Cultural Studies*, 17: 3, pp. 251–56.

Auden, W.H. (1966), *The Collected Poetry of W.H. Auden*, New York: Random House.

Australian Bureau of Statistics (ABS) (2006), '2006 Census QuickStats', http://www.abs.gov.au. Accessed 21 January 2008.

Australian Ethnic Affairs Council (AEAC) (1977), *Australia as a Multicultural Society*, submission to The Australian Population and Immigration Council on The Green Paper, 'Immigration Policies and Australia's Population', Canberra: Australian Government Publishing Service.

Badiou, A. (2001), *Ethics: An Essay in the Understanding of Evil*, trans. P. Hallward, London: Verso.

Baker, M. (2006), 'Our Favourite Enemies', *The Age*, 13 April, http://www.theage.com.au/news/opinion/our-favourite-enemies/2006/04/12/1144521396957. Accessed 4 July 2007.

Barker, C. (2004), *The Sage Dictionary of Cultural Studies*, London: Sage.

Basarin, H. and Basarin, V. (1993), *The Turks in Australia*, Melbourne: Turquoise Publications.

Bataille, G. (1985), *Visions of Excess: Selected Writings 1927–1939*, trans. A. Stoekl, Manchester: Manchester University Press.

Bataille, G. (1991), *Eroticism: Death and Sensuality*, trans. M. Dalwood, San Francisco: City Lights.

Batrouney, T. (2006a), 'Family, Business and Community', *Agora*, 41: 4, pp. 24–28.

Batrouney, T. (2006b), 'Arab Migration from the Middle East: From "White Australia" to "Beyond Multiculturalism"', *Agora*, 41: 4, pp. 5–17.

Batrouney, T. (2006c), 'A History of the Lebanese in Australia', *Agora*, 41: 4, pp. 32–34.

Bauman, Z. (1998), *Globalization*, Cambridge: Polity Press.

Bauman, Z. (2001), *The Individualized Society*, Cambridge: Polity Press.

Beauvoir de, S. (1971), *The Second Sex*, trans. and ed. H.M. Parshley, New York: Alfred K. Knopf.

Beck, U. (2006), 'Risk Society Revisited: Theory, Politics and Research Programs', in James F. Cosgrave (ed.), *The Sociology of Risk and Gambling Reader*, London: Routledge, pp. 61–85.

Bennett, J. (2007), '*Head On*: Multicultural Representations of Australian Identity in National Cinema', *Studies in Australasian Cinema*, 1: 1, pp. 61–78.

Bennetto, C. (1986), 'Dutch T(h)reat' (interview with Paul Cox), *Cinema Papers*, 59, pp. 18–21.

Berry, C. (1992/93), 'These Nations Which are Not One: History, Identity and Postcoloniality in Recent Hong Kong and Taiwan Cinema', *Span*, 34/35, pp. 37–49.

Berry, C. (1999), 'The Importance of Being Ari', *Metro Magazine*, 118, pp. 34–37.

Berry C. and Farquhar, M. (2006), *China on Screen: Cinema and Nation*, New York: Columbia University Press.

Bertone, S., Keating, C. and Mullaly, J. (2000), *The Taxidriver, the Cook and the Greengrocer: The Representation of Non-English Speaking Background People in Theatre, Film and Television*, Report for the Australia Council, Melbourne: Victoria University of Technology.

Bertrand, I. (1999), 'The Anzac and *The Sentimental Bloke*: Australian Culture and Screen Representations of World War One', in M. Paris (ed.), *The First World War and Popular Cinema: 1914 to the Present*, Edinburgh: Edinburgh University Press, pp. 74–95.

Betts, K. and Healy, E. (2006), 'Lebanese Muslims in Australia and Social Disadvantage', *People and Place*, 14: 1, pp. 24–42.

Bhabha, H. (1994), *The Location of Culture*, 2nd ed., New York: Routledge.

Bhabha, H. (2004), *The Location of Culture*, 1st ed. reprint, London: Routledge.

Blunt A., and Dowling, R. (2006), *Home*, London: Routledge.

Blunt, A. (2007), 'Cultural Geographies of Migration: Mobility, Transnationality and Diaspora', *Progress in Human Geography*, 31: 5, pp. 684–94.

Bordwell, D. and Thompson, K. (1997), *Film Art: An Introduction*, New York: McGraw-Hill.

Boyum, J.G. (1983), 'A Sweet, Quirky Little Movie', *Wall Street Journal*, 7 January, p. 17.

Bradshaw, P. (2007), 'Jindabyne', *The Guardian*, 25 May, http://film.guardian.co.uk/News_Story/Critic_Review/Guardian_review/0,,2087207,00.html. Accessed 15 June 2007.

Brearley, D. (2002), 'Ethnicity and Bad Publicity a Volatile Mix – the Cultural Divide', *The Australian*, 9 May, p. 12.

Brennan, F. (2003), *Tampering with Asylum: A Universal Humanitarian Problem*, Brisbane: University of Queensland Press.

Brewster, A. (1995), *Literary Formations: Postcolonialism, Nationalism, Globalism*, Melbourne: Melbourne University Press.

Bristow, W. (1991), 'Time and the Life of Paul Cox', *The Australian Magazine*, 16–17 February, pp. 38–42.

Broinowski, A. (1992), *The Yellow Lady: Australian Impressions of Asia*, London: Oxford University Press.

Brown, S., Johnson, K., Jackson, A. and Wyn, J. (1998), 'Healthy, Wealthy and Wise? The Health Implications of Gambling for Women', *Australian Journal of Primary Health*, 4: 3, pp. 156–62.

Brubaker, R. (2005), 'The "Diaspora" Diaspora', *Ethnic and Racial Studies*, 28: 1, pp. 1–19.

Bruzzi, S. (2006), *New Documentary*, 2nd ed., New York: Routledge.

Bulgakowa, O. (2005), 'The "Russian Vogue" in Europe and Hollywood: The Transformation of Russian Stereotypes Throughout the 1920s', *The Russian Review*, 64, pp. 211–35.

Bunbury, S. (1987), 'Everything is Not Roses: The Press and Women's Independent Film', in A. Blonski, B. Creed and F. Freiberg (eds), *Don't Shoot Darling!* Richmond: Greenhouse Publications, pp. 230–48.

Burgess, S. (2008), Telephone interview with Brian Yecies, Melbourne, 3 January.

Burke, A. (2001), *In Fear of Security: Australia's Invasion Anxiety*, Sydney: Pluto Press.

Buruma, I. and Margalit, A. (2004), *Occidentalism: A Short History of Anti-Westernism*, New York: Penguin.

Butcher, M. (2003), 'Revisioning Sydney', *Space and Culture*, 6: 2, pp. 187–94.

Butler, K. (2001), 'Defining Diaspora, Refining the Discourse', *Diaspora*, 10: 2, pp. 189–219.

Butters, P. (1998), 'When Being a Man is All You've Got: Masculinity in *Romper Stomper*, *Idiot Box*, *Blackrock*, and *The Boys*', *Metro*, 117, pp. 40–46.

Caillois, R. (1984), 'Mimicry and Legendary Psychasthenia', *October*, 34, pp. 17–32.

Callahan, D., 'His natural whiteness: Modes of ethnic presence and absence in some recent Australian films' in Craven, I., (ed.) *Australian Cinema in the 1990s* (London and Portland, Or, Frank Cass 2001), pp. 95–114.

Cameron, D., 'Our sun, sand and surf image remade for Japan', *Sydney Morning Herald*, 4 October 2006. Available at http://www.smh.com.au/news/arts/our-sun-sand-surf-image.html (accessed 4 October 2006).

Caputo, R. and Danks, A. (2007), 'They're a Weird Mob', in G. Mayer and K. Beattie (eds), *The Cinema of Australia and New Zealand*, London: Wallflower Press, pp. 91–99.

Caputo, R. and Urban, A. (1993), 'Paul Cox: Self Portrait of an Exile' (interview with Paul Cox), *Cinema Papers*, 94, pp. 4–10, 60–61.

Carniel, J. (2006), Who Josie Became Next: Developing Narratives of Ethnic Identity Formation in Italian Australian Literature and Film, PhD thesis, The Australian Centre and the Department of History, University of Melbourne.

Carter, P. (1992), 'Lines of Communication: Meaning in the Migrant Environment', in S. Gunew and K.O. Longley (eds), *Striking Chords*, Sydney: Allen & Unwin, pp. 9–18.

Carver, R. (1977), *Furious Seasons*, Santa Barbra, CA: Capra Press.

Castles, S. and Miller, M.J. (2003), *The Age of Migration: International Population Movements in the Modern World*, 3rd ed., New York: The Guilford Press.

Cavafy, C.P. (1998), 'Ithaka', in G. Savidis (ed.), *C.P. Cavafy Collected Poems*, trans. E. Keeley and P. Sherrad, London: Chatto and Windus, p. 29.

Chambers, I. (1996), 'Signs of Silence and Listening', in I. Chambers and L. Curtis (eds), *The Post-colonial Question*, London: Routledge, pp. 47–62.

Chambers, I. (2008), *Mediterranean Crossings*, Durham, NC: Duke University Press.

Chartier, R. (1989), 'Texts, Printings, Readings', *The New Cultural History*, ed. B. Lynn Hunt, Berkeley, CA: University of California Press, pp. 154–75.

Chauvel, E. (1973), *My Life with Charles Chauvel*, Sydney: Shakespeare Head Press.

Chipperfield, M. (1989), 'The Burning Fuse', *The Australian*, 2–3 September, p. 12.

Choi, J. (2006), 'National Cinema, the Very Idea', in N. Carroll and J. Choi (eds), *Philosophy of Film and Motion Pictures: An Anthology*, Malden, MA: Blackwell, pp. 310–19.

Chow, R. (1998), *Ethics after Idealism*, Bloomington: Indiana University Press.

Chow, R. (2004), 'Toward an Ethics of Postvisuality: Some Thoughts on the Recent Work of Zhang Yimou', *Poetics Today*, 25: 4, pp. 673–88.

Chua, S.K. (1993), 'Reel Neighbourly: The Construction of Southeast Asian Subjectivities', *Media International Australia*, 70, pp. 28–33.

Clammer, J.R. (2001), *Japan and Its Others: Globalization, Difference and the Critique of Modernity*, Melbourne: Trans-Pacific Press.

Clammer, J.R. (2002), *Diaspora and Identity: The Sociology of Culture in Southeast Asia*, Subang Jaya, Selangor: Pelanduk Publications.

Clarsen, G. (2002), 'Still Moving: *Bush Mechanics* in the Central Desert', *Australian Humanities Review*, March, http://www.australianhumanitiesreview.org/archive/Issue-March-2002/clarsen.html. Accessed 10 June 2008.

Clifford, M. (1999), '"You Have to Make Some Sort of Commitment": Polish Migrant Women Taking Australian Citizenship in Western Australia 1947–1997', *Studies in Western Australian History*, 19, pp. 155–65.

Cohen, R. (1997), *Global Diasporas: An Introduction*, Seattle: University of Washington Press.

Cohen, S. and Hark, I.R. (1997), *The Road Movie Book*, London: Routledge.

Colbert, M. (1987), 'Zubrycki Zooms in on Social Inequalities and Worthy Causes', *Times on Sunday*, 20 September, p. 31.

Collins, F. (2000), 'Heaven's Burning aka You Don't Know What Love Is (Craig Lahiff 1997)', *Senses of Cinema*, 9, http://www.sensesofcinema.com/contents/00/9/heaven.html. Accessed 10 June 2008.

Collins, F. (2003a), 'Brazen Brides, Grotesque Daughters, Treacherous Mothers: Women's Funny Business in Australian Cinema from *Sweetie* to *Holy Smoke*', in L. French (ed.), *Womenvision: Women and the Moving Image in Australia*, Melbourne: Damned Press, pp. 167–218.

Collins, F. (2003b), '*Japanese Story*: A Shift of Heart', *In Film*, November, http://www.infilm.com.au/reviews/japanese.htm. Accessed 30 May 2006.

Collins, F. (2006), 'The Hedonistic Modernity of Sydney in *They're a Weird Mob*', *Senses of Cinema*, 40, http://www.sensesofcinema.com/contents/06/40/theyre-a-weird-mob.html. Accessed 10 June 2008.

Collins, F. (2007), 'Kenny: The Return of the Decent Aussie Bloke in Australian Film Comedy', Metro, 154, pp. 84–90.

Collins, F. and Davis, T. (2004), Australian Cinema After Mabo, Cambridge: Cambridge University Press.

Colvin, M. (2007), In conversation with Robert Manne on ABC Radio National, 'Professor Outlines Armenian Connection to Gallipoli', 12 February, transcript available at http://www.abc.net.au/pm/content/2007/s1846039.htm.

Connell, R.W. (1995), Masculinities, Sydney: Allen & Unwin.

Conomos, J. (1992), 'Cultural Difference and Ethnicity in Australian Cinema', Cinema Papers, 90, pp. 10–15.

Corrigan, T. (1983), New German Film, Austin, TX: University of Texas Press.

Cottle, S. (2007), 'Mediatised Recognition and the "Other"', Media International Australia, 1, pp. 34–48.

Cox, P. (1998a), Reflections: An Autobiographical Journey, Sydney: Currency Press.

Cox, P. (1998b), Three Screenplays: Lonely Hearts, My First Wife, A Woman's Tale, Sydney: Currency Press.

Coyle, R. (2000), 'Speaking Strine: Locating "Australia" in Film Dialogue', in P. Brophy (ed.), Cinesonic: Experiencing the Soundtrack, Sydney: AFTRS.

Coyle, R. (2004), 'Pop Goes the Music Track: Scoring the Popular Song in the Contemporary Film Sound Track', Metro Magazine, 140, pp. 94–98.

Cremen, C. (1984), 'Sophia Turkiewicz', Cinema Papers, 47, pp. 236–39, 287.

Cunningham, S. (1991), Featuring Australia: The Cinema of Charles Chauvel, Sydney: Allen and Unwin.

Cunningham, S. and Sinclair, J. (eds) (2000), Floating Lives: The Media and Asian Diasporas, Brisbane: University of Queensland Press.

Curthoys, A. (1993), 'Identity Crisis: Colonialism, Nation and Gender in Australian History', Gender and History, 5: 2, pp. 165–76.

Curthoys, A. (2000), 'An Uneasy Conversation: The Multicultural and the Indigenous', in J. Docker and G. Fischer (eds), Race Colour and Identity in Australia and New Zealand, Sydney: UNSW Press, pp. 21–36.

Dale, D. (2005), 'Australia by Numbers', Griffith Review, 8, pp. 37–44.

Davis, C. (2006), 'Diasporic Subjectivity', French Cultural Studies, 17: 3, pp. 335–48.

Dayal, S. (2002), 'Inhuman Love: Jane Campion's The Piano', Postmodern Culture, 12: 2, http://muse.uq.edu.au.dbgw.lis.curtin.edu.au/journals/postmodern_culture/v012/12.2dayal.html. Accessed 10 December 2007.

Dell'Oso, A. (1984a), 'A New Insight into the Migrant Experience', Sydney Morning Herald, 27 September, p. 10.

Dell'Oso, A. (1984b), 'A Star is Born: It Couldn't Happen in Poland', Sydney Morning Herald, 29 September, p. 50.

Dempsey, M. (1986), 'The Fragility of Meaning: Three Films by Paul Cox', Film Quarterly, 39: 3, pp. 2–11.

Dennison, J. (2008), Telephone interview with Brian Yecies, Sydney, 7 January.

Dermody, S. (1977), 'Journey Among Women', Cinema Papers, 14, pp. 173–74.

Dermody, S. (1980), 'Action and Adventure', in S. Murray (ed.), New Australian Cinema, Melbourne: Nelson, pp. 79–97.

Dermody, S. and Jacka, E. (1988a), *The Imaginary Industry: Australian Film in The Late '80s*, Sydney: Australian Film Television and Radio School.

Dermody, S. and Jacka, E. (1988b), *The Screening of Australia: Volume 2: Anatomy of A National Cinema*, Sydney: Currency Press.

Downing, L. (2007), 'Re-viewing the Sexual Relation: Levinas and Film', *Film-Philosophy*, 11: 2, pp. 49–65.

Dreher, T. (2003), 'Speaking Up and Talking Back: News Media Interventions in Sydney's 'Othered' Communities', *Media International Australia*, 109, pp. 121–37.

Dresner, J. (2007), 'Japanese Diaspora at ASPAC', in Frog in a Well – The Japan History Group Blog, http://www.froginawell.net/japan/2007/06/japanese-diaspora-at-aspac. Accessed 25 Jan 2008.

Driscoll, K. (1996), 'Gambling with Cities: Cultural Life as a Political and Economic Jackpot', *Social Alternatives*, 15: 2, pp. 15–18.

Elkin, A.P. (1941), *Our Opinions and the National Effort*, Sydney: Australasian Medical Publishing Company.

Elsaesser, T. (1994), 'Putting on a Show: The European Art Movie', *Sight and Sound*, 4, pp. 25–26.

Fewster, K. (1982), 'Ellis Ashmead Bartlett and the Making of the Anzac Legend', *Journal of Australian Studies*, 1: 10, pp. 17–30.

Fleishman, A. (1992), *Narrated Films: Storytelling Situations in Cinema History*, Baltimore, MD: John Hopkins University Press.

Foucault, M. (1997), *Ethics: Essential Works of Foucault 1954–1984, Volume One*, ed. P. Rabinow, trans. R. Hurley, London: Penguin.

Freebury, J. (1987), 'Screening Australia: Gallipoli: A Study of Nationalism on Film', *Media Information Australia*, 43, pp. 5–8.

Frei, H.P. (1991), *Japan's Southward Advance and Australia. From the Sixteenth Century to World War II*, Melbourne: Melbourne University Press.

Freiberg, F. and Damousi, J. (2003), 'Engendering the Greek', in L. French (ed.), *Women Vision*, Melbourne: Damned Publishing, pp. 211–22.

Fuery, P. (2000), *New Developments in Film Theory*, Basingstoke: Macmillan.

Galligan, B. and Roberts, W. (2003), 'Australian Multiculturalism: Its Rise and Demise', refereed paper presented to the Australasian Political Studies Association Conference, University of Tasmania, Hobart, 29 September–1 October, http://www.utas.edu.au/government/APSA/GalliganRoberts. pdf. Accessed 5 January 2006.

Gibson, R. (1993), *South of the West: Postcolonialism and the Narrative Construction of Australia*, Bloomington, IN: Indiana University Press.

Gilbert, H., Khoo, T. and Lo, J. (eds) (2000), *Diaspora: Negotiating Asian-Australia*, Brisbane: University of Queensland Press.

Gilroy, P. (1994), 'Black Cultural Politics: An Interview with Paul Gilroy by Timmy Lott', *Found Object*, 4, pp. 46–81.

Goering, E. (2005a), '(Re)presenting Russia: A Content Analysis of Mages of Russians in Popular American Films', Russian Communication Association, http://www.russcomm.ru/eng/rca_biblio/g/goering_eng.shtml. Accessed 3 June 2008.

Goering, E. (2005b), 'Still Enemy at the Gate? The Changing Iconography of Russia and Russians in Hollywood Films', *The International Journal of the Humanities*, 3: 7, pp. 13–20.

Goldsmith, B. (forthcoming), 'Settings, Subjects and Stories: Creating Australian Cinema', in A. Sarwal and R. Sarwal (eds), *Creative Nation: Australian Cinema and Cultural Studies*, New Delhi: Authorspress.

Goldsmith, B. and O'Regan, T. (2008), 'International Film Production: Interests and Motivations', in J. Wasko and M. Erickson (eds), *Cross-Border Cultural Production: Economic Runaway or Globalization?* Youngstown, NY: Cambria Press, pp. 13–40.

Govor, E. (1997), *Australia in the Russian Mirror, Changing Perceptions, 1770–1919*, Melbourne: Melbourne University Press.

Govor, E. (2005), *Russian Anzacs in Australian History*, Sydney: UNSW Press in association with NAA.

Gray, J. (2003), *Al Qaeda and What It Means to Be Modern*, London: Faber and Faber.

Grosz, E. (1995), *Space, Time and Perversion: Essays on the Politics of Bodies*, New York: Routledge.

Guilliatt, R. (2003), 'Ohmoy Gourd!', *The Age*, 26 August.

Gullett, H.S. (1939), *Official History of Australia in the War of 1914–18 – Vol. VII: Sinai and Palestine*, Sydney: Angus & Robertson.

Gunew, S. (1994), *Framing Marginality: Multicultural Literary Studies*, Melbourne: Interpretations.

Gunew, S. (2003), 'Multicultural Sites', in N. Papastergiadis (ed.), *Complex Entanglements*, London: Rivers Oram Press, pp. 176–204.

Haddad, R. (2005), 'Treat Us Like Dogs and We'll Bite Back', *The Age*, 17 December, p. 24.

Hage, G. (1998), *White Nation: Fantasies of White Supremacy in a Multicultural Society*, Sydney: Pluto Press/Comerford and Miller.

Hage, G. (2003), *Against Paranoid Nationalism: Searching for Hope in a Shrinking Society*, London: The Merlin Press.

Hall, S. (1999), 'Cultural Identity and Diaspora', in N. Mirzoeff (ed.), *Visual Culture and Diaspora: Representing Africans and Jews*, London: Routledge, pp. 21–33.

Hall, S. (2003), 'Cultural Identity and Diaspora', in J.E. Braziel and A. Mannur (eds), *Theorizing Diaspora*, Malden, MA: Blackwell, pp. 233–46.

Hallebone, E. (1999), 'Autobiographical Interpretations of the Development of Harmful Gambling in Victoria: Cultural Context and Gender', *Just Policy*, 16, pp. 11–20.

Haltof, M. (1993), 'In quest of self-identity: Gallipoli, mateship and the construction of Australian national identity', *Journal of Popular Film and Television*, 21: 1, pp. 27–38.

Haltof, M. (2001), *Autor i kino artystyczne. Przypadek Paula Coxa* [*Author and Art Cinema: The Case of Paul Cox*], Kraków: Rabid.

Haltof, M. (2005), *Kino australijskie: O ekranowej konstrukcji Antypodów* [Australian Cinema: The Screen Construction of Australia], Gdansk: stowo/obraz terytoria.

Hannerz, U. (1996), *Transnational Connections: Culture, People, Places*, London: Routledge.

Hanrahan, J. (1983), 'Aussie Jolt: Romantic Drama in Migrants' Struggle for Acceptance', *The Sun*, 10 November, p. 29.

Harrison, R. (2003), 'The Archaeology of 'Lost Places': Ruin, Memory and the Heritage of the Aboriginal Diaspora in Australia', *Historic Environment*, 17: 1, pp. 18–23.

Haslem, W. (2007), '*The Goddess of 1967*', in G. Mayer and K. Beattie (eds), *The Cinema of Australia and New Zealand*, London: Wallflower.

Hayward, P. and Konishi, J. (2001), 'Mokuyo-to no ongaku: Music and the Japanese Community in the Torres Strait (1890–1941)', *Perfect Beat*, 5: 3, pp. 66–74.

Henderson, A. (2007), 'Islam and Australia – the Next Phase', *The Sydney Institute Quarterly*, 30, pp. 9–12.

Hessey, R. (1988), 'Why SBS is Our Cultural Conscience', *Sydney Morning Herald: The Guide*, 31 October, p. 3.

Higson, R. (2004), 'Filming on Trust', *The Australian*, 17 January, p. 16.

Hill, M. (2000), 'Cross-cultural Animation – Japanese Punks Versus the Lizards of Oz', *Perfect Beat*, 5: 1, pp. 42–55.

Holmgren, B. (2005), 'Cossack Cowboys, Mad Russians: The Émigré Actor in Studio-Era Hollywood', *The Russian Review*, 64, pp. 236–58.

Honig, B. (1998), 'Immigrant America? How Foreignness "Solves" Democracy's Problems', *Social Text* 56, pp. 1–27.

hooks, b. (1996), *Reel to Real: Race, Sex, and Class at the Movies*, New York: Routledge.

hooks, b. (2001), *All About Love: New Visions*, New York: Perennial.

Hoorn, J. (2005), 'Comedy and Eros: Powell's Australian Films *They're a Weird Mob* and *Age of Consent*', *Screen*, 46: 1, pp. 73–84.

Hugo, G. (2006), 'Defining Australia's National Population in the Era of Globalization', *People and Place*, 14: 4, pp. 26–33.

Humphrey, M. (2007), 'Culturalising the Abject: Islam, Law and Moral Panic in the West', *Australian Journal of Social Issues*, 42: 1, pp. 9–25.

Hynes, L. (2000), 'Looking for Identity: Food, Generation and Hybridity in *Looking for Alibrandi*, *Metro Magazine*, 24, pp. 30–37.

Iordanova, D. (2001), 'Displaced? Shifting Politics of Place and Itinerary in International Cinema', *Senses of Cinema*, 14, http://www.sensesofcinema.com/contents/01/14/displaced.html. Accessed 3 June 2008.

Irigaray, L. (2000), *Democracy Begins Between Two*, trans. K. Anderson, London: The Athlone Press.

Irigaray, L. (2002), *The Way of Love*, trans. H. Bostic and S. Pluhácek, London: Continuum.

Jacka, E. (1989), 'Island', *Filmnews*, October, p. 11.

Jackson, P. and Sullivan, G. (eds) (1998), *Multicultural Queer*, London: Haworth Press.

Jacobsen, L. (2006), 'The Polysemous Coathanger: The Sydney Harbour Bridge in Film-making 1930–1982', *Senses of Cinema*, 40, http://www.sensesofcinema.com/contents/06/40/sydney-harbour-bridge.html. Accessed 27 March 2008.

Jayasuriya, L. and Pooyong, K. (1999), *The Asianisation of Australia? Some Facts about the Myths*, Melbourne: Melbourne University Press.

Jennings, K. (1993), *Sites of Difference: Cinematic Representations of Aboriginality and Gender*, Melbourne: Australian Film Commission.

Johnson, B. and Poole, G. (2005), 'Scoring: Sexuality and Australian Film Music 1990–2003, in R. Coyle (ed.), *Reel Tracks: Australian Feature Film Music and Cultural Identities*, Eastleigh, UK: John Libbey, pp. 97–121.

Johnston, R. (1965), *Immigrant Assimilation (A Study of Polish People in Western Australia)*, Perth: Paterson Brokensha.

Jones, A. (2004), 'A Note on Atatürk's words about Gallipoli', *History Australia*, 2: 1, pp. 1–10.

Jones, P. and Oliver, P. (2001) (eds), *Changing Histories: Australia and Japan*, Melbourne: Monash University Press.

Jones, R. (1995), 'Far Cities and Silver Countries: Migration to Australia in Fiction and Film', in R. King, J. Connel and P. White (eds), *Writing Across Worlds: Literature and Migration*, London: Routledge, pp. 248–62.

Jones, T.A. (1990), 'The British Coin', *British History* 19: 1, pp. 98–121.

Jupp, J. (2001), *The Australian People*, Melbourne: Cambridge University Press.

Jurkiewicz, W. (2003), 'Embracing a New Culture and Keeping Another', *Canberra Historical Journal*, September, pp. 23–28.

Kalra, V.S., Kaur, R. and Hutnyk, J. (2005), *Diaspora and Hybridity*, London: Sage.

Kaluski, M. (1985), *The Poles in Australia*, Melbourne: AE Press.

Katz, C.E. (2001), 'Reinhabiting the House of Ruth: Exceeding the Limits of the Feminine in Levinas', in T. Chanter (ed.), *Feminist Interpretations of Emmanuel Levinas*, University Park, PN: Pennsylvania State University Press, pp. 145–70.

Kawin, B.F. (1978), *Mindscreen. Bergman, Godard, and First-Person Film*, Princeton: Princeton University Press.

Keen, S. (1986), *Faces of the Enemy – Reflections of the Hostile Imagination – The Psychology of Enmity*, San Francisco: Harper and Row.

Kelly, D. (1985), 'Love Amid a Foreign Culture', *The Globe and Mail*, 17 September.

Kent, D.A. (1985), 'The Anzac Book and the Anzac Legend: C.E.W. Bean as Editor and Image-Maker', *Historical Studies*, 21: 84, pp. 376–90.

Khoo, O. (2004), 'The Sacrificial Asian in Australian Film', *RealTime OnScreen*, 59, p. 15.

Kitson, M. (2003), 'The Great Aussie Car Smash at the End of the World', *Australian Screen Education Online*, 31, pp. 64–69.

Kraicer, S. (1996), '*Floating Life*: Australia 1996', reviewed at the 1996 Toronto International Film Festival [Online], http://www.chinesecinemas.org/floating.html Accessed 11 March 2008.

Kuna, F. and Strohmaier, P. (2002), 'Australian Film: Policy, Text and Criticism', in X. Pons (ed.), *Departures: How Australia Reinvents Itself*, Melbourne: Melbourne University Press 2002, pp. 112–25.

Kyu-jung Lee, M. (2001), 'Sex, Drugs and Degenerate People', *Metro*, 131/132, pp. 270–72.

Lai, L. (2001), 'Film and Enigmatization: Nostalgia, Nonsense and Remembering', in Esther Yau (ed.), *At Full Speed: Hong Kong Cinema in a Borderless World*, Minneapolis, MN: Minnesota University Press, pp. 231–50.

Lane, T. (2001), Article (no title available), *The Age*, 9 September, http://www.sbs.com.au. Accessed 2 April 2008.

Lange, C., Kamalkhani, Z. and Baldassar, L. (2007), 'Afghan Hazara Refugees in Australia: Constructing Australian Citizens', *Social Identities*, March, pp. 31–50.

Langfield, M. (1999), 'Recruiting Immigrants: The First World War and Australian Immigration', in R. Nile (ed.), *War and Other Catastrophes*, Brisbane: University of Queensland Press, pp. 55–65.

Latour, B. (1993), *We Have Never Been Modern*, trans. Catherine Porter, Cambridge, MA: Harvard University Press.

Latour, B. with Kastrissianakis, K. (2007), 'We are All Reactionaries Today', *Re-Public: Re-Imagining Democracy – English Version*, http://www.re-public.gr. Accessed 22 March 2007.

Lee, G. and Tapp, N. (eds) (2004), *The Hmong of Australia: Culture and Diaspora*, Canberra: Pandanus Books.

Lee, S. (2004), 'Performing Community: A Comparison of Korean-Language Newspapers in Beijing and Sydney', *Diaspora*, 13: 2/3, pp. 227–52.

Levey, G.B. (2007), *Political Theory and Australian Multiculturalism*, Oxford: Berghahn.

Lévinas, E. (1998), 'Philosophy, Justice, and Love', *Entre Nous: Thinking of the Other*, trans. M.B. Smith and B. Harshav, New York: Columbia University Press.

Lévinas, E. (1969), *Totality and Infinity: An Essay on Exteriority*, Pittsburgh, PN: Duquesne University Press.

Lionnet, F. and Shih, S. (eds) (2005), *Minor Transnationalism*, Durham, NC: Duke University Press.

Lohrey, A. (1982), 'Australian Mythologies – Gallipoli: Male Innocence as Marketable Commodity', *Island Magazine*, 9: 10, pp. 29–34.

Longley, K. (1992), 'Fifth World', in S. Gunew and K. Longley (eds), *Striking Chords*, Sydney: Allen & Unwin.

Lopez, M. (2000), *The Origins of Multiculturalism in Australian Politics 1945–1975*, Melbourne: Melbourne University Press.

Loshitzky, Y. (2006), 'Journeys of Hope to Fortress Europe', *Third Text*, 20: 6, pp. 745–54.

Lubelski, T. (2000), *Strategie autorskie w polskim filmie fabularnym lat 1945–1961*, Kraków: Rabid.

McLean, I. (1998), *White Aborigines: Identity Politics in Australian Art*, New York: Cambridge University Press.

Madan, M. (2000), 'Bollywood Down Under: Imagining New neighbourhoods', *South Asia: Journal of Asian Studies*, 23: 1, pp. 21–30.

Manne, R. (ed.) (2004), *The Howard Years*, Melbourne: Black Inc Agenda.

Manne, R. (2007), 'A Turkish Tale', *The Monthly*, 20, http://www.themonthly.com.au/tm/node/459. Accessed 10 June 2008.

Manning, P. (2003), 'Arabic and Muslim People in Sydney's Daily Newspapers, Before and after September 11', *Media International Australia*, 109, pp. 50–70.

March, R. (1997), 'A Marketer's Perspective of Current Tourism Forecasting', presentation at the Australian Tourism and Hospitality Research Conference, Sydney, 9 July, http://inboundtourism.com.au.article_two.html. Accessed 25 January 2008.

Marks, L.U. (2001), *Under the Skin of the Film: Intercultural Cinema, Embodiment, and the Senses*, Durham, NC: Duke University Press.

Marshall, D. and Baker, R. (2001), 'Clubs, Spades, Diamonds and Disadvantage: The Geography of Electronic Gaming Machines in Melbourne', *Australian Geographical Studies*, 39: 1, pp. 17–33.

Marshall, R. (1984), 'A Luminous Beauty Brings Passion to Moving Story', *Manly Daily*, 5 October, from personal archives of Sophia Turkiewicz, no page number available.

Martin, A. (2001), 'The Seconds Pile Up', in *Do Not Fear Thought Provoking Art*, http://www.16beavergroup. org/monday/archives/002145.php. Accessed 20 April 2008.

Martin, A. (2003), *The Mad Max Movies*, Sydney: Currency Press.

Mason, V. (2004), 'Strangers Within the 'Lucky Country': Arab-Australians After September 11', *Comparative Studies of South Asia, Africa and the Middle East*, 24: 1, pp. 233–43.

McFarlane, B. (1987), *Australian Cinema 1970–1985*, London: Secker and Warburg.

McFarlane, B. (2007), 'A Road Movie Without a Road: An Interview with Michael James Rowland', *Metro Magazine*, 153, pp. 22–28.

McLennan, G. (1993), 'Australia and Japan: From Enemies to Mates?', *Metro Magazine*, 92, pp. 28–33.

McNamara, D., and Coughlan, J.E. (1992), 'Recent Trends in Japanese Migration to Australia and the Characteristics of Recent Japanese Immigrants Settling in Australia', *Japanese Studies*, 12: 1, pp. 50–73.

Miller, T. (2007), 'Culture, Dislocation, and Citizenship', *Global Migration, Social Change, and Cultural Transformation*, (eds) Emory Elliott, Jasmine Payne and P. Ploesch, New York: Palgrave Macmillan, pp. 166–86.

Mirzoeff, N. (1999a), *Introduction to Visual Culture*, London: Routledge.

Mirzoeff, N. (ed.) (1999b), *Visual Culture and Diaspora: Representing Africans and Jews*, London: Routledge.

Mitchell, T. (2000), 'Kylie Meets Misato: Bridging the Gap Between Australian and Japanese Popular Culture', in I. Ang, S. Chalmers, L. Law and M. Thomas (eds), *Alter/Asians: Asian Identities in Art, Media and Popular Culture*, Melbourne: Pluto Press, pp. 183–200.

Mitchell, T. (2003), 'Clara Law's *Floating Life* and Hong Kong-Australian "flexible citizenship"', *Ethic and Racial Studies*, 26: 2, pp. 278–300.

Molitorisz, S. (2004), 'The New Seekers', *Sydney Morning Herald*, 30 January, p. 3.

Molloy, B. (1990), *Before the Interval: Australian Mythology and Feature Films 1930–1960*, Brisbane: University of Queensland Press.

Moore, T. (2005), *The Barry McKenzie Films*, Sydney: Currency Press.

Moran, A. and O'Regan, T. (eds) (1985), *An Australian Film Reader*, Sydney: Currency Press in association with the Australian Film Commission.

Moran, A. and Vieth, E. (2005), *Historical Dictionary of Australian and New Zealand Cinema*, Lanham, MD: Scarecrow.

Moran, A. and Vieth, E. (2006), *Film in Australia: An Introduction*, Cambridge, MA: Cambridge University Press.

Morris, M. (1984), 'Long Hits Gold in *Silver City*', *The Australian Financial Review*, 5 October, p. 41.

Morris, M. (1998), 'White Panic or *Mad Max* and the Sublime', in Kuan-Hsing Chen (ed.), *Trajectories: Inter-Asia Cultural Studies*, London: Routledge), pp. 239–62.

Mousoulis, B. (2000), 'Is Your Film Language Greek? Some Thoughts on Greek-Australian Film-makers', *Senses of Cinema*, 1, http://www.sensesofcinema.com/contents/00/1/greek.html. Accessed 27 June 2008.

Much Ado Films (2002), *The Projectionist* – Credits, Muchadofilms.com, http://www.muchadofilms.com/mod.php?mod=userpageandpage_id=6andPHPSESSID=b8725622ef15b323dab69fbb2d888ffe. Accessed 13 March 2008.

Muecke, S. (1997), *No Road: Bitumen All the Way*, Fremantle: Fremantle Arts Centre Press.

Murray, S. (ed.) (1980), *The New Australian Cinema*, Melbourne: Nelson and Cinema Papers.

Nader, C. (2005), 'Young Men Behaving Badly Span All Races', *Age*, 17 December, p. 25.

Naficy, H. (2001), *An Accented Cinema: Exilic and Diasporic Film-making*, Princeton, NJ: Princeton University Press.

Nagata, Y. (1996), *Unwanted Aliens: Japanese Internment in Australia*, Brisbane: University of Queensland Press.

Nairn, T. (2003), 'Democracy and Power: American Power and the World', openDemocracy.net, 9, 16, and 23 January, 4 and 20 February.

Nattaporn, T., Jackson A.C. and Thomas, S.A. (2004), 'Gambling Among Young Thai People in Melbourne, Australia: An Exploratory Study', *International Gambling Studies*, 4: 2, pp. 189–203.

New South Wales Parliamentary Debates, Legislative Assembly (2003), 'Anzac Cove World Heritage Listing', *Hansard*, 1 July, http://www.parliament.nsw.gov.au/prod/parlment/hansart.nsf/V3Key/LA20030701022. Accessed 2nd March 2008.

Nichols, B. (1991), *Representing Reality: Issues and Concepts in Documentary*, Bloomington, IN: Indiana University Press.

Nichols, B. (2001), *Introduction to Documentary*, Bloomington, IN: Indiana University Press.

Nicoll, F. (2001), *From Diggers to Drag Queens: Configurations of Australian National Identity*, Sydney: Pluto Press.

Nourry, D. (2005), 'Body-Politic (National Imaginary): 'Lest We Forget... Mateship (Empire) Right or Wrong', *Continuum: Journal of Media and Cultural Studies* 19: 3, pp. 365–79.

Nussbaum, M.C. (2001), *Upheavals of Thought: The Intelligence of Emotions*, New York: Cambridge University Press.

O'Brien, C. (ed.) (2001), *The Life and Death of Sandy Stone*, Sydney: Pan Macmillan.

O'Dwyer, E. (2005), 'Questions for Sejong Park', *Sun-Herald*, 30 January, p. 73.

O'Regan, T. (1989), 'Cinema Oz: The "Ocker" Films', in A. Moran and T. O'Regan (eds), *The Australian Screen*, Ringwood: Penguin, pp. 75–98.

O'Regan, T. (1996), *Australian National Cinema*, London: Routledge.

Pakulski, J. (1985), 'Polish Migrants in Hobart: A Study of Community Formation', in J. Zybrzycki and R. Sussex (eds), *Polish People and Culture in Australia*, Canberra: Australian National University, pp. 82–107.

Papastergiadis, N. (2000), *The Turbulence of Migration*, Cambridge: Polity Press.

Papastergiadis, N. (2003), 'Cultural Identity and Its Boredom', in Nikos Papastergiadis (ed.), *Complex Entanglements*, London: Rivers Oram Press, pp. 171–77.

Pew Research Center for the People and the Press (2003), *Views of a Changing World, June 2003*, Washington, DC: Pew Research Center.

Pew Research Center for the People and the Press (2004), *A Global Generation Gap: Adapting to a New World*, Washington, DC: Pew Research Center.

Pike, A. and Cooper, R. (1980), *Australian Film 1900–1977: A Guide to Feature Film Production*, Melbourne: Oxford University Press in association with the Australian Film Institute.

Pollak, A. (1985), 'First Person: Sophia Turkiewicz', *Sydney Morning Herald Metro*, 8 February, p. 3.

Poppenbeek, P. (1994), 'Inside Images by Outsiders: Stereotypes of and by Both Black and White Australians', in D. Grant and G. Seal (eds), *Australia in the World: Perceptions and Possibilities, Papers from the Outside Images of Australia Conference, Perth 1992*, Curtin University: Black Swan Press, pp. 34–39.

Porteous, J.D. (1985) 'Literature and Humanist Geography', *Arena*, 17, pp. 117–22.

Poynting, S. (2002), ''Bin Laden in the Suburbs': Attacks on Arab and Muslim Australians Before and After 11 September', *Current Issues in Criminal Justice*, 14: 1, pp. 43–64.

Poynting, S. (2007), 'Multiculturalism at the End of the Line?' in S. Velayutham and A. Wise (eds), *Everyday Multiculturalism Conference Proceedings, Macquarie University 28–29 September 2006*, Centre for Research on Social Inclusion, Macquarie University, Sydney.

Poynting, S. and Mason, V. (2006), '"Tolerance, freedom, justice and peace"? Britain, Australia and Anti-Muslim Racism Since 11 September 2001', *Journal of Intercultural Studies*, 27: 4, pp. 365–91.

Poynting, S. and Noble, G. (2003), ''Dog-whistle' Journalism and Muslim Australians Since 2001', *Media International Australia*, 109, pp. 41–49.

Poynting, S., Noble, G. and Tabar, P. (1998), ''If Anyone Called Me a Wog, they Wouldn't be Speaking to Me Alone": Protest Masculinity and Lebanese Youth in Western Sydney', *Journal of Interdisciplinary Gender Studies*, 3: 2, pp. 76–94.

Poynting, S. Noble, G., and Tabar, P. (2001), 'Middle Eastern Appearances: "Ethnic Gangs", Moral Panic and Media Framing', *The Australian and New Zealand Journal of Criminology*, 34: 1, pp. 67–90.

Praz, M. (1951), *The Romantic Agony*, trans. A. Davidson, London: Oxford University Press.

Probyn, F. (2005), 'An Ethics of Following and the No Road Film: Trackers, Followers and Fanatics', *Australian Humanities Review*, 37, http://www.australianhumanitiesreview.org/archive/Issue-December-2005/Probyn.html. Accessed 10 June 2008.

Pulleine, T. (1985), 'Inside Looking Out', *Monthly Film Bulletin*, 52, pp. 207–08.

Rando, G. (2007), 'Expressions of the Calabrian Diaspora in Calabrian Australian Writing', *Faculty of Arts Papers*, Wollongong: University of Wollongong, http://ro.uow.edu.au/cgi/viewcontent.cgi?article=1167andcontext=artspapers. Accessed 18 June 2008.

Rankin, P. (1998), 'Making Headlines', *Rave Magazine*, 22 February, p. 3.

Rattigan, N. (1991), *Images of Australia: 100 Films of the New Australian Cinema*, Dallas: Southern Methodist University Press.

Rattigan, N. (1998), 'Ethnicity and Identity in the New Australian Cinema', *Metro Education*, 13, pp. 22–26.

Reis, M. (2004), 'Theorizing Diaspora: Perspectives on "Classical" and "Contemporary" Diaspora', *International Migration*, 42: 2, pp. 41–60.

Reith, G. (1999), *The Age of Chance: Gambling in Western Culture*, London: Routledge.

Renov, M. (1993), 'Towards a Poetics of Documentary', in M. Renov (ed.), *Theorizing Documentary*, New York: Routledge.

Reynaud, D. (1996), Celluloid Anzacs: Representations of the Great War in Australian Cinema and Television Dramas, PhD thesis, University of Newcastle.

Reynaud, D. (2005), *The Hero of the Dardanelles and Other World War I Silent Dramas*, Canberra: Research and Academic Outreach National Film and Sound Archive Monographs.

Rosenbaum, J. (1998), 'The Color of Paradise', *Chicago Reader*, http://www.chicagoreader.com/movies/archives/1998/0198/01168b.html. Accessed 3 June 2008.

Rueschmann, E. (ed.) (2003), *Moving Pictures, Migrating Identities*, Jackson, MS: University Press of Mississippi.

Rundle, G. (2007), 'Jindabyne: A Guilt Trip from Down Under', *Spiked*, 24 May, http://www.spiked-online.com/index.php?/site/article/3403. Accessed 15 June 2007.

Rushdie, S. (1988), 'Songs Doesn't Know the Score', in K. Mercer (ed.), *Black Film Black Cinema*, London: ICA Documents 7, p. 16.

Rutherford, J. (2000), *The Gauche Intruder: Freud, Lacan and the White Australian Fantasy*, Melbourne: Melbourne University Press.

Rutland, S.D. (2005), *The Jews in Australia*, Cambridge: Cambridge University Press.

Safran, J. (2006), 'Interview with Heng Tang', *Sunday Night with Safran*, ABC Radio Triple J, 22 October.

Safran, W. (1991), 'Diasporas in Modern Societies: Myths of Homeland and Return', *Diaspora: A Journal of Transnational Studies*, 1: 1, pp. 83–99.

Said, E. (2003), *Reflections on Exile and Other Essays*, Cambridge, MA: Harvard University Press.

Sarris, A. (1983), 'Lonely Hearts', *Village Voice*, 13 September, p. 43.

Sauer, A.E. (1999), 'Model Workers or Hardened Nazis? The Australian Debate about Admitting German Migrants 1950–1952', *Australian Journal of Politics and History*, 45: 3, pp. 422–37.

Siemienowicz, R. (1999), 'Globalisation and Home Values in New Australian Cinema', in F. Murphy (ed.), *Writing Australia: New Talents 21C*, Journal of Australian Studies, 63, pp. 49–55, 187–89.

'Silver City' (1985), *Ms London*, 10 June, from private archives of Sophia Turkiewicz, no page numbers available.

Silverman, M. (1996), *The Threshold of the Visible World*, New York, Routledge.

Simpson, C. (2000), '"Turkish Delights?': An Analysis of the Media Reception to the First Turkish Film Festival in Australia', *Metro Magazine*, 124–5, pp. 60–3.

Simpson, C. (2006), 'Antipodean Automobility and Crash: Treachery, Trespass and Transformation of the Open Road', *Australian Humanities Review*, 39–40, http://www.lib.latrobe.edu.au/AHR/archive/Issue-September-2006/simpson.html. Accessed 10 June 2008.

Simpson, C. (2007a), 'Bonds of War: Tolga Örnek on *Gallipoli: The Frontline* and Australian-Turkish Relations', *Metro*, 153 pp. 92–95.

Simpson, C. (2007b), 'Taking the "Nation" Out of Gallipoli – Tolga Örnek's *Gallipoli: The Frontline*', *Metro*, 153, pp. 86–90.

Sissons, D.C.S. (1977), 'Karayuki-San: Japanese Prostitutes in Australia 1887–1916 – I', *Historical Studies*, 17: 68, pp. 323–41.

Sissons, D.C.S. (1988), 'Japanese', in J. Jupp (ed.), *The Australian People: An Encyclopedia of the Nation, Its People and Their Origins*, Sydney: Angus & Robertson, pp. 635–37.

Smaill, B. (2005), 'Three Australian Documentaries: Diaspora and Subjectivity', *Post Script*, 24: 2/3, pp. 22–35.

Smaill, B. (2006), 'Diasporic Subjectivity in Contemporary Australian Documentary: Travel, History and the Televisual Representation of Trauma', *Continuum: Journal of Media and Cultural Studies* 20: 2, pp. 269–83.

Smith, N. (2004), 'Investigating the Consumption of 'Asianness' in Australia: Culture, Class and Capital', paper presented to the 15th Biennial Conference of the Asian Studies Association of Australia, Canberra, 29 June–2 July.

Smolicz, J.J. and Harris R.M. (1984), *Australijczycy polskiego pochodzenia*, Wroctaw: Zaklad Narododowy Imienia Ossolinskich.

Speed, L. (2005), 'Life as a Pizza: The Comic Traditions of Wogsploitation Films', *Metro Magazine*, 146–47, pp. 136–44.

Stein, M. (2002), 'Dir. Clara Law, *Floating Life* [Fu sheng]', *Intersections*, 8, http://wwwsshe.murdoch.edu.au/intersections/issue8/stein_review.html. Accessed 11 March 2008.

Steiner, G. (1971), *Extraterritorial*, New York: Antheneum.

Stone, J. (1985), 'A Love Story of Poles Who Go to Australia', *San Francisco Chronicle*, 6 September, p. 72.

Stratton, D. (1990), *The Avocado Plantation: Boom and Buts in the Australian Film Industry*, Sydney: Pan Macmillan.

Stratton, J. (1998), *Race Daze: Australia in Identity Crisis*, Sydney: Pluto Press.

Stratton, J. and Ang, I. (1994), 'Multicultural Imagined Communities: Cultural Difference and National Identity in Australia and the USA', *Continuum: The Australian Journal of Media and Culture*, 8: 2, http://wwwmcc.murdoch.edu.au/ReadingRoom/8.2/Stratton.html. Accessed 11 March 2008.

*Sunday Press* (Vic) (1984), 7 October, p. 31.

Tada, M. (2000), 'Japanese Newspaper Representations of Australia 1970–1996', in R. Nile and N. Moore (eds), *The Vision Splendid*, special issue of *The Journal of Australian Studies*, 66, Brisbane: API Network/University of Queensland Press, pp. 170–79.

Tascón, S. (2001), 'Refugees in Australia: Border-crossers of the Postcolonial Imaginary', *Australian Journal of Human Rights*, 8: 1, pp. 125–35.

Tascón, S. (2008), 'Narratives of Race and Nation: Everyday Whiteness in Australia', *Social Identities*, forthcoming.

Teo, S. (2001), '*Floating Life*: The heaviness of moving', *Senses of Cinema*, 12, http://www.sensesofcinema. com/contents/01/12/floating.html. Accessed 11 March 2008.

Thompson, K. (1986), 'The Concept of Cinematic Excess', in P. Rosen (ed.), *Narrative, Apparatus, Ideology: A Film Theory Reader*, New York: Columbia University Press, pp. 130–42.

Thompson, K. (1999), *Storytelling in the New Hollywood: Understanding Classical Narrative Technique*, Harvard, MA: Cambridge University Press.

Tivey, B. (1984), 'A Breath of Fresh Hope', *Daily Telegraph*, 28 September, p. 61.

Tsavdaridis, D. (2006), 'We Own This Beach – Court Hears the Words that Sparked Cronulla Riots', *Daily Telegraph*, 21 June, p. 5.

Tuccio, S. (2006), 'Transcending the Stereotype: An Interview with Franco di Chiera', *Metro Magazine*, 151, pp. 132–35.

Turkiewicz, S. (1974), *Treatment for a Feature Film Script. Working Title*, unpublished manuscript, July.

Turner, G. (1997), 'Australian Film and National Identity in the 1990s', in G. Stokes (ed.), *The Politics of Identity in Australia*, Melbourne: Cambridge University Press, pp. 185–92.

Turner, G. (2003), 'After Hybridity: Muslim-Australians and the Imagined Community', *Continuum: Journal of Media and Cultural Studies*, 17: 4, pp. 411–18.

Vasconcelos, J. (1925), *La Raza Cósmica*, n.p.

Verhoeven, D. (2007), 'Twice Born: Dionysos Films and the Establishment of a Greek Film Circuit in Australia', *Studies in Australasian Cinema*, 1: 3, pp. 275–98.

Walker, D. (1999), *Anxious Nation: Australia and the Rise of Asia 1850–1939*, Brisbane: University of Queensland Press.

Warneke, R. (2001), 'Take Away Pizza or I'll Do It Myself', *The Age*, 30 August.

Webster, W. (2006), 'Transnational Journeys and Domestic Histories', *Journal of Social History*, Spring, pp. 651–66.

Weise, K. (2004), 'Social Engagement: The 21st St Kilda Film Festival, *Senses of Cinema*, 32, http://www. sensesofcinema.com/contents/festivals/04/32/st_kilda2004.html. Accessed 22 December 2007.

White, R. (1981), *Inventing Australia: Images and Identity*, Sydney: Allen & Unwin.

Willemen, P. (1994), *Looks and Frictions: Essays in Cultural Studies and Film Theory*, Bloomington, IN: Indiana University Press/British Film Institute.

Williamson, K. (1984), 'Love in a Nissan Hut', *The National Times*, 21–27 September, p. 29.

Wilson, J. (2001), 'Hollowing Out the Romantic Comedy: *Russian Doll*', *Senses of Cinema*, 14, http:// www.sensesofcinema.com/contents/01/14/russian_doll.html. Accessed 3 June 2008.

Wolska, B., Saggers, S. and Hunt, L. (2004), '"Now We Can Drink, Too": Changing Drinking Practices Among Polish-Australian Women', *Health Sociology Review*, 13: 1, pp. 65–73.

Yamine, R. and Thomas, S.A. (2000), *The Impact of Gaming on Specific Cultural Groups*, Melbourne: The Victorian Casino and Gaming Authority.

Yecies, B. and Shim, A. (2007), 'Hallyuwood Down Under: The New Korean Cinema and Australia 1996–2007', *Screening the Past*, 22, www.latrobe.edu.au/screeningthepast/22/new-korean-cinema-australia.html. Accessed 27 March 2008.

You, D. (2008), Telephone interview with Brian Yecies, 3 January.

Yudice, G. (2003), *The Expediency of Culture: Uses of Culture in The Global Era*, Durham, NC: Duke University Press.

Yue, A. (2000), 'Asian-Australian Cinema, Asian-Australian Modernity', in H. Gilbert, T. Khoo and J. Lo (eds), *Diaspora: Negotiating Asian-Australia*, Brisbane: University of Queensland Press, pp. 190–238.

Yue, A. (2006), Interview with Heng Tang on *The Last Chip*, 27 October.

Yue, A. (2008), Email interview with Heng Tang on *The Last Chip*, 2 February.

# NOTES ON CONTRIBUTORS

## The Editors

**Catherine Simpson** teaches in media and convenes the Honours program at Macquarie University, Sydney, Australia. She has organized film festivals in Australia and Turkey, and has written on the cinema of both countries in various publications, including *Womenvision* (ed. Lisa French), *Metro, Senses of Cinema, Australian Humanities Review, SCAN, M/C, Journal of Australian Studies* and *Studies in Australasian Cinema*. Her research and teaching interests include nationhood, gender and geography in the cinema; automobile cultures; film festivals; transnational cinemas and the work of Australian female film-makers.

**Renata Murawska** lectures in film, media and public relations at Macquarie University. She has published a number of articles on Polish cinema and presented papers on migrant and diasporic films and film-makers. Her most recent publications include two chapters in *After Kieslowski* (ed. Steven Woodward) on the legacy of Krzysztof Kieslowski's film-making in Poland. She immigrated to Australia in 1994 and has been researching and writing on Polish and émigré cinema for five years, including her PhD on Polish (post)transitional cinema from 1989–2004.

**Anthony Lambert** lectures in the Department of Critical and Cultural Studies at Macquarie University. Recently published works include articles and chapters in *Postcolonial Text, Crime Media Culture* and the book *Gendered Outcasts*. He is working on a book about Australian visual culture, and further collections devoted to mobility and space in Australian cinema. His research and teaching interests include Australian film and culture, representations of gender and sexuality, critical methodologies, and the politics of identity and space.

## Contributors

**Felicity Collins** teaches cinema studies at La Trobe University, Melbourne and is the author of *The Films of Gillian Armstrong* (Melbourne Press 1999) and *Australian Cinema After Mabo* (Cambridge University Press 2004, with Therese Davis). She is project leader/chief investigator of an Australian Research Council Discovery project on Australian screen comedy with Sue Turnbull and Susan Bye.

**John Conomos** lectures at the Sydney College of the Arts, University of Sydney. He is a media artist, critic and author of the book *Mutant Media* (Artspace/Power Publications 2008). He is currently working on a 'postcolonial' memoir, *Milkbar*, and a book called *The Cinema Century*, and is co-editing (with Brad Buckley) the forthcoming anthology *Re-thinking the Contemporary Art School* (NASCAD University Press 2009). A New Media Fellow of the Australian Council for the Arts, his new video *Lake George (After Mark Rothko)*, is being screened at the Tate Modern, London this year while his radio essay on Luis Bunuel ('The Bells of Toledo') is in production for ABC Radio National, Sydney.

**Rebecca Coyle** has published two anthologies and several articles and chapters on cultural production and Australian cinema related to documentary, and to screen music and sound. Her most recent book is *Reel Tracks: Australian Film Music and Cultural Identities* (John Libbey/Indiana 2005). She is currently researching the Australian film music industry with assistance from an Australian Research Council Discovery Project grant, and editing an anthology on animation film music and sound for Equinox (UK). She teaches in the Media Program at Southern Cross University, Lismore, Australia.

**Greg Dolgopolov** is a lecturer in film at the University of New South Wales, Sydney, Australia. He completed his PhD on the transformations of post-Soviet television culture at Murdoch University in 2003. He has worked as an actor, director and 'spin doctor'. His primary areas of interest are Australian cinema, Russian cinema, screen theory, video production, short films, mobile devices and documentary. Greg runs a production entity called BadDad, focused on hybrid documentary and cinema theory put into practice.

**Garry Gillard** has been teaching Australian cinema at Murdoch University since 1998. His textbook, *Ten Types of Australian Film* was published by Murdoch University in 2007. He has also published a number of articles in the journals *ATOM*, *Metro* and *Screen Education*.

**Antje Gnida** is a PhD candidate in Macquarie University's Media Department. Her thesis investigates the portrayal of the German enemy in Australian visual culture in World Wars I and II, the subject of her papers for the Conference of the Film and History Association of Australia and New Zealand in 2006, and the online postgraduate journal *NEO*.

**Ben Goldsmith** is a senior researcher at the Australian Film, Television and Radio School (AFTRS). He has written extensively on Australian film and television production, international media policy and international film production. He has authored or co-authored four books, including *The Film Studio: Film Production in a Global Economy* (Rowman and Littlefield 2005, with Tom O'Regan). His current research interests include changes in Australian film and television production since the introduction of subscription television, the future of television and the history of television ratings.

**Marek Haltof** is Professor of Film in the English Department at Northern Michigan University in Marquette. His recent books include *Historical Dictionary of Polish Cinema* (Scarecrow Press 2008), *The Cinema of Krzysztof Kieslowski: Variations on Destiny and Chance* (Wallflower Press 2004), and *Polish National Cinema* (Berghahn 2002). He also published on Australian cinema, including two books in Polish, *Australian Cinema: The Screen Construction of Australia* (Lodz, 1996; revised and expanded edition published in 2005 in Gdansk) and *Authorship and Art Cinema: The Case of Paul Cox* (Rabid 2001), as well as *Peter Weir: When Cultures Collide* (Twayne 1996).

**Susie Khamis** is a researcher and teacher in Macquarie University's Media and Music Departments. Her interest is in the branding process – how people, places, ideas and goods are invested with imagery and associations and the consequences of this on individuals, communities and nations. She has published in the *Journal of Australian Studies*, *Shima*, *M/C: A Journal of Media and Culture*, *Australian Cultural History*, *SCAN: Journal of Media Arts Culture*, *History Australia*, *Food, Culture and Society*, the *International Journal of Entrepreneurship and Small Business*, and *Altitude*.

**Sonia Magdalena Tascón** teaches media studies at Curtin University, Western Australia, where she is an adjunct staff member of the Centre for Human Rights Education. Her academic interests are in the areas of cross-cultural encounters, ethics (across difference and embodied ethics), cross-cultural film, human rights and the border, with a major interest in thinkers such as Levinas, Irigaray, Derrida, Sontag, Nancy, Baudrillard and Bauman. Sonia organizes an ongoing human rights film festival in Perth, promotes the arts in Perth and is an advocate of refugee rights.

**Brian Yecies** is a senior lecturer in media and cultural studies at the University of Wollongong. He teaches and researches issues surrounding Asian screen cultures with a focus on cinema in colonial Korea (1910–45) and postcolonial South Korea (1945 to the present). His current research, which involves a 2008 Advanced Research Grant from the Korea Foundation, investigates strategies being used by the South Korean film industry to overcome new modes of censorship, domestic competition and piracy/downloading. His forthcoming book, *Korea's Occupied Cinemas* (with Ae-Gyung Shim), will be published in the Routledge Advances in Film Studies Monograph Series.

**Audrey Yue** lectures in cultural studies at the University of Melbourne. She is the co-editor of *AsiaPacifiQueer: Rethinking Gender and Sexuality* (University of Illinois Press 2008) and *Mobile Cultures: New Media in Queer Asia* (Duke University Press 2003). Her most recent essays on queer Asian diasporas, and Asian-Australian and Hong Kong cinemas appear in *Sexualities*, *GLQ*, *Studies in Australasian Cinemas* and *Cultural Theory in Everyday Life* (Oxford University Press 2008). She is working on a collaborative project on Asian-Australian cinema and completing a monograph on queer Asian migrations in Australia.

# INDEX